ED STEWART
OUT OF THE STEWPOT

ED STEWART

OUT OF THE STEWPOT

MY AUTOBIOGRAPHY

JOHN BLAKE

Published by John Blake Publishing Ltd,
3, Bramber Court, 2 Bramber Road,
London W14 9PB, England

www.blake.co.uk

First published in hardback in 2005

ISBN 1 84454 086 3

British Library Cataloguing-in-Publication Data:

A catalogue record for this book is available from the British Library.

Design by www.envydesign.co.uk

Printed in Great Britain by CPD, Wales.

1 3 5 7 9 10 8 6 4 2

Papers used by John Blake Publishing are natural, recyclable products made from
wood grown in sustainable forests. The manufacturing processes conform to the
environmental regulations of the country of origin.

Every attempt has been made to contact the relevant copyright-holders,
but some were unobtainable. We would be grateful if the appropriate people
could contact us.

To my brother Mike, a wonderful writer,
sadly cut off in his prime.

CONTENTS

INTRODUCTION

I'VE ALWAYS tried to make my radio programmes a 'good listen', and I've tried to follow that through by making this book a 'good read'. It was a strange experience at first, sitting in front of a blank screen on my computer. It was stranger still having a computer at all – until recently, I have been computer illiterate. As with many first-timers, there was a mini disaster when I thought I'd lost over 5,000 words. Thanks to computer whiz Ron Barrett, we eventually found the missing chapter. At least I hadn't lost it all, unlike TE Lawrence, better known as Lawrence of Arabia, who left his entire manuscript for the *Seven Pillars of Wisdom* on a platform at Reading Station, whereupon a cleaner promptly binned it. He then had to rewrite the *Seven Pillars* from memory.

Poor old Isaac Newton didn't fare much better. The work of a lifetime went up in flames when his dog, Diamond, leapt on to his desk and knocked over Isaac's reading candle while he was out. The old boy returned to find his papers transformed into a pile of ashes. Thank goodness an apple falling on his head hadn't affected his memory!

It has amazed me how much I have been able to remember when looking back over my life. Sometimes, I can't remember why I've walked upstairs, but the floodgates of my memory have opened to the events of a lifetime. For a man not noted for his organised mind, writing this book has been the biggest challenge of my life. But I have enjoyed it – honestly!

Ed Stewart, February 2005

1

WAR BABY

*My family still tell me off when I wipe my
plate clean with a piece of bread. I just laugh
and explain, 'I was a war baby ...'*

THE GERMAN pilot gave a smug smile as he wheeled away towards the English Channel. It had been a good night's work. His snarling pack of bombers had jettisoned their loads over Cardiff and Swansea and even further north above Manchester and Liverpool. Now they were on their way back to their homeland. But for one Fokker pilot (and he was probably known as a right one in the Officers' Mess) the temptation was too strong. After ordering the others to stay in formation, he flew down over the huddled buildings below, strafing the houses on the main Exeter to Exmouth road. He saw the bright flashes and the spurts of smoke, and then flew triumphantly away avoiding the searchlights and flak that were desperately seeking him out. The attack missed Caroline House, thank goodness, or I wouldn't be writing this book!

My father, Ray Mainwaring (pronounced 'Mannering', except in Wales where it is pronounced as written), was a solicitor for the Treasury in London but, as the war had progressed and the capital had become too dangerous a place in which to live, he and my mother, Peggy, with 18-month-old John, had moved in with her parents who lived in Fleet, Hampshire.

Granny Fraser was a very independent person and didn't take kindly to having a boisterous baby around the house. Her main activity was golf – she was an exceptional golfer with a handicap of two, which in those days made her a leading lady amateur. She was nothing if not cunning. To make sure she kept her golf handicap up to scratch during the war, she became a Senior Air Raid Warden, which entitled her to extra petrol – that way she could visit the nearby North Hants Golf Club more often. When she became Captain of Sunningdale Ladies, she discreetly dropped her Christian name of Doris and became Diana – she believed it to be much more classy!

Golf was her passion, and it was on the golf course that Granny Fraser would help a young flying officer who had lost both legs in a flying accident. His name was Douglas Bader. His wife Thelma used to carry his bag for him, and Granny Fraser would help him back on his feet again every time he took a swing at the ball and fell over! But Bader, a hero to many, wasn't liked by everyone. He used to roar up the golf club drive in his sports car, slam on the brakes and scatter the gravel into the members' gin and tonics. 'Bloody chap, Bader!' they would mutter.

I was to meet Douglas Bader years later at a golf day at Silvermere in Surrey. I reminded him that he used to pinch my mother's bottom at the North Hants Golf Club, which didn't go down too well with the members since she was just 15 at the time. Then I told him we'd been educated at the same school – St Edward's, Oxford.

'And what do you do now?' he enquired, not knowing who I was, and possibly not caring either.

'I'm a disc jockey with Radio 1,' I replied.

'A chap from Teddies ...' our nickname for St Edward's, '... a *disc jockey*?' He spat the words out in the same tone of voice that Lady Bracknell had used when enquiring about 'a *haaaandbaaaaag*?' He laughed mischievously and, as I turned away, I started humming Andy Fairweather Lowe's famous hit 'Wide-Eyed and Legless'. I think the relevance was lost on him!

Although she had had three children, Granny Fraser was the sort of person who shouldn't have had children at all – my mother, her brother Ian and her sister Gill had all been brought up by nannies, whose main criterion for a quiet life was the convenient saying, 'Little girls that ask, don't get ... and little girls who don't ask, don't want.' What a load of rubbish! No wonder, then, that Mum never took up golf. She was determined that, when she married, she would be a full-time mother – which she always has been.

Granny Fraser was only too glad when a wonderful opportunity arose to move her daughter and lively grandchild elsewhere. Her house was so close to the North Hants Golf Course that the day a bomb landed in a bunker by the 18th green, Fleet was deemed too dangerous for a young mother to bring up a small child. By this time, she also had another on the way – me! It was a shame I wasn't born in Granny Fraser's house – some of her golfing talent might have rubbed off, and it was talent that I sorely needed as golf started to take up an increasingly large part of my life in my later years. It's strange how my love of golf started with a bomb in a bunker!

I was eventually born in Caroline House in Devon, on 23 April 1941. As the war unfolded, it was unique in that it was to be the first war in which the civilians at home were to play as important a part in its victory as the men and women who were sent abroad to fight it.

Unfortunately for my father, my brother John soon reached that level of awareness that other fathers must have dreaded. He asked, 'What do you do in the war, Dad?'

'I don't fight, son.'

Dad saw our look of disappointment.

'I'm part of the war effort,' he said proudly.

We smiled, relieved that my father was so important! Little did I know then that he had been too young for the First World War and too old for the Second, so had never lifted a rifle in anger in his life. As a joke, he used to suck his teeth, roll his tongue around the inside of his mouth, and then he would stop, feign surprise, and exclaim, 'Ham ... ham ... haven't had ham for weeks!' referring to the dreadful conditions and lack of hygiene in the trenches of the First World War. He'd also contracted TB, and spent some of the war in a convalescent home, so Dad was not exactly prime fighting material. Yet the image we had was that everyone went to war – 'Will the last person leaving Dover please switch off the light?' That was so far from the truth. Recognising the civilian efforts at home, Churchill wrote in his history of the Second World War, 'Men and women toiled at the lathes and machines in the factories till they fell exhausted to the floor, and had to be dragged away and ordered home, while their places were occupied by newcomers ahead of time.' You can hear Churchill's voice in those words, and it was no small wonder that he was voted The Greatest Briton in the BBC poll in 2002.

So my father was part of the war effort, travelling into London every day to the Ministry of Fuel and Power to fufil his duties as a solicitor. Life had to go on, however ineffective it might have seemed at the time.

So, in the aftermath of the bunker bombing at Granny Fraser's, were Peggy and her growing family sent somewhere really safe like the north of Scotland perhaps? Oh no. Mum had a great friend living in Devon, whose husband was serving with the Royal Marines, so off we went to Lympstone ... and jumped straight out of the frying pan into the fire. That part of the country, with its important naval bases of Plymouth, Devonport and Exeter, were heavily bombarded, so we would probably have been safer living next to the bombed-out bunker. I never got to play on the streets of Exmouth, though. When I was six months old, my mother moved back to Fleet – again!

My only recollection of the war was when a doodlebug went over our house in Fleet on its way to London. 'When the whining stops,' they said, 'hide under something solid – like your Dad!'

After months of treatment for his TB at King Edward's Hospital in Midhurst, Dad had been advised to recuperate by the sea, so Mum and Dad found a place very quickly and very cheaply in Aldwick Bay in Sussex. It wasn't surprising that it was so cheap – they soon realised why they'd got such a bargain when they noticed that the house was only a couple of miles south of Tangmere, one of the busiest airfields on the south coast.

One day, Mum was pushing John and me in the pram near the beach, to breathe in the healthy sea air and listen to the calls of the gulls and cormorants. She heard some activity above her, and looked up to see several dogfights between the buzzing Spitfires and Messerschmitts overhead, and quickly raised the hood on the pram! Suddenly, she saw a plane screaming towards her with spurts of flame across both wings. Surprising herself with her speed of foot, she made for the nearest object and flung herself and the pram behind it – a good old-fashioned red pillar box, and it saved our lives.

Crouching there with her arms around us and fearing the worst, she heard a huge explosion, and felt cascades of water all over her head, arms and legs, running in mini-waterfalls down the sides of the pram hood. While plummeting to earth, the plane had lost a wing and had spiralled out of control into the sea. Everything within a hundred yards was soaked with salty water and oily debris. Sadly, the plane had been a Spitfire and the dead pilot's body would later be found still strapped to his seat. He hadn't baled out, even though his wings had caught fire, as he knew he was doomed. Mum had told us later, when we were old enough to understand the story, that the pilot had seen us all rushing towards that pillar box and wanted us to survive. And we had ... just.

I'm glad I wasn't any older during those war years. By the time it had finished, I was four and a half and hadn't really appreciated the privations of rationing, because our parents had always tried to feed us the best of what was available. Mum was fortunate in that she was an impressive 6ft tall, and attracted quite a bit of attention, notably down at the grocer's. So much so, in fact, that when she went to the grocer's one week to buy our ration entitlement, the shopkeeper took one look at her and said, 'We can see who eats all the rations in your house!' Looking down at my brother and me, two rather puny objects clinging to Mum's skirt, he smilingly slipped two sausages and a couple of rashers of bacon into her shopping bag. That was a real treat. The dried egg that followed wasn't too popular in the house, and neither was my most hated food of all time – liver. The pig's liver we were force-fed put me off it for life and I still can't stand the smell and taste today.

By the age of three, we had moved from the south coast to our own house in Fleet, about half a mile from Granny Fraser's. The previous owners had cultivated their own kitchen garden, so now we would be able eat our own fresh vegetables. All we needed were some hens for fresh eggs. Mum had an Aunt Marty, her mother's sister, who had an old bike. It was as old as she was – about 50. But it was sturdy and its wheels went round, so off Mum cycled to Farnham, ten miles away. She bought some hens, stuffed them in two large shopping bags with their heads popping out over the handlebars, and rode home. I can hardly imagine how she did it, but when she got back, and had shooed the hens into their pen, Granny Fraser asked, 'Where's the cock? You've got to have a cock, you know.' And so Mum got right back on her bike, knowing she only had one bird to carry this time – and it would be a rooster, noisy enough to wake Granny Fraser up in the mornings. Mind you, any mother who gave their child the names of Peggy Isabella Stewart with their obvious initials deserved to be woken up at the crack of dawn!

At least three members of the family were part of the armed and affiliated forces during the war – and they all survived. Grandpa Fraser was brought out of retirement to help mastermind the retreat of the forces from Dunkirk. He was Chief-of-Staff to Admiral Ramsey and they spent days in the hollowed-out operations headquarters within the white cliffs of Dover. He loved the song, which Vera Lynn was to make famous, about the white cliffs of Dover. He never saw a bluebird, though, despite the famous song – it had been written by an American, Walter Kent, for whom a bluebird had just been a figment of his imagination.

Grandpa Fraser was a typically dour Scot, and any show of affection was to him unmanly. On one occasion, when a visiting French Admiral came to review the fleet, he made a quick excuse when the Frenchman, as was customary, went to kiss him on both cheeks. 'I'm sorry, I can't kiss you, I've got a cold!' he said stiffly. I've used the same line myself ever since!

My mother's brother, my Uncle Ian, was the only one who fought throughout the war. He had had a very difficult relationship with his father because, among other things, he hadn't wanted to follow in his father's footsteps and join the Navy. He wanted to become a soldier, and went to Woolwich College for Gunnery officers. And there was something else that didn't endear him to his father. After leaving Woolwich, he was posted to Singapore and promptly fell in love with his CO's wife … and later married her! Unfortunately, she was married to someone else at the time. If it hadn't been for the war, he'd have been thrown out of the regiment for ungentlemanly behaviour, but attitudes had become more relaxed because of the conflict. Luckily for them both, they were posted back to Britain just before the Japanese invasion. Even on his return, he insisted that the British guns should not have all been pointing out to sea, but inland as well. He was right; months later, the Japanese attacked from the Malayan Peninsular – and Singapore fell.

Ian soon found himself back in action in the desert at El Alamein and then pushing up and through Italy to eventual victory there. That was his war, and he survived to tell the tale. Ironically, after it was over, he was posted back to Singapore to command a Malay regiment of the Royal Artillery and became known locally as the King of Blakamati, a small island in the middle of Singapore Bay, which was home to his group of soldiers. Years later, he and Auntie Joan (who was still asking my mother, 'When is Edward going to get a proper job?' Whilst at the same time basking in the reflective glory of a famous relative!) were thrilled to see Anneka Rice presenting an edition of *Treasure Hunt* from that same island of Blakamati – which had now become the theme resort of Sentosa.

And there was also my Auntie Gill, my mother's younger sister – if things had worked out differently for her, she would have been an active member of a group of people made famous by the film *Enigma* – the élite team of military decoders. Auntie Gill is the clever-clogs of the family, one of those people who can race through *The Times* crossword in 20 minutes and then half an hour later complains that the *Telegraph* puzzle is too easy! She had married an army officer of the cloth, Padre Glyn Lewis, and the ceremony was held in St George's Cathedral in Jerusalem. The British mandate still controlled Palestine then – Jews weren't fighting Arabs; they were both fighting the British. That day in 1938, their driver was a Jew, and the Best Man was a major in the Royal Army Medical Corps and arrived for the ceremony driving an army ambulance. The happy couple were escorted by a Bren-gun carrier, as well as Granny Fraser, who had flown out for the ceremony. It was a toss-up as to who was the more formidable – Granny Fraser or the Bren-gun carrier!

After the reception in the King David Hotel, Glyn and Gill returned to their home in Haifa. On the way back, they had to stop as they saw a landmine in the middle of the road. 'Too stupid, really,' recalls Auntie Gill (or AG as we were to call her). 'We got out of the Jeep and took pictures of it. Crazy, absolutely crazy. There could have been an enemy in the surrounding hills who could have detonated that landmine by remote control. Sure enough, a couple of minutes later, there was a huge explosion. Too late for us, thank goodness.'

After Haifa, there was Cairo and, in 1940, my cousin Anthony was born, six months before me. By this time, it was thought Cairo was going to be taken by General Rommel, so all wives and offspring were sent to South Africa for safety. AG was not to return to the UK for another three and a half years.

As with so many couples separated for long periods during the war, when AG and Glyn met up again they realised that the chemistry in their marriage had evaporated. And so they split up and went their different ways. AG, for so long out of it, was determined to contribute something to the war effort and an opportunity soon arose. The First Aid Nursing Yeomanry were better known as the FANYs, and AG was a member. They had their own HQ in London and, on her first day, AG was manning the phones. As usual, she greeted each caller with, 'FANY Club – how can I help?'

A man's voice at the other end asked in a strong American accent, 'The "FANY" Club – that sounds interesting … can anybody join?'

'No, sir,' said AG, 'ladies only.'

'That sounds even more interesting!' replied the American. The word 'fanny' means two different things in America and the UK, but both pertain to parts of a woman's anatomy. AG had to acclimatise fast!

As the war ground its way to an eventual conclusion, the

government advertised for a special forces unit of coders and wireless operators. AG applied, was accepted and went on a training course to Chicheley Hall in Newport Pagnell. The chief coder there was Leo Marks, who had become very famous in his field, but by all accounts was not too popular. He used to test the reactions of his new recruits by being particularly rude to them, and then leave the room, keeping a secret tape recorder switched on to listen to their reaction and comments about him. With the exception of AG, everyone was very rude about him, and when he played their comments back to them, they turned different shades of grey and puce. But they had learnt their first lesson – be extremely careful about what you say about anything to anybody; you never knew who was listening.

Although the war in Europe was nearly over, Marks saw AG's potential and she was sent out to join Mountbatten's staff in Ceylon. While there, she spent the rest of the war decoding and scrambling messages sent by spies who were still hiding in the jungles of Southeast Asia, helping to fight the war against the Japanese.

These stories show in a small way how we as a family, like many others at that time, survived those six years of war and privation. Nearly 30 years later, when I married Chiara, she brought with her many different stories and memories from her mother Ginetta Veronese, providing a valuable alternative perspective from the viewpoint of a country that experienced both invasion and occupation – Italy.

In the winter of 1942, a group of German and Italian fascist officers was slowly wandering the streets of the walled Italian town of Este, a few miles south of Padova in the Veneto region of northeast Italy. They had eaten well again in the large villa, which had been taken over by the German military to become their home. Ginetta's mother, Signora Veronese, had been responsible for their full stomachs – she was such a wonderful cook, whom they, too, called 'Mama', once she had been coerced into working for the German officers. There was a great deal of humiliation in that service to the German and Italian oppressors, but she was to find out later that it was a blessing in disguise.

The officers were patrolling the hours of the *coprifuoco*, the curfew. Suddenly, one of them stopped, gesticulating to the others to keep quiet. Out of an upstairs window came the faint but unmistakable sound of the first few bars of Beethoven's 'Fifth Symphony' – *dot-dot-dot-daaashhh* – the Morse code for the letter 'V', 'V' for victory. It came from the BBC's Radio Londra. Listening to it was against the law, punishable by death or imprisonment.

Barging their way through the doors, the officers caught the man red-handed as he was listening for his instructions from the wireless. He never heard the men enter, so engrossed was he in the words streaming out of his headphones. He was bundled to the floor, with his hands quickly bound behind him. 'Please,' he begged, 'take me to my mother in the kitchen – you know her well!' They dragged him along the passage to the kitchen, and cried out in amazement as they saw who was sitting at the table.

'Mama!' they gasped and, indeed, sitting in front of them was their wonderful cook, La Signora Veronese. 'Please, tell no one,' they implored as they set the man free. His name was Gino Veronese, and he was Mama's son. He was also the brother of Ginetta Rosa, who, 30 years later, would become my mother-in-law.

Life in occupied Italy from 1943 until the day that Germany surrendered in April 1945 was never easy. Ginetta and her brothers joined *la resistenza* – the resistance movement. Ginetta would make daily visits from the family restaurant 'Il Leon d'Oro' to the villa where the German officers were living, with pots and bowls of milk. Then she would return with those same pots filled with grenades and shells, which her brother Gino would defuse, making them inoperable when the Germans needed to use them.

She now realises that although they were brave to do it, they were also stupid. Gino nearly killed himself one day when one of the grenades blew up, blinding him permanently in one eye. Ginetta herself made a large overcoat out of blankets – she was, and still is, a marvellous seamstress – and sewed secret pockets into it, inside which she hid the bullets and magazines she had 'borrowed' from the munitions room. How the Germans never stopped and searched her she will never know. She would flash one of her beautiful smiles at them, and they were like putty in her hands! This didn't stop them on one occasion, though, from bundling many of the civilians into lorries and driving them over to the city square in Padova to witness a public execution. Two *partigiani* (resistance fighters) and a priest were hanged for being members of the underground and everybody was forced to watch.

As the bodies were still twitching, a burst of machine-gun fire hit the arch against which Ginetta had been leaning, still in shock from what she had just witnessed. To her horror, the bullets had decapitated the man she had been standing next to; he was still holding an unexploded grenade, which an ever-watchful German sniper had spotted from a window opposite. The bodies were left hanging until they were putrid, as a warning to others who may have been daring enough to stand up to the might of the Third Reich.

The Germans never bombed Este, even when they were retreating. A local Contessa had become the mistress of the German Kommandant and had persuaded him that she had many relatives living there who would be killed or wounded in an attack. La Contessa became a heroine because of this, but many other girls who had consorted with the enemy – or, even worse, had had a child by them – did not fare so well. Their heads were shaved and the community ostracised them. But the Veronese family had survived and Mama became the cook for the American officers when they arrived.

And then there was the oldest son of the family, Delmo – the artist, the dreamer, the poet and painter. When, in 1940, Mussolini ordered the mobilisation of all males over the age of 14, Delmo was sent on an abortive attempt to capture Greece. Like all officers, he was supplied with a revolver. The attack was an unmitigated disaster, but the Italian Army had retreated in an orderly fashion, with very few casualties. On his return, Delmo's revolver was still in its case, unopened and unused.

SW19

IN THE immediate post-war years, many houses could be bought easily and cheaply if they had been damaged in the bombing. Such was the case of 16 Parkside Gardens in Wimbledon. A five-bedroom, two-bathroom house, it had survived the bombing around it, but the ceilings and windows had to be repaired, and were, by the Ministry of Defence. A snip at £3,000. One of the more recognisable of London's postal districts, SW19 is closely associated with the All-England Tennis Championships at Wimbledon. As kids, we used to turn down the volume knob on our radio so that we could listen to the actual applause from the courts half a mile away. What a thrill – but then we were very young, we four Mainwarings.

No sooner had we moved in, than my sister Sue was born in July 1946, and Mr and Mrs Mainwaring's brood was complete – John Weston, Michael James, Edward Stewart and now Susan Fraser. I only became Ed Stewart when I joined the 'pirates'. My passport, driving licence and even some of my pensions are in my real name, so anybody from MI5 reading this will know how to find me!

There was another brood in the house as well, fine healthy chickens, one of which was to become the centrepiece of our first post-war Christmas table a few months later. So, despite the continuing heavy rationing, we still had our home produce – and the food parcels from our relations in Canada. Ooooh, the excitement of the day they arrived, with their tins of pineapple chunks, mandarin oranges, peaches and … marshmallows! Mum had packed everything away in preparation for a Christmas lunch that would give us all a rare treat of roast chicken, Brussels sprouts and roast potatoes. I have to admit, though, I've never touched a Brussels sprout since – I couldn't stand the taste then, and don't now. This was to be followed by Mother's Crowning Glory – all the tinned fruit was made into a huge fruit salad with the marshmallows on top and served in a huge crystal bowl, which had been given as a wedding present nine years before. That, too, had survived the packing, the moving and the bombing.

With great ceremony, Mother's Crowning Glory approached the table, my father ready with the largest spoon we'd ever seen. Unfortunately, in the excitement, nobody had noticed two-year-old Michael crawling under the table and, as Mother's Crowning Glory floated majestically towards the table like a large battleship, youngest son Michael's smaller frigate suddenly hove into view alongside. Trying to take evasive action, Mother tripped, and the crystal bowl, complete with fruit salad and marshmallows, crashed to the floor, shattering into thousands of pieces. Hitler's Heinkels couldn't have done a better job, the tiny slivers of broken glass making it impossible to rescue the fruit. But if there was now one less chicken in the run (yes, I could count by then – I was a grown-up five!) at least it had given us all half a Christmas meal.

Food has always played an important part in my life. In those days, I ate to live, whereas, with Chiara and Genetta, I'd live to eat their wonderful cooking. Not that my mother was not a good cook – she just had fewer ingredients to work with. I dreaded going to friends' houses, in case their mothers, like mine, had bought pig's liver because it was cheaper than anything else. I would not put any sort of offal, Spam or swedes and turnips anywhere near my mouth, let alone in it. And that wasn't all I dreaded as a child – there was also the dentist.

Surprisingly, despite a comparatively sugar-free diet, visits to the dentist were frequent and were filled not with fun, but with fear and amalgam. Only once did I have an injection to ease the pain. Our dentist was a former Italian PoW named Genzerolli – or Gorgonzola as we called him – who, at the end of the Second World War, was given back his credentials and a licence to practise. Maybe he should have practised more. Instead of waiting for the injection to take effect, he extracted the tooth immediately. My screams were heard halfway up the street. In the waiting room my brother John turned a whiter shade of pale, and his pallor hadn't changed when he was eventually released from the chair.

In those days, there were no high-speed drills or pain-killing injections. You just clutched the arms of the chair until your knuckles went white, and the tears streamed down your cheeks and into your open mouth.

After my tooth-pulling experience with Mr Gorgonzola, we changed to another dentist in London, Mr Harvey, who was forever laughing, especially when it came to presenting the bill. The ever-climbing pencil marks on the door frame bore testimony to the fact that he would measure our heights every time we paid a visit. It was only when I got to 35 and 6ft 2in that we decided that we had been playing that game long enough.

If you had an injection in those days, you were considered a sissy, so, to take your mind off the pain of the drill, Mr Harvey would stick a piece of cotton wool on the cord so that you could watch it go round and round. How on earth could a piece of cotton wool stop you blubbing? We were invariably kept waiting for what seemed like hours for his call to his torture chamber. When, many years later, I was caught in traffic and was late for my appointment, he had a real go at me for keeping him waiting. I reminded him of the times he had kept *me* waiting in fear as a child, and walked out, leaving the pencil marks on the door frame as a memory for him.

And it wasn't only dentists who aroused my feelings of dread as a child – there was also Andy Sandham. Mr Sandham was a partner in the Alf Gover Indoor Cricket School in Wandsworth in South London. I never understood why he became a teacher. While Alf Gover was the friendliest and most encouraging of men, Andy Sandham was the complete opposite, and almost put me off playing the game for life. I dreaded the times in the nets having my cover drive 'coached' by Mr Sandham, while dear old Alf would content himself with, 'Good shot, old boy. You could play for England with that stroke!'

Years later, when I had begun to play in the celebrity matches, Alf would often be there, still bowling occasionally, and umpiring as well. I reminded him of the times when Andy Sandham's strict manner struck fear into his young pupils, and Alf admitted that he'd realised what a poor teacher he was. 'Not a well man, old boy, not a well man.' That's all he would say.

And from dentists and teachers, to one doctor who had a bearing on a small part of our childhood – our family doctor believed that learning to ride a horse might be a way of strengthening muscles and limbs, so we were all packed off to Major Walker to learn to ride. The major had been a teacher in the cavalry during the First World War, but from the way he shouted at us and his horses, he sounded more like a sergeant-major! We were terrified of him – except my sister Sue. He treated her with a compassion that brought out the very best in her riding talents, and she was cantering, galloping and jumping better than any of us. I have often wondered whether the marvellous cartoonist Thelwell ever based any of his characters on her. Sue has battled against some serious physical disabilities to lead as near a normal life as possible. She brings great joy to those around her.

The Major was a firm disciplinarian, not only with us, but with his horses as well. You would be trotting around the cinder track, when he would yell out 'About turn!' Before the second syllable of 'About' had escaped from his lips, the ponies – Rusty, Squibs, Vanity and Paintbox – had turned a full semi-circle, throwing you, if you hadn't been concentrating, straight to the ground. But this sort of discipline made us all decent riders, Sue particularly. We even owned a horse together, a beautiful Arab called Sultan.

Although I managed to master horseriding relatively proficiently, it was a different matter when it came to riding bikes. 'Steady, Ed!' shouted my brother John. If it hadn't been for his hand on the back of my saddle, I'd have been in the middle of Mum's prize roses. Suddenly, out of the drawing-room window came the sound of music ... exciting music. It was the 'Devil's Gallop', the theme music to *Dick Barton, Special Agent*, our favourite programme on the BBC. John let go of the saddle and ran off towards Dick Barton, while my bike and I continued in ever-decreasing circles towards the scented blooms.

With my knees still bleeding from the prickly stemmed roses, I tore back to the radio, just as Snowy, Jock and Dick were stopping the dastardly Russian spy, Ivor Nastikov, from blowing the world up. The 'Devil's Gallop' is one of my first musical memories, and hearing it today takes me back to those days when we were huddled around the radio, laughing and shouting at whatever was coming out of the speaker. *Children's Hour*, Uncle Mac, *Toytown* and Laaarry the Laaamb – that's who kept you company with your toast and Marmite, and a cup of warm milk. Then off to bed, snuggling down beneath the blanket, arguing as to who was going to drive which train that night. Typical boyhood dreams – we all wanted to be train drivers, and the only way was to let our imaginations take over. We hadn't ever been on a steam train by then, but had been to London on Southern Electric and the Tube. Invariably, John, being the eldest, had first choice. He drove the chuff-chuff, I had the lang-a-lang, and Mike, being the youngest, was a guard. Even at the age of four, Mike really got into his role, and began reciting his own poetry:

'When I grow up, I want to be a guard upon a train,
And when I wave my little flag, the train will be in vain.'

Mum and Dad thought Mike was to a future Poet Laureate. John and I just laughed and Mike burst into tears. I've got to say that all four children used to get quite emotional when we heard sad music; even our new baby sister Susan would cry at anything, even 'Baa Baa Black Sheep', especially when her three big brothers sang it to her.

When it comes to sport, I've always been like a kid in a sweet shop, though I would have to wait until several years after the war to understand what being a kid in a sweet shop really meant. I've never really grown up when it comes to meeting other celebrities, and I've been fortunate to have been blessed with two gifts which have enabled me to meet some really fascinating and exciting people – a God-given talent to communicate with my voice, and an ability to turn my hand to various sports. My brothers John and Mike were equally adept, and our earliest recollections have all been connected with sport.

Our mother had taken us to Bentall's in Kingston to do some shopping. John and I were running up the down escalator and Mike was playing with his marbles by the lifts; not the best way to endear yourself to the madding crowds. Gathering us up with a Stentorian 'Boys!' she dragged us off to the cafeteria, and sat us down in front of a slice of walnut cake and lemonade. What a treat.

Then Mum noticed a couple with a cuppa in the corner. She had recognised them as two famous sportsmen of their generation and, better still, two of brother John's heroes. One was Roy Bentley, centre-forward for Chelsea and England, and the other was the Surrey wicket-keeper, Arthur Macintyre. She found an old envelope in her handbag and told us to go over and ask for their autographs. As we nervously approached the table, another two men suddenly appeared. They looked like giants to us, and appeared to be identical. It was the famous Bedser twins, cricketing legends Alec and Eric. They sat down and, seeing these little pink faces and puny outstretched arms, knew exactly what to do. 'Are you cricketers, lads?'

'Oh, yes, sir ... we play in the back garden, and against the wall in the road!'

'And,' said John, getting braver by the second, 'I've seen you on the television.'

It was true. We had a friend called Billy Trinder, whose father was somebody Big in the City, and who could afford one of these boxes with fuzzy pictures and what seemed to us blizzards of snow every so often. Despite the dodgy reception on those early sets, and the tendency for the picture to roll up or down the screen, until you fiddled with the vertical hold, we had still seen Alec Bedser bowling, and here he was sitting next to us in the café at Bentalls.

The men couldn't have been more gracious to we three nippers and, as we were leaving, Roy Bentley said to John, 'Do you play football, son?'

'Yes, sir,' said John.

I don't think Mr Bentley had been called 'sir' before, and a broad grin appeared on his face as he asked, 'Where's that then?'

'Over by the bushes, sir!'

The four men roared with laughter, and gave us the rest of their cakes. 'That's a good answer, son,' replied Roy, and looking over at my mother said, 'Why don't you come to Stamford Bridge next Saturday, and watch us play Everton?' He handed my mother two player's tickets, and hoped we enjoyed the match.

So began my lifelong love affair with Everton FC, which gets stronger as the years go by. That Saturday in September 1948 saw a score which a psychologist might be able to identify as the source of one of my character traits. Everton lost 6–0 and I felt sorry for them! And, as my brother John says, I have been ever since. But the very name in print still seems to hypnotise me – *Everton*. If they lose, it almost ruins my weekend; when they win, life seems to take on a new meaning. This might seem sad to those not afflicted in this way, but I'm sure many of you will relate to those feelings, wherever your allegiances lie!

My father then had to explain to me where Everton was, how Dixie Dean, before the War, had become the greatest centre-forward, and why they were called the Toffees. Having chosen our English teams, we two brothers then decided we wanted to support a Scottish team as well. John chose Dumbarton – it was the nearest he could get to Dick Barton, his hero of the airwaves. I went for Queen of the South. I liked the name, and it was also the first quiz question to which I knew the answer, and it was a sure-fire way of winning a wager. I bet my friend Ian Whitcomb his pudding at school that he couldn't tell me Queen of the South's home town. He couldn't, and – joy of joys – I won his jelly. He won the next time he asked some unsuspecting fool the same question. And what is Queen of the South's home town? Dumfries. In the words of Michael Caine: 'Not many people know that!'

Ian Whitcomb and I shared a common affliction, stuttering, which could, in my case, have been as a result of a childhood accident. Both Ian and I somewhat ironically went on to make careers out of using our voices. Ian later went to Los Angeles to become a record producer. His most noticeable claim to fame was putting Mae West in a recording studio to belt out 'Great Balls of Fire'. I don't suppose she needed much persuasion!

Although we had a decent-sized garden, we were forever playing in the road. Mike was in goal, and John and I were scoring at random. Mike's knees were always bleeding from falling on the tarmac trying to save our thunderbolt shots. He was only five. Once again, we heard the resounding cry of 'Boys! To the bathroom … IMMEDIATELY!' We went running inside and up to the bathroom, where Mother had already rolled up her sleeves, ready to dispense the necessary punishment. She always told us that she closed the windows so that the neighbours wouldn't hear the screams!

We all stood there shaking, and Mike started blubbing – he always was the most sensitive. Mum tapped me on the hand, and gave John a sharp smack on the bottom. If mothers do that today, there's every risk of getting arrested, but that smack worked for us and we never played in the road again.

Thank goodness we had parents who were themselves very sports-minded. Dad had played ice hockey in Newfoundland to quite a high standard and, when he moved to England, joined a prominent team called The Exiles. A keen skier and toboggannist, he had conquered the Cresta Run on several occasions. A very quick sprinter, he was given his athletics Blue at Oxford. Mum had also shone at sports, and had been Captain of lacrosse at school.

Little did I know then that sport was to play a major part in the enjoyment of my life and career, although I've never been tempted to take up any sport professionally. Apart from a bash on the head at a cricket match at Blenheim (thank you, Fred Rumsey!), I've not had to endure the headaches of being a full-time sportsman. Missing a putt to pay for lunch is a bit less painful than missing one for £10,000!

Along with our love of physical activity and competition, we were brought up in a house which seemed filled with music, veering between Semprini's 'Mediterranean Concerto', the 'Warsaw Concerto' and 'Sparky's Magic Piano'. Mum would listen to Hutch, Fats Waller, Fred Astaire, Crosby and Sinatra. Dad, who had played the bugle in the school band, would listen to Glenn Miller and Harry James, and try and kid us that he could whizz through the 'Flight of the Bumble Bee' just as Harry James had. Dad was a character, though, and used to tell us he was the 'Greatest Man in Wimbledon'. Years later, on his seventieth birthday, I played 'Moonlight Serenade' for him and told the listeners that story about his telling us that he was the 'Greatest Man in Wimbledon', and that when I asked around, nobody had ever heard of him! He took it in good heart as he always did, but in actual fact he was highly respected in SW19. Years later, as the churchwarden of St Mary's, he had to appease a parishioner who thought it disgraceful that the churchwarden had a son who was a pirate disc jockey! While I was working for Radio London, Dad would often come back from the Sunday service at St Mary's to find that his house had been invaded by sundry DJs and musicians whom I'd invited back for a jam session on my odd Sunday ashore.

If laughter is the best medicine, then you hardly needed the NHS in my childhood days. With *Workers' Playtime*, *Variety Bandbox*, *Take It from Here*, *Much Binding in the Marsh*, the *Al Read Show* and *Ray's a Laugh*, your life really was made happier by the sound of laughter from the Light Programme. If today there are Gold Channels for TV comedy, why on earth isn't there one for radio comedy? Radio 7 has some output, but that's on digital radio, and how many of us have that? Radio 2 has some comedy slots, but not enough to my mind.

We were privileged to have listened to radio in those earlier days and nights, though we might not have realised it at the time.

Out of the multitude of radio stations today, there are two which I listen to the most – Radio 2 and Classic FM. But when I was a kid, there was the Light Programme, the Home Service, the Third Programme – or nothing, except your gramophone. We loved our seventy-eights, but they went round and round so fast, you had to keep turning them over and starting them again! We had quite a pile – 'Teddy Bear's Picnic' and 'Hush, Hush, Hush, Here Comes the Bogeyman' on the B-side. We filthy-minded kids liked that one better because they were singing about 'bogeys'. And I was living proof of the truth of the old joke: What's the difference between bogeys and Brussels sprouts? You can't get your kids to eat Brussels sprouts!

We also had a bit of class, too, with Charles Trenet's 'La Mer', Ethel Smith's 'Tico–tico', Jimmy Durante's 'Lost Chord' and Fats Waller with my mum's favourite, 'When Somebody Thinks You're Wonderful'.

I was preparing myself for a life in radio already by crawling behind the wireless and pretending to be an announcer. Just like Terry Scott in 'My Brother', nobody knew what I was talking about, but they had a pretty good idea. Certain catchphrases and famous lines still reverberate from those days: Uncle Mac saying 'Goodnight, children, everywhere ...' and Bill Kerr, the Australian comedian, starting his act with 'I'm only here for four minutes'! Every time he appeared on *Workers' Playtime*, he would say those same words, 'I'm only here for four minutes,' and I used to think, 'Where does he go for the rest of the time?'

When I started wearing glasses, one of Max Wall's lines made us all laugh: 'I wouldn't say I was short-sighted but, on a clear day, I can see my specs!' And then there was Al Read, the comedian who was so much loved in our house that sometimes we would sneak away from Sunday service to get back home in time for his programme. 'You'll be lucky ... I said, you'll be lucky!' we laughed as we pedalled furiously to reach the house. Then there was good old Tony Hancock, and especially *A Sunday Afternoon at Home*. And who can forget Kenneth Williams as the boring next-door neighbour, dropping in on Hancock, Sid James and Hattie Jacques to practise his animal impersonations? When, six hours later, everybody has had enough, Kenneth Williams decides it's time for him to go. 'Oh, so soon?' Hancock dryly exclaims. Anybody who has been to our house always gets the same reaction when they get up to leave – 'Oh, so soon?'

Another of my heroes when I was growing up was Jack Benny, the famous American comedian. My father loved him and, when he appeared on the radio, and later on TV, he would always encourage us to appreciate Jack Benny's humour. At first, we would laugh at his attempts at playing the violin but, as I grew older, Jack's way with money and not spending it made me howl. His act was masterful in its timing, but I might have been too young to have appreciated that. It was the jokes about his apparent meanness that would make me laugh. As I grew older, I cultivated this, and have become a butt of many a joke from my peers. Jimmy used to tell me I had an impediment in my reach! Jack Benny, whose act was partly based on being less than generous with his money, once famously joked that it had cost him a fortune being mean.

* * *

The war had been over for a couple of years as the army ambulance crawled its way along Parkside next to that most beautiful stretch of countryside south of the River Thames, Wimbledon Common.

'That bloke's a bit noisy in the back, Sarge,' said the driver.

The sergeant and his driver were taking a young officer from the Atkinson Morley in Wimbledon to another hospital in Hertfordshire, who would take over the care of this shell-shocked soldier. There were still many in this sad condition, despite the amount of time since the last significant action of the war.

'Take it easy, Corporal,' said the sergeant, 'there seems to have been an accident ahead.' Indeed, there had been. A couple of people were looking down at a small body lying in the middle of the road. It was me. My face was turned blankly to the sky, as the drivers and their passengers pressed their faces against the windows to have a better look. Nobody stopped, so thank God for that army ambulance which did, or little Edward might not have survived to tell his tale.

It was a winter morning in 1947, and my brother John and I had been on our way to school at Glengyle in Putney. No cars or school buses then – just the good old 93 double-decker. Every day was a scramble to see who could get to the top deck first and grab the window seat. The half-hour journey was an adventure in itself. 'Windmill!' shouted the conductor, as we reached the next stop, and we would gaze out at the woods and heath and the distant outline of the old windmill. It only had half a sail left from the bomb that had fallen close by. The next stop sounded like 'Arl-arl' – it wasn't until I could learn to read that I could understand what the conductor had been saying. Behind the bus stop there was a posh block of flats called Albemarle. That conductor needed elocution lessons! Next stop was Tibbett's Corner. Tibbett was a highwayman who used to hide behind two large oak trees, to rob and pillage his unfortunate victims. Those trees are gone now and the whole area holds a huge roundabout and underpass for the A3. Two stops later, Putney Hill, and off we got for the daily grind at Glengyle School.

The headmaster at the time was Mr Wallace. My brother John had been given a picture book for his birthday called *The Adventures of Wallace the Worm* and that very day he had excelled himself with a good mark for his arithmetic test. As Mr

Wallace handed him back his paper, he said, 'Well done, John!' who replied, quite innocently, 'Thank you, Wallace the Worm.' The other boys sniggered at this unexpected humour, and then froze in silence as the Worm stopped in his tracks. 'What did you say, John?'

'I said that I had a worm in my pocket, sir!'

My brother is not telling the truth, I thought, when suddenly John put his hand in his blazer pocket and produced a worm he had found in the garden.

'Ooohs,' 'Aaaahs', 'Squirmy!' 'Disgusting!' and even a 'Lovely!' littered the classroom conversation, and Mr Wallace laughed resignedly at his new school nickname – Wallace the Worm! That was the first time that I realised teachers had to have a sense of humour. I stuck close to my brother after that.

At lunch, everything was written on a blackboard, so John used to read to me what was on the menu. Menu? You ate what was put in front of you, or lumped it. On the blackboard that day were mince and mashed potato, and for sweets ... John stopped. 'We're going to get sweets!'

Stupid boy – sweets were still rationed. What he hadn't seen was 'Sweets – tapioca or jelly'! Apart from the marshmallows in the food parcels from Canada, we were happy to get a gobstopper a week. I settled for the jelly, by the way.

But now a term had passed since my first day at school, and we were into a daily routine of cereal, a boiled egg and soldiers, and whatever they dished up at school.

On that fateful morning, as the ambulance was still crawling along Parkside, I had been a bit slower than usual, having dropped a birthday present off to my first-ever girlfriend, Fiona, our doctor's daughter. She was six and I was seven. By the time I caught John up, he had already crossed the road and was waving at me to hurry – the bus was about to go. I didn't see the car that had turned out of the side road into Parkside. The protruding door handle, (they weren't fixed into the doors then) hit me on the right temple, and I was out for the count – a very long count; 48 hours to be exact. The army ambulance then stopped, and because the poor officer in the back was moving about and shouting so much, they strapped him into his strait-jacket while they laid me gently on the floor. The driver then tore back to the hospital he had left just ten minutes earlier. In the meantime, a policeman had rung the doorbell of our house in Parkside Gardens, just a few hundred yards from where the accident had happened, and asked my mother whether the bloodstained blazer in his arms belonged to her son, Mainwaring E?

When the officer had picked my mother up from the floor (there must have been a better way of bringing news like that), she called my father, who, for the first and only time in his career, took time off work. As for me, I stayed in hospital for four weeks with a fractured skull, had lots of ice cream and jelly in the children's ward, and felt like I was on holiday! But at least I had survived ... again.

In some ways, having had that crack on the head has given me a wonderful excuse for things not quite going according to plan when I've tried my hardest to make sure they do. My most embarrassing memory loss was when, as a schoolboy, I went to summer camp with the combined cadet force to Thetford. Being part of the advance party, we travelled via Tube and train to arrive a day ahead of the main party to prepare the site. As we marched proudly down the platform, I was aware of people staring at us and wondering to themselves, 'I hope we're not going to be defended by that rabble!'

On arrival at camp, I packed my battle dress away somewhere really safe, thinking that it would be out of the way, and I'd just unpack it when I needed it. By the time the Sunday parade came around, I was in a flat panic – I had lost my uniform, which we had all been instructed to wear. Our Sergeant, Sam Tero, ordered me to stand to attention throughout the parade as punishment, and there I was, in my fatigues, feeling slightly sorry for myself, and starting to wilt in the sunshine ... when I remembered where I had put the uniform. I slipped away, ran back to my bunk, and opened up my palliasse (a straw mattress), and there was my beautifully creased best uniform. Unfortunately, it was creased in all the wrong places. I quickly undressed and scrambled into the heavy khaki dress suit, just before the rest of the platoon returned from the parade. I was still picking off the pieces of straw when Regimental Sergeant Major Samuel Tero returned to the billet with his group of sweaty, grumbling cadets.

'Good news, sir.'

'Don't call me sir ... I am not an officer!' he shouted. He took one look at me, all straw and creases, and I thought he was going to cry. He just turned his eyes towards the heavens and, surprising all of us with his knowledge of poetry, whispered, 'Why should England tremble when made of men like these?'

3

THE HAPPIEST DAYS
OF MY LIFE

THE TITLE of the first film I remember seeing was *The Happiest Days of Your Life*. The antics of Alistair Sim, Margaret Rutherford and Joyce Grenfell still make me fall about.

How lucky I was to have had such a good education. My strengths were encouraged and they built the foundation for a happy life and career. Eagle House and St Edward's, Oxford, were fee-paying schools, and how indebted to our parents we were for the enormous sacrifices they made to send us there. The most difficult period for most of us was the teenage years when we lost the innocence of childhood and started to confront the realities of growing up. Academically, I was quite gifted, though a bit idle. But do we insist too rigidly on academic qualifications? I have never needed them to get a job, but the qualities of honesty and good manners were instilled into me, and I hope they have remained to this day.

Eagle House – homework tonight: write an essay of 100 words on the subject 'Is Tipping Necessary?'

I stared at the paper without fear – this was a subject on which

I had definite views, and at 11 years old I was going to make those views felt to Mr Huxtable, our English teacher. Of course tipping was necessary. If we didn't have tipsters, how could we know which horses to back? I wrote and wrote extolling the virtues of horse racing, point-to-points, the advice of Gulli Gulli and the Scout, my favourite tipsters, and the excitement of watching the horses sweep by at Tattenham Corner on the Epsom Downs. Always being one for an outsider, my father once let me put sixpence of my pocket money as part of his bet on the Pink Horse – it came in third at 66–1, and the Scout had tipped it as a good each-way bet. So, Mr Huxtable, that is why tipping is necessary.

My essay was returned the next day, with two marks for putting my name on the paper, but a note from Mr Huxtable saying, 'In this case, the word "tipping" meant leaving those few coins on the saucer for the waiter after a meal, and not about racehorses. But,' added Mr Huxtable as he handed my essay back, 'it was a jolly good effort on the wrong subject. By the way,' he added, with a twinkle in his eye, 'you should have followed the tip – I was given the winner!'

Eagle House was a wonderful prep school, with two masters who spotted and nurtured the two talents that were to form the basis of my life and career – sport and music. Their names were William Bean and John Watson. The BBC used to produce a series of programmes called *Adventures in Music*, telling the stories of the lives of the great composers like Mozart, Bach, Beethoven and Tchaikovsky. It was transfixing to listen to the stories of Beethoven's deafness, and how he was able to write some of his 'Pastoral Symphony' from the vibrations he felt from a thunderstorm; to wonder whether Tchaikovsky was mad or brave to drink water contaminated with cholera; and then to marvel at how a boy of one's own age could write music as Mozart had. I took up the piano, but my own efforts at 'Für Elise' and 'The Peasants' Frolic' would have given Sparky and his magic piano nightmares. Aaaah, Sparky ... I always wished Uncle Mac would play 'Sparky's Magic Piano' every week, little knowing that 20 years later I would be playing him on *Junior Choice* myself.

Paul Wootton was the headmaster of Eagle House. Although a strict disciplinarian, he had a sense of humour that offset the initial loneliness of the boarding school. We were to call him Mr Paul and his wife Mrs Paul – that was much less frightening to a new boy than Sir or Madam. From your first term, the day after you arrived, you had to write home to tell your anxious parents that you were fit and well, and that you weren't blubbing any more. One boy, Featherstonehaugh, pronounced 'Fanshaw', presented his letter to Mr Paul. On it he had written, 'Dear Mummy and Daddy, I'm all right, but I've got a boil on my neck, Love from Giles.'

'That's not good enough, Featherstonehaugh,' Mr Paul said. 'Your parents will want to read a little more than that.'

We went back to dipping our nibs in the Quink and, after an eternity, we saw Featherstonehaugh raise his hand and call out, 'Finished, sir.'

'All right, Featherstonehaugh, would you like to read your letter home to the rest of the class?'

He obliged immediately. 'Dear Mummy and Daddy, I'm all right but I've got a boil on my neck, Love from Giles. P.S. It's just burst.'

All three Mainwarings (Major, Minor and Minim) went to Eagle House. John, as I have hinted, was somewhat limited academically but was a good sportsman and Captain of boxing – nobody messed with him. I was keen on sport and music – 'Could do better if he tried' was the usual report. Then there was Michael. He was the cleverest by far, a writer, pianist and excellent sportsman – and Head Boy! His all-round qualities were recognised so early in his life, and naturally raised expectations for his future way above those of mine or John's.

Perhaps one reason I was struggling a bit in the classroom in my early teens was because I was finding it increasingly difficult to focus on my work – literally. I remember Mr Lough, my maths teacher, asking me what he had written on the blackboard. 'What blackboard, sir?' I asked. The rest of the class burst out laughing, and it was then I found out two things about myself: one, I was short-sighted; and two, I, intentionally or otherwise, could make other people laugh.

My short-sightedness didn't do much for my street cred. I was standing in Ely's, a traditional department store in Wimbledon, while my mother was shopping. Two youths passed by, one nudged the other and muttered, 'Look – a moron!' I was wearing my new basic National Health glasses, like the ones worn by Prime Minister Clement Attlee. They were less than impressive, I could tell.

An endearing quality in anybody is a sense of humour; without one life is dull, and with one you can see the funny side of anything. This even went as far as cold showers in the morning, especially when you were laughing at each other's willies – not that they could get any smaller in the cold. You'd stand in line, and when the master clapped his hands, it was your turn for ten seconds of purgatory.

In the summer, it was a length of the outdoor pool to wake you up. But they were pretty fair with you – outdoor swimming only began when the temperature had reached 60°F, otherwise it was back in the showers which were ten degrees cooler.

At the Haven Hotel's outdoor pool in Sandbanks where I swim these days, the pool is never less than 80°F, otherwise nobody will go in. Having said that, there is a group of madmen who swim in the sea every day, summer and winter. So those cold showers did work for some!

Thankfully, life at Eagle House was fun, but Spartan. Food rationing was still in place, which has meant that various meals have lingered long in the digestive memory. Now, having being married to a brilliant and inventive cook, it makes me wonder how the chefs of the early 1950s managed to produce wholesome school meals at all. Wholesome? Spam or Marmite fritters, cod in thick batter, stew (a quarter meat, and three-quarters fat and gristle) and tapioca (or 'frog spawn' as we called it). Then, twice a week, two ounces of sweets and chocolate. Unfortunately for us, food rationing didn't end until 1954.

How we can refer to them as 'the good old days' escapes me! But 'the good old days' meant that children from certain backgrounds were sent away from home to spend their formative years apart from their parents and, under the guidance of people who, initially, were perfect strangers. It was the accepted way to be educated and very few parents gave it a second thought. We were lucky at Eagle House, and later at St Edward's, that we had headmasters who were enlightened, encouraging and who set down standards of discipline that we respected.

My original Mr Bean was not Rowan Atkinson's creation, but our music master at Eagle House. William Desmond Bean nurtured anybody who had a musical inclination, and it was thanks to him that I have enjoyed a lifetime's appreciation of having a musical ear. Our French master, John Watson, who was able to instil in us the semblance of a good French accent, was a fine pianist, playing mostly by ear. His musical talent went even further. He wrote 'Looking High, High, High', which became the British entry for the Eurovision Song Contest in 1960. Teddy Johnson's brother, Bryan, recorded it and, although it only came second that year, John Watson's composition made the UK Top 20, not bad for a French teacher at an English prep school!

It's fascinating what we remember as we get older … and what we don't, as well. It's a struggle to remember what I'm doing from one day to the next, but I can distinctly remember my old headmaster at Eagle House telling me what the shortest-ever telegram was in Latin. A university don sent his friend a telegram asking him whether he could swim. The Latin word he used was '*Nare?*' meaning 'to swim', in this case 'Do you swim?' The answer came back: '*No*' – which meant either 'I swim', or 'No, I don't!' Why can't I memorise the important things, like what the golf professional taught me in my last lesson? Instead, I can tell you who the winning jockey was in the 1953 Derby, or who the opening bowlers were for the West Indies in 1950. Useful, eh?

I also loved my four years at St Edward's, where I could indulge my passion for music and sport. My third would have been girls, but there were none there! So it was boys, or nothing. I made do with nothing.

Eventually, the dreaded O-levels reared their ugly heads, and we had to apply ourselves a little more seriously to our academic studies. John and I took our O-levels in the same summer term of 1957. As was the custom then, at the end of the exams, you filled in a postcard with a list of the subjects you had taken, from top to bottom, so that the examiner could put a 'pass' or 'fail' against each one. Then you would address the card to yourself – rather like digging your own grave, I suppose. And you had to put a stamp on it as well, which then was 2d – the equivalent of 1p today. Then came the summer holidays, and you forgot all about exams, and went off to enjoy the long break. As the second week in August approached, you remembered two really important events – the start of the football season and O-level results day, 8 August.

I lay in bed waiting for the mail to plop through the letterbox. The postman was later than usual, his mailbag swollen by those extra postcards of doom and delight, so I quickly got dressed and went down to the end of the drive to intercept him. I was sure the bundle would include the dreaded postcards. I was right. As my eyes ran down the list, I felt my blood grow cold. Being considered fairly bright, I was expected to pass all eight exams. Brother John would have been happy with passing half of that!

I woke John, suggesting we run down our lists one after the other, and that John, being the elder, should read first. 'Fail … fail … fail …' he started, and his voice became fainter as he read out a further five fails. 'Your turn, Ed,' he whispered dejectedly, as I began with a couple of passes; then my voice fell as I read out four fails, and then rose an octave with two final passes.

I suppose I shouldn't have been surprised, really. My energies had gone into cricket, hockey, rugby, football, squash, tennis, golf, swimming and singing. I hadn't had much energy or enthusiasm for Elementary Maths, English Literature, Physics and Biology – they were my fails. My passes were French, Spanish, English Language and History. So, at least I had four O-levels. Dad was not too pleased, and we had to stay at home that day and not go to the American tennis tournament at the home of John's current girlfriend. He was gutted, and so was I – she had a pretty sister too. She was, he assured me, the 'real thing' – like all the others. What a shame for John – Ann's mother said he had such a wonderful service … and her daughter didn't complain either!

But it's simply a fact of human nature that we'll put more effort into what we enjoy, and are good at. I've always loved singing, and spent all of my years at school in the choir. St Edwards is Church of England, but in my time it was what was termed 'High Church'. Three services on a Sunday, Holy Communion on every saint's day and long sermons turned an impressionable teenager into a cynic. Nothing has changed my views since, so when I go to church these days, it's usually for weddings, funerals and carol services at Christmas, and I'm more interested in the notes sung than the words spoken.

The CCF, or the Combined Cadet Force, was another form of discipline from which there was no escape, unless you had flat feet. Being a conscientious objector had no effect, otherwise there would have been no 'corps', as we called it. A master plan to get out of square-bashing and cleaning equipment worked for me, though – I joined the military band.

By this time, the musical part of my career was beginning to take shape. Noting there was no double bass in the school orchestra, and wanting to take it up, the school found a teacher in Oxford, a Mr Hall, who started me off with great enthusiasm. But you don't lug a large double bass around a parade ground, so the music master, Ted Manning, suggested the euphonium as a simpler way of joining the band. Another teacher was found, and soon, instead of marching to the music, I was playing it.

It was just as well I did give up on the soldier's life; the summer before the band was reformed, the CCF was sent to Summer Camp at Thetford in Norfolk, together with about 5,000 other cadets and their regular instructors. I was sent as part of the advance guard, which meant travelling to London by train, Tube and then train again from Liverpool Street to Thetford. We were sitting on our rucksacks and holdalls, waiting for the train to pull in, when along the platform came a very important-looking officer in full regalia, accompanied by a large retinue of other soldiers. We just sat there watching him walk past, when he suddenly barked out, 'CAAA-DETS … ATTENTION!'

We jumped up, terrified, as he tore us off a strip for lounging about in public. He then closed with the words, 'You always salute an officer!'

We were too stunned to realise that it was Field Marshal Montgomery, until our accompanying RSM pointed it out to us. He also reminded us that the Field Marshal was coming to the prize-giving at St Edward's the following summer, and hoped we would be better disciplined than we were that afternoon. As it was, Monty did attend, and began his speech by saying how nice it was 'to be here at St Mary's'. We wouldn't have put it past him to have remembered seeing us in London, and then decided to get his own back by calling us the name of a girls' school!

St Edward's had a strong school orchestra, and it wasn't long before I was lugging the double bass to and from rehearsals for the school concert in the summer of 1958. The main piece chosen to play before an adoring audience of parents and friends was Schubert's 'Unfinished Symphony', which has a long and moving introduction featuring the cellos and double basses. There were already two cellists – all they needed now was a bassist, and that soloist was going to be me! I practised hard, but it wasn't easy. There were other temptations for me to resist at the time – skiffle, jazz and rock 'n' roll!

Here's a Top Ten from my years as a teenager at school:

1. **'Rock Island Line' – Lonnie Donegan**
   My introduction to skiffle and the joy of playing the double bass in a band. I never tried a tea chest, though it was considered more trendy.
2. **'Rock Around the Clock' – Bill Haley**
   Everybody's anthem but, looking at the photos, the Comets were hardly pin-ups or heart-throbs. But Bill Haley started it all for most of us.
3. **'Tutti Frutti' – Little Richard**
   The most outrageous of them all to me. Forty years later I saw him at Wembley and he hadn't changed a bit.
4. **'It's Now or Never' – Elvis Presley**
   It's difficult to choose a favourite because all of his early stuff was brilliant. I was working at Keith Prowse Records in Kensington at the time, and we were told to sell only this record on the Saturday it was released in December 1960. It went straight to Number One. People were queuing down the road and, in three hours, we sold

nearly 500 copies at 6s 3d each, about 30p in today's money.

5. **'Tammy' – Debbie Reynolds**

   What went on in the back row of the movies that evening was nobody's business. The others were very jealous when I told them.

6. **'Mack the Knife' – Bobby Darin**

   He was like a chameleon, changing effortlessly from 'Splish, Splash!', 'Eighteen Yellow Roses' and 'Dream Lover' to his finest hour, 'Mack the Knife'. A sad loss at the age of 37.

7. **'Only You' – The Platters**

   My favourite slow-dancing record of the time, especially when a girl asked me why I had a torch in my pocket. I was so embarrassed, I left the dance floor!

8. **'On the Street Where You Live' – Vic Damone**

   The most successful of the My Fair Lady songs. I remember it was great snob value to have a copy of the original Broadcast cast recording of the show. It wasn't allowed to be released in the UK until the show itself was on the London stage. A friend of ours brought a copy over from New York, and we had a special party at home to play it.

9. **'Ying Tong Song' – The Goons**

   Their radio programmes were a must, and we all tried to imitate their voices. This record was made when many of us were growing up. Or were we? The Goons certainly hadn't started to!

10. **'Little Darling' – The Diamonds**

    Just a great record, with everybody wanting to join in on the falsetto bits and then aping the deep, deep voice in the middle.

4

GO EAST,
YOUNG MAN

'RADIO WAVE' – a technical definition: 'Electromagnetic wave by a transmitter. The *Light Programme* is on 1,500 metres, being the length of that wave.' My definition to a BBC personnel officer in 1960 differed slightly: 'It sort of bounces, from the atmosphere back to the earth's surface.'

'How?'

'I've no idea.'

There was a pause and an audible sigh ... from the personnel man. 'Thank you, Mr Mainwaring. You don't seem to have the sort of technical knowledge required to become an ASM [Assistant Studio Manager]. We have no openings for presenters or newsreaders at the moment, so I'm sorry, there's nothing I can offer you. By the way, you didn't write on your application form which university you attended.'

'I didn't go to university.'

'Oh.' He seemed to be losing interest. 'You have to have a bit more experience to join the BBC.'

'Where can I find that experience then?'

'You'll have to go abroad.'

So I did, but not intentionally as a broadcaster, but as a bass player in a band. Though what I thought would be for three months at the most turned into nearly four years. But I didn't complain – I was about to experience life in 'The World of Suzy Wong'.

On leaving school, I had gone to work with Keith Prowse Records. I was still playing the double bass and, on the spur of the moment, I agreed to join a band in Hong Kong. The year was 1961, the Berlin Wall was being built and JFK was President of the USA. Two years later, I was reading the news about his assassination on Hong Kong Radio.

Hong Kong – where I became a man, and spent my 21st birthday in the very hotel where Richard Mason had written *The World of Suzie Wong*. It was where I established my radio career, interviewing diverse characters ranging from the Indonesian Foreign Minister Subandrio to Danny Kaye, Ella Fitzgerald and the Beatles. But all of that lay ahead of me. For the time being, it seemed as though I had limitless possibilities, as I saw the tongue of land that was Kai Tak Airport rushing towards me. This was it – the World of Suzie Wong for real.

I'd seen the show on stage in London and now I would be entering that world, full of lascivious and sensuous adventure, and me still a virgin! Public school was not the place to experience awakening sexual feelings unless you enjoyed the attentions of another boy, which I did once much to my pleasant surprise and subsequent guilt. So my exploration of any sexual feelings was limited to masturbation (you met a nicer class of person), snogging, or fondling girls' breasts. Below the navel was out of bounds! Lynn, Jane, Muriel and Françoise, are you blushing now at the memory of what went on in the back row of the movies? There was definitely 'no first base' for Edward, so it was a timid but excited 20-year-old who landed in Hong

Kong in July 1961. What on earth would I find there ... and how long would it be before I became a *man*?

It was down to one of my friends, Richard, who was doing his national service that I was here at all. He had urged me to come out and sample the delights of the Orient, adding, 'About the bass ... I really would advise you to bring it with you. There is only a hire system here, which is very expensive. All the clothes you need are the ones you travel in – a really good suit out here will only cost, at the most, £8. The joke is that the Chinese tailors can have it ready for you in 24 hours!'

The plane skimmed the dirty, huddled buildings of old Kowloon and the garish high-rise blocks of the New Territories, before pulling up with what seemed like inches to spare from the end of the runway. Kai Tak might have been an immense feat of airport design and engineering, but, boy, was it scary! My BOAC Sky Coach (British Airways had not been named yet) had left Heathrow on Monday night and, after stopping off at Rome, Bahrain and Kuala Lumpur, had arrived in Hong Kong around lunchtime on Wednesday. Obviously, no one was in a hurry to get there.

Sky Coach was a service that BOAC had devised for British ex-pats and their children. As my brother John was working for Thomas Cook then, he was able to book me on for a £149 single fare. My father paid for this as a way of saying 'good luck' and presumed that I had a return ticket written into the contract. Little did he know that there was no contract and no return ticket. Being desperate to go, I had made it all up. How naïve of me. It would be another four years before I was to return home with just ten *pfennig* in my pocket and £100 in the bank. But all I had with me as I entered this new land of opportunity was my double bass on my shoulder and a little wicker case of underpants, hankies and a spare pair of cavalry twills (I knew what to wear in the tropics). I had arrived and was ready to start work as a professional musician.

I looked for a familiar face in the crowd waiting in the Arrivals hall, and realised at once this would be fairly simple as 99 per cent of the faces peering at me from behind the barrier were oriental. The Chinese say that all Westerners have big noses and large ears. My friend Richard went along with that philosophy, and told me that even if he had never met me, he would have recognised me from the Chinese way of spotting a foreigner. Charming!

That day, the temperature was in the high 90s and the relative humidity was 95 per cent. I'd never heard the expression 'relative humidity' before, but it sure made me sweat! Whatever it was, I was steaming in it, and my cavalry twills were making me itch.

As I strode through the airport, my double bass on my shoulder, I spied Richard, and standing next to him was someone who looked like Buddy Holly and who turned out to be the pianist in our trio. His name was Tony, and where he is today I know not, but he was wasted in the Army doing his National Service. Many young men of the day would argue that their lives were disrupted by the two years they had to spend in the armed forces. Today, those same people would probably agree with reinstating National Service as an antidote to the boredom and frustration of today's youth, which has brought about so much crime, violence and unhappiness for society generally.

The first words I learnt in Cantonese, the main language of Hong Kong, were not 'I love you, I want to sleep with you', or 'How much?' No, in true male fashion, in next to no time I could ask for a Tiger beer (*lo-fu bay-jow*) or a plate of chow mein (*a play-of-chow-mein*). In fact, before you could say 'fried rice', I was enjoying my first Tiger beer. It was superb. As I ran my finger up and down the drops of condensation on the outside of the bottle, I thought of John Mills and his expression of pure delight when he had reached that bar in Alexandria in the movie *Ice Cold in Alex*. Mind you, he had spent weeks crossing the Sahara in a rusty old ambulance, while I'd only spent a few hours in a steel

tube crossing a couple of continents. But the result was the same
– a sublime quenching of a deep thirst. By the time we had left the
bar, I could order a beer in phonetic Chinese. That way, you were
served much quicker.

After the beer, we hailed a taxi to take us to the club where we
would be playing. We somehow squeezed ourselves in, with the
neck of the bass on my shoulder and the other two squashed
behind the rest of it in the back. The driver was none too pleased
– he was only licensed to carry three people and he classified the
bass as an extra body!

'So what time are we on?' I started, barely able to turn my head
because of my cramped position. There was a pause. 'Where's the
club and how far have we got to travel like this?' I continued. By
now, the sweat was pouring off me so much that if I had peed
myself nobody would have noticed.

'Sorry, Eddie, the gig's been cancelled.'

'What?' I cried.

'We've been posted to Aden. We could leave at any time, so the
club owner has cancelled the contract.'

I was lost for words, a dull panic enveloping me. There might
have been a tropical heatwave outside, but inside I was turning
very, very cold. Twelve thousand miles in a Sky Coach for this! I
was numb.

'So where are we going now?'

'To the YMCA in Kowloon. You can spend a couple of nights
there, and then you can move into Mai-lei's place.'

'Who is Mai-lei?'

'Tony's girlfriend.'

Things were looking up, I thought. A nice flat and a wardrobe
full of *cheongsams*.

'As long as you teach her children to speak English, you won't
have to pay any rent. She's a bar girl, though, and you might have
to put up with a few nocturnal comings and goings!'

With a bit of luck, I thought.

The journey from the airport to Kowloon was an education in itself. There were more people in one street than I had seen in an entire rush hour in the West End of London. This was Nathan Road, built by the then Governor in the 1930s. It was the size of a dual carriageway, the first in Asia, and had been jokingly called Nathan's Folly. But in 1961, this was the hub of life in Kowloon. At the northern end of it was the Star Ferry, and the culmination of that journey was Hong Kong Island itself. This was the island that gave the colony its name, and was the most spectacular and exciting place I'd ever seen – the bustling road and the climbing ladder streets, the stalls and tables where you could order anything from snake and dog to fried rice and noodles to be cooked before your very eyes. Then there were the girls, unbelievably exotic or unexpectedly plain, but many available. The noises, the sounds and the smells – did they make a heaven or a hell? To me, at that moment, it was all too engrossing to be anything but heaven – but the hell was just around the corner.

'Let's stop and have something,' we said, and we sat ourselves at one of the tables on the side of the road, and called over a *fokay* (waiter). Realising we wouldn't understand anything since it was all written in Chinese, we gesticulated to the *fokay* that he could choose for us. But first I said in my recently acquired Cantonese, 'Three beers, please.' Six turned up, but at least I'd tried – and no one was complaining!

Before we knew it, three steaming bowls of rice and a large tureen of soup were served with bits of white meat and noodles floating around on top. 'And this is just for starters!' the boys added with a knowing wink. I was so ravenous, I knew I could eat anything.

'Nice bit of chicken,' I said.

Just then, a better-dressed Chinese man appeared and asked politely, 'You eat dog before?'

'Dog?' I gulped, swallowed hard … and threw up.

Now, I've always been a dog lover. As kids, we had Sammy and Jet, the cocker spaniels, followed by Willie, Sid and Myrtle, the dachshunds. When I married, I took on Sacha and Kelly, the Afghans, and Buster the German Shepherd, and finally Wellington the Great Dane. Dogs have been an important part of my life, but I'd never had to imagine what they taste like. So how was I to know I was eating one?

Dogs had a tough time of it in Hong Kong. There was another story going about at the time, which was straight out of Ripley's *Believe It or Not*. A European woman went to eat at a well-known Chinese restaurant in Aberdeen in Hong Kong, the floating town so beloved of tourists. Taking her pet Chihuahua with her, she managed to communicate to the waiter that she would like him to take the dog out and feed it some scraps. Twenty minutes later, the waiter returned, lifted the lid on the beautiful silver tray and there was the Chihuahua, perfectly roasted. The only tip he got that night was the end of her umbrella, and a suggestion as to where he could stick his silver tray!

That first night in Hong Kong was spent on the balcony of the YMCA, underneath the Milky Way, but the way I was feeling after my stewed dog and half-a-dozen San Miguels made me wish I had never left the UK. We had crept up the stairs while the night porter was away from his desk and saved ourselves the two HK dollars (25p) it would have cost us if we had booked in normally. After two more nights of tiptoeing up the stairs, we were spotted, thrown out and eventually spent the night on one of the benches outside the Star Ferry. But help was at hand, in the shapely form of Tony's girlfriend Mai-lei.

The room was ready in her flat and I could move in immediately. My wildest dreams were coming true after all, and what better way to learn the ways of the world than on the 14th floor of Far East Mansions, Kowloon?

Mai-lei had a very voluptuous figure for a Chinese girl ... but a less-than-pretty face. If I hadn't been a gentleman, I might have casually asked, 'Why look at the mantelpiece when you're poking the fire?' but I thought better of it. There was another girl in the flat as well, the mistress of a high-ranking British police officer. They had had a daughter together, and she was one of the little girls I was to teach.

Two possibilities came to mind – I had a great opportunity to sample the wonders of womankind with all the energy of youth, but there was also the possibility of bringing some unwanted attention in the form of the police boyfriend, and I had no desire to experience the consequences. The simple truth was, I had no job and no prospects, but I wasn't going to slink home with my tail between my legs. So I decided to phone home and tell the family a white lie. I said that the job with the band had been postponed for a month, so I was a bit short of cash. And, just in case it didn't happen at all, didn't Dad have an old schoolfriend at Jardine Matheson, the great Hong Kong shipping company, who might find me something?

Obviously, panic set in in SW19 and, within a week, I had a call from Sir Hugh Barton's office at Jardine Matheson – would I like to come in for a chat? Sir Hugh was the Chairman. I had never thought of working at Kai Tak Airport, but since Jardine Matheson were handling agents for BOAC and Qantas, I had to take the first offer that had come along.

I was employed as a trainee traffic clerk on HK$100 a week, which was the equivalent of about £6, a fortune to me. The job entailed filling out the forms for the passenger and cargo manifests, bureaucratic paperwork that required tidiness and accuracy, qualities which I lacked considerably ... and still do! But it was a lot of fun, whizzing around the runways on my little Lambretta, running up the ramp to deliver the satchel to the flight deck – and chatting up the air hostesses.

It was one such Filipino beauty who was to prove my downfall. Her name was Lucy, but she was so sexy, I called her Juicy Lucy. There was an obvious mutual attraction, so much so that she persuaded me to stay on board when we took off for Manila so that we could spend the stop-over together, and then come back the next day. Did I have my passport or a ticket with me? 'Yes,' I foolishly lied. She sat me down in a spare seat, and the plane took off. Talk about young and foolish.

In the meantime, the flight deck had been radioed from Kai Tak that there was a stowaway on board, as I hadn't returned with the completed manifests. It was all done as a joke, but the captain was not amused. When we arrived at Manila, he refused to let me leave the plane. I spent the night alone. There was no Juicy Lucy for me that night, and she didn't appear the next morning for the return trip. I often wondered what had happened to her. She never called … she never wrote!

When I got back to Kai Tak, I was summoned to the office of the station manager, Paddy Cussans. He was in the middle of dealing with an irate and very drunk American tourist who had missed his plane. 'It wasn't our fault you were asleep in the john,' said Paddy.

'Oh, kiss my arse!' shouted the American.

'Well, sir,' Paddy replied, 'you'd better mark the spot, 'cos to me you're all arse!' Now that's a classy put-down in my book!

We laughed as he came back into his office, but I soon became serious. I had told Paddy about my previous experiences on the World Service with the BBC and he suggested I tried radio as a career – I wasn't cut out for airline work. Why didn't I try airwaves! So my mind was made up for me. It was radio or nothing – and off I went to try my luck at Radio Hong Kong.

Tony, the pianist with our soon-to-be extinct trio, knew the jazz producer there – his name was Ray Cordeiro – and we fixed up a meeting. To get to the studios, which were in the Cable & Wireless building on Hong Kong Island, you had to cross by the Star Ferry, one of the most beautiful and exciting ferry trips in the world. There were two decks. On the top, it was slightly more expensive at 30 cents, but cleaner and less crowded. Then there were seats on the lower deck for just 10 cents; that was more like the steerage section! You jostled with the local Hakka women with their wide-brimmed hats and baskets full of hens and ducks. You could find yourself crammed tight with the peddlars and their trays of rice and sweetmeats, and push bikes laden with fruit and vegetables ready to sell on the streets of Kowloon and Hong Kong Island. Most Europeans went on the top deck – you got strange looks, even then, when you travelled with the Chinese. And you could avoid getting covered in feathers as well.

I decided to tell Radio Hong Kong that I had worked for the BBC at Bush House and was immediately welcomed with open arms. 'Pull up a chair ... have a cup of tea ... how many sugars?' My first assignment was to go and review a show. Which blockbuster was that going to be? I think they were testing me when they sent me to see *Snow White and the Seven Dwarfs on Ice*, starring the world-famous skater Sonja Henie.

My review was broadcast. I was paid HK$30, which seemed like a fortune, and the Great Film Critic waited patiently by the phone for the next booking. In due course, my financial resources had dwindled to my last few Hong Kong dollars, and I was rationing myself to one meal a day. There was a restaurant nearby frequented by what were still known as White Russians – those Russians who had escaped Communist rule in the 1920s and had set up enclaves all over China. When the Communists had taken over in mainland China, the Russians had moved to Hong Kong, and were then recognisable by their white beards and long hair. They still liked to eat their old food from the motherland, so there were several Russian restaurants around the place. It was in one of these, called the Marseille, because it cooked French food as well, that I took my daily bread – literally. They served a daily menu for HK$5 – three courses, but the portions were small, and bread was extra. One day, I noticed at the next table a man with a tureen of soup, and a whole loaf of thick brown bread.

'What's he eating?' I asked the waiter.

'He's having the bortsch soup from the à la carte,' he replied. I scanned the menu, and there it was: 'Bortsch soup with loaf of bread – HK$3'. Soon, I was feasting my eyes on the soup, the beetroot, the slice of meat with a dollop of sour cream – and the loaf of bread. There were a good two-and-a-half bowls in a tureen – it was meant for two people! I ate the lot and became a regular customer. For 40p a day, what else could a poor boy do?

Behind the bar was a turntable and, as well as the Chinese music he played, the manager was also a fan of Johnny Mathis. He used to play Johnny's *Warm* album non-stop. Whenever I hear him singing 'What'll I Do?' and 'I'm Glad There Is You', I'm transported back to those days at the Marseille and the bortsch soup floods my taste buds once again.

But I wasn't working, so I went back to the studios to see what was happening. 'Oh, we don't phone you … you've got to come in every day to see us!' Important lesson learnt. So I went in every day after that and soon there were interviews and rugby reports, and eventually a permanent announcer's job. But then, another disappointment – they didn't think that my delivery was suited to being an announcer or newsreader. 'Too up and down, old boy. Not flat enough!'

I turned to my original contact, Ray Cordeiro, for help. He said, 'I'll give my brother Armando a call at Rediffusion – he's in charge of the English-speaking Blue network there. They had two different colours for their Chinese services – Silver for Cantonese and Gold for Mandarin and Shanghainese. So this was to be my first appearance on a Blue channel!

'Armando, I've got a young English broadcaster here, and he's desperate for work. Have you got anything?'

I held my breath, but even in the air-conditioned office I could feel the sweat running down my neck. Ray's face lit up. 'You have? Tony Myatt's leaving and you need somebody now? I'll send him right over!'

Talk about being in the right place at the right time. I started that weekend and threw myself into the job, loving every minute of it. One evening, I would sit waiting for the strains of Duke Ellington's 'Satin Doll' to fade away, before starting to read the script for Voice of America's *World of Jazz*. The following afternoon, there would be requests to read out from Paul Elvis Wong or the various fan clubs like the Paul Anka Lonely Boy or the Ricky Nelson Hallo Mary Lou and Travelling Man Fan Club. Every programme was different with a daily news and personality show called *Rediffusion Byline*.

The next day, I'd be at the airport grabbing a quick interview with Nat 'King' Cole as he was about to board his plane for Japan, for yet another concert. He had two worldwide hits to promote at the time – 'Rambling Rose' and 'Let There Be Love'. What a singer – even though he was feeling the effects of the lung cancer that was eventually to take his life, he still stood up there and belted out his pop and jazz standards or gently crooned his romantic love songs. His fans from his early jazz days hated those pop hits and called them 'corn'. Nat himself said he was just moving with the times. 'But as soon as you start to make money in the popular field, they scream about how good you were in the old days and what a bum you are now.' But Nat cut across all the musical boundaries, with his pop hits such as 'Those Lazy, Hazy, Crazy Days of Summer', to the romantic ones like 'When I Fall in Love' and 'Unforgettable', on which he played the piano intro, and there were also the more jazzy ones such as 'Sweet Lorraine' and 'Route 66'. Today, he is still the most requested singer on my Sunday afternoon programme on Radio 2.

It was a cool November morning, and I awoke with a start, looked at the alarm clock, and realised there were still a few minutes before it was due to shatter my peace. I was on the early shift that morning, opening up the studios to read the news and then play some records. I'd stayed the night at Joe Macmillan's house – he was the pianist with the band I'd played with the night before, Pete O'Neill's Dixie Landers. His *amah*, the Chinese maid, had a cup of tea ready for me as I was leaving, and mumbled something at me in Cantonese and broken English. The only word I understood sounded like Kennedy. It was only a short walk to Rediffusion's studio, on the Waterfront in Wanchai, and was a great place for a radio station, right in the middle of the bars and red-light district! I passed groups of excited Chinese, and kept hearing the name Kennedy over and over again. When I opened up the studio, there was a long strip of printed paper literally falling off the teleprinter. There was a black line down one of the edges – were we running out of paper? I asked myself. As soon as I began to read, I realised the gravity of the situation. John F Kennedy had been shot dead, and I was about to read the news to the hundreds of thousands of listeners tuning in for the 7.00am bulletin. Running round to the record library, I grabbed a handful of classical music albums, hoping these would reflect the sombre mood of the moment. I'd never read the news so carefully in my life. It wasn't easy with the emotion of the story. JFK had been a true icon of the 20th century.

Most of us can remember where we were or what we were doing at the time of the death a major world figure. I remember JFK's more vividly than those of Elvis Presley, John Lennon or even the Queen Mum. It must have been the mark of the person as well as the moment in time.

My third move in as many years, and I was off to the most

popular radio station at that time in Hong Kong, called simply Commercial Radio. Not that the Blue network was a bad station, but it was only on cable and, anyway, I was ambitious enough to want to be where most people were listening, a feeling that has persisted to this day.

Musically, our tastes changed more dramatically in the 60s than in any other decade. The Beatles, the Searchers, the Hollies and the Rolling Stones all became the dominant names of the decade yet, ironically, it started and ended with two singers whose names didn't conjure up the 60s at all – Michael Holliday and Rolf Harris. Michael, a Bing Crosby soundalike, had the decade's first Number One in Britain with 'Starry-Eyed', showing that, despite the emergence of Elvis Presley and Little Richard in the 50s, the public still liked a good tune sung by someone clean-cut and wholesome.

In July 1960, we were introduced to a young Australian singer called Rolf Harris. If you hadn't known what a wobble board and a didgeridoo sounded like before, you did by the end of July – Rolf had a Top Ten hit with 'Tie Me Kangaroo Down, Sport'. Rolf has been part of our lives ever since, and even had the last Number One of the 60s with 'Two Little Boys'. You have to admire his versatility. Who else would be able to turn 'Stairway to Heaven' into a hit? Not even its originators, Led Zeppelin, could do that, even if their recording has become a rock anthem. But Rolf managed it in 1993 with a version that shocked the purists, but rose to Number Seven in the charts. Robert Plant, who wrote it, might have felt like throwing up at the adulteration, but still would have laughed all the way to the bank. Rolf has become a national institution, and anyone who suggests he should be in one deserves a didgeridoo firmly inserted where the Aussie sun don't shine!

The first Hong Kong Lottery was to be held at the new City Hall as part of its opening celebrations. It was newly built, with arguably the best acoustics in Southeast Asia, and was to hold two prestigious concerts featuring Frank Sinatra on the opening night, with Igor and David Oistrakh in a classical concert the following Saturday. The lottery was to be broadcast live by Commercial Radio that opening morning, with Tony Myatt and Eddie Mainwaring presenting. When I knew I'd be on air that morning, I went out and bought – with my own money – a ticket for the draw. It cost HK$5.

When the Head of the Legislative Council, the body that governed Hong Kong in those days, started the draw, I confirmed the numbers into the microphone, while keeping an eye on my own ticket. '6 … 5 … 5 … 6 …' My voice rose discernibly – the numbers were matching my own, and there were only three to go: '… 7 … 9 …' mine again! The tension was unbearable as I waited for the final ball to drop from the drum; I needed a 3 to win HK$100,000! 'And the last number is … zero.' I could hardly say the word as I handed the microphone over to Tony, who was completely unaware of the situation, and was babbling about where the lucky winner might be listening at that precise moment. That lucky winner could so easily have been sitting two yards away from him, and was now in complete shock! And I could have announced my own winning ticket live on air. That's the closest I've ever come to winning the Big One. I won £45 on our own National Lottery recently – small consolation, eh?

Commercial Radio was situated to the south of Kowloon, on the way to the New Territories, which were themselves the last bit of British territory before you reached China. I used to travel from the apartment in Kowloon by bus on the top deck, since it gave you an uninterrupted view of the real city and the day-to-day lives of the population. I was sharing the flat with a Eurasian guy called John, who ran a very successful hi-fi business. His Swedish fiancée was friends with a Chinese nurse I was going out with at the time called Oi-Luen. She had Westernised her name to Ellen.

Ellen wouldn't allow me anywhere near her, unless I married

her. No way, José! So she had to go. Luckily for me, she was keen to go to London to further her nursing career, so I encouraged her all I could and told her that my mother would meet her off the plane. When she arrived, and my mother was there as promised, Ellen flung her arms around her and cried, 'Mummy!' It took my mother years to forgive me for that one.

As I waved Ellen off at the airport, she had promised that I could enjoy her 'intimately' on her return, (if nobody else had in the meantime, I thought to myself). I stopped off at a bar on the way back, and supped half a dozen San Miguels with some vodka chasers to get me in the mood for John and Erica's engagement party at the flat that night. Her parents were flying in especially from Stockholm for the event.

Hong Kong at that time had a chronic water shortage, and an antiquated distribution system, and every so often rationing would have to be introduced. That week we had filled every possible container with water, knowing that the supply would not be turned on again for another four days. The bath would hold our main supply, with various other bottles and jugs filled to the brim. From the bar, I made my way, extremely carefully, trying to look as sober as possible, back to the flat. With the utmost difficulty, I found my door key, turned the latch and staggered in. I didn't see or –to be more precise – I couldn't see John and his family-to-be with their glasses of champagne, one of which had been left for me. My bladder and sphincter both sighed with relief as I emptied an hour's steady drinking into what was, I thought, the lavatory bowl, until, to my horror, I realised I was peeing into four days' worth of water ... in the bath. There was a loud gasp and, as I turned around, still with my dick in hand, I noticed the assembled party.

'Cheers!' I cried, and promptly fell towards my own room and my welcoming *tatami* mattress. The next morning, there was a note on my door asking me to leave immediately. I went round a week later, having summoned up the courage to apologise – but they had all gone back to Sweden. So I'll say it now: so sorry, John. I hope you had a happy marriage, and that your wife didn't think all your friends were like that! If ever there was a time to have signed the pledge, that was it. But I never did.

Frank Fonseca came to my rescue. A brilliant guitarist, Frank had been brought up in Shanghai but, like many who had fled after the Communists took over in China, he had settled in Hong Kong. Frank had heard of this crazy guy who had lugged a dirty great double bass all the way to Hong Kong and then found he had no job. And worse than that, he wasn't even a professional. Frank had been born with a quarter of a left arm, with just a finger for a hand. He laid the guitar on his lap, playing the chords with his complete right hand, and using his finger to pick out the individual notes. He played the double bass the same way, and when he sat behind the drums you'd never know he was missing anything. We became, and still are, good friends and when he said that he needed someone to take his spare room to help pay the rent, I jumped at the chance.

His apartment was on Hong Kong Island, halfway up the Peak, in an area known as Mid Levels. The views were amazing, and gave me a completely different picture of the colony from what I had seen in Kowloon, where you were looking at the Island in the distance, as opposed to taking in the whole picture from several hundred feet up.

Frank had bought an old Ford Zephyr, with a specially adapted gear lever for his arm and finger, but I always preferred to walk to the city centre. This was another adventure in itself. You could walk down to the Peak tram station, and then get whisked up to the top of the Peak, over 1,000 feet up. The views were really spectacular, but you needed a few more dollars than I had to afford a place up there. But if I continued walking past the tram station, then I would soon find myself in the real Hong Kong, the

Hong Kong where the bustle and the noise, the people and the smells made me realise that I was walking through one of the most densely populated places on earth. Chinese, Indians, Filipinos and Westerners lived side by side, each living their own lives in apparent harmony.

It was a part of Hong Kong that I'd grown to know well when I was having to take on any job that came my way. One of these was selling space in a large commercial directory called *Owen's European and Middle East Business Directory*. The company was then setting up in Hong Kong, and was looking for salesmen. I applied for a job and was taken on very quickly, which gave my self-esteem a big boost. I soon realised why they were so desperate for staff. The deal with *Owen's* was that you received 15 per cent of what you sold. For a business to advertise with a quarter of a page might have cost HK$400, so I would receive HK$60. That was on a good day. And I didn't have many of those. The business community, I found, was visited daily by salesmen with similar products. My publication was the newest and the most difficult to sell – and I was finding it harder day by day to cope with the rejection. The agent for *Owen's* was an Indian called Murjani, and the day that I handed in my notice, he sent me off to one more potential customer, who turned out to be his cousin, another Murjani. He bought a full page worth HK$1,500! My cut – $225. He had realised my impecunious plight, had felt a bit sorry for me and had asked me to go on this last sales effort, having asked his cousin to put some business my way. What a heart he had. We had become quite friendly by this time, and he, his wife and myriads of kids, would invite me to their tiny flat and delight in showing me how to eat my curry with my hands. That same family went on to make Murjani jeans – I've often wondered why they never asked me to be one of their salesmen!

I was still mad keen on pursuing as many double bass-playing opportunities as I could, and was delighted to accept an offer to join the Hong Kong Philharmonic Orchestra, a fine semi-professional outfit which played many concerts, attracting some of the world's foremost soloists like David and Igor Oistrakh. My fellow double bass players were a full-time Filipino called Tommy Ignacio and a Chinese player, Jiang Cheng Tao. Jiang had paddled his double bass down the Pearl River, escaping from the communist regime, singing 'I'll String Along With You'!

He had been picked up by one of the ferries, which sailed between the Portuguese enclave of Macao and Hong Kong. He didn't speak a word of English and his dialect was Shanghainese. How far he had travelled to play in an orchestra shows you how desperate educated Chinese were to get to Hong Kong. Even at his audition, he was wearing that dull grey Chairman Mao suit which conjured up such dismal pictures for those of us living in the West. He soon fell in love with a pretty Aussie viola player who, with typical dry humour, said they had moved in together with no strings attached. It was a dreadful line – and could easily have been one of my own!

Although my sales skills were clearly lacking, at least I could be confident about my music. Or so I thought. 'You can't tell a crotchet from a bleeding hatchet!' my first band leader in Hong Kong screamed at me. Those encouraging words came from the mouth of Pete O'Neill, whose Dixielanders were a group of expatriate musicians. Of course I could tell a crotchet from a hatchet, but I could also tell after that engagement just how good you had to be to become a full-time pro musician. And I wasn't good enough. But at that point, I didn't mind too much – I was just as happy being a semi-pro and to still be able to earn a living doing something else – like working in radio.

At the end of the Second World War, Pete O'Neill had been posted to Hong Kong with the 53 Repair Unit of the RAF and, after demob, had joined the police. Having played with the RAF Band, he was able to form his own Dixieland Band and had become a firm favourite with the British and European communities. After my two mates, Richard and Tony, had been posted to Aden, Pete asked me to join his band at HK$50 a gig. So I remember that evening at Kai Tak well. Our band uniform was black trousers (the pianist Joe Macmillan leant me a pair of his) and a bright-red jacket that came with the job. It also made us look like waiters. Most of the time, we played jazz, but our trombonist, Alan Hare, had written some fine arrangements of Porter, Berlin and Gershwin dance numbers. I thought I was a good enough reader, until I inadvertently played a crotchet (one beat) instead of a minim (two beats). Hence Pete's outburst, but I took it in good heart – Pete complained more with humour than venom. I was working at something I loved, and I was going to be paid for it – or so I thought.

After the dinner-dance ended, Pete was given a wad of Hong Kong dollars, which he stuck in his back pocket, assuring us he would be paying out when we had found a bar with some Suzie Wongs and San Miguels. Chubby Checker was 'Twisting Again' over on the jukebox, and I'd pulled a real dolly with a *cheongsam* up to her armpits, when I was aware of a commotion at our table. Pete couldn't find the money he had put in his back pocket, and couldn't pay for the drinks he had bought. Worst of all, though, he couldn't pay us. The wad had fallen out of his jeans in the taxi … all HK$400 of it!

My first paid gig in weeks and nothing to show for it, and no way of getting home. Pete said not to worry – we'd take a couple of rickshaws back to his place, and his wife, Slim, could put a sheet on the sofa for me. Unfortunately, the up and down movement of the rickshaw made me feel decidedly queasy, and I was sick down the back of the driver. Another day in paradise!

Soon, I was a full-time member of the band, and we became the support musicians for many of the big names who came through the colony. Tony Scott, who had just been voted the world's number-one clarinettist by the readers of the jazz magazine *Downbeat*, was a regular visitor. Although he was playing in a more modern idiom, he loved to join us on our Dixieland sessions, always bringing the house down with his amazing technique. On one occasion, the jazz flautist Herbie Mann was also performing. When he and Tony got together for a jam session with us, I thought this really *was* another day in paradise – for real! Then Kenny Ball and Acker Bilk came through. I didn't actually get to play with them, but Kenny's bass player, Vic Pitt, had left his bass behind in Singapore, so I lent him mine. It was an education for me, seeing my own double bass being played the way it should be. Although aware by now that I didn't have the talent for a career as a pro, I still continued to play along with the best of them – a bit like my golf, really.

Ray Lawrence was a brilliant tenor saxophonist who had played most famously with the Harry James Band. Pete O'Neill got wind of this, and invited him to play on one of our gigs. The cheek of it – but he did. 'Where's a good hairdresser? I want to look good tonight for the gig,' he asked. So I took him along to a place which gave a haircut with a difference. When you went in, they asked you whether you wanted just a simple haircut, or one of their – here the eyebrows were raised invitingly – 'special offers'.

'Take the special offer, Ray,' I said, with the voice of experience. He did. He came out with a smile on his face that you don't normally get from a simple haircut. After the gig, Ray wanted to go and get laid. I thought he'd already had just that, but apparently it had only been a manual effort. At this time, I was still a virgin, believe it or not, but together with the rest of the band, we strolled around Wanchai until we found Madam Chiu's Emporium – the word 'brothels' wasn't ever used.

'Fools rush in where angels fear to tread' – but I was not afraid. My hopes were high that this finally was to be *the moment*. No such luck. The others were all ahead of me ... and all the girls were taken. Only the *mama-san* was left. She looked about 60 going on 140.

'AAAAAH ... you too big!' she screamed as I positioned myself delicately for entry. I kid you not. Those of you who've seen me in the showers will think I'm lying. 'TOO BIG ...' she screamed again, '... but I give you blow job!' With that, she took her false teeth out, and the memory of what happened next has not been lost to any sign of impending dementia ... I did gain my proper spurs a little later.

When Annie Lam and I first met, I thought 'This is it!' I knew she was a bar girl, on the game, but she was sooooo beautiful – a mixture of Chinese and Japanese. She invited me back to her place. There was no mention of money. I had already assured her I wasn't in the Army, and neither was I a tourist. I was just a penniless musician. We spent a night of wild passion, and I realised what I had been missing all these years. Boy, was I going to make up for it! In the morning, though, her mood had changed. 'Where my dollar?' she asked rather forcibly.

'Dollar, what dollar? I told you I had no money. I thought this was a love match!'

'Love match – I love only dollar!'

With that, she picked up my clothes and threw them out of the window. Unfortunately, her flat was five storeys up, and since most fire escapes then were blocked by vagrant sleepers and other debris, I had to go down in the lift to rescue my clothes. I covered myself with both hands, and looked straight ahead as the lift made its way to the ground floor. I rushed out against the incoming tide of people, who were too shocked to scream, and made for the nearest T-shirt and shorts I could see. They were mine, thank goodness – how many other people had had their clothes thrown out of the window the night before?

Annie Lam, in the meantime, had called the police to say there was a naked intruder outside her block of flats. As they arrived, Annie was leaning out of her window, screaming, 'KWEI-LO! KWEI-LO!' (Foreign devil, foreign devil!) By this time, I had found safety in numbers, and mingled with a group of American tourists. To the Chinese, foreign devils all look the same, with their big noses and funny features. I glanced up at the beautiful Annie, but she had lost me in the crowd by then. Hell hath no fury like a woman scorned, I thought, and wandered untroubled along the crowded streets.

The great composer Hoagy Carmichael was in the colony, and had been booked to play at a private party for the millionaire George Ho at his mansion in Fanling, which is a very wealthy part of the Island. Frank Fonseca was asked to take his guitar along, the top Filipino drummer Celso Carrillo took his drum kit, and 'guess who' took his double bass. One of Hoag's compositions, 'Hong Kong Blues', was appropriate for the occasion, and would have been a showstopper had the band not been slightly drunk. Somebody had definitely spiked our drinks. We staggered through 'Stardust', 'Two Sleepy People' and 'Lazybones' with Mr Carmichael shouting the chord sequences at me. When we got to 'I Get Along Without You Very Well', he slammed the piano lid shut and walked off the stage. The mainly Chinese guests applauded wildly – they thought it was part of the act!

Exit Hoagy Carmichael. Enter another singer, whose name escapes me, as black as night with teeth to match. Before we could say, 'Come back, Hoagy, all is forgiven,' this guy hit the first chord of 'Don't Get Around Much Any More', but with his own lyrics.

'Missed the bucket last night,
Went all over the floor,
Mopped it up with my toothbrush –
Don't clean my teeth much any more!'

We all fell about, although the subtlety of the lyric was lost on the Chinese. But whoever you were, thank you. I've never forgotten those lyrics. That evening convinced me finally to hang up the bass. I took Frank's advice – stick to the day job.

As 1964 turned into 1965, I felt it was time to leave Hong Kong and go home. Home ... I'd been away for over three years and I was feeling homesick. I wanted to explore further my career in broadcasting, and felt that perhaps the BBC would be more interested now that I'd taken their advice and gone abroad to gain experience. I'd done that all right, and not just in broadcasting! In the time I'd been away, I'd only spoken to the family on the phone at Christmas and birthdays. My father had told me his mother, my Granny Ida, had died, and I was fortunate not to have seen her, because she had become senile and then dementia had overtaken her; Alzheimer's Disease had not been heard of then, though clearly that was what she had had. My parents had built an extension to the house in Wimbledon so that they could look after her. That old comedy line, 'Be nice to your children, because they're the ones to decide where to put you when you're past it,' couldn't have been truer.

But enough was eventually enough. Granny Ida said to her daughter-in-law one morning, 'I didn't like that man who brought me my cup of tea this morning. Who was he?'

'That was your son, Ray.'

'I did tell him that I didn't like the food much any more and he should get a new cook.'

That was it. However sad it might have been, Granny Ida had to go to a new home. Even though they had to prise her fingers off the door handle of her old one she was soon in a new room, in a new place and quite oblivious to the change. Countless families have found themselves in situations similar to ours, and although I'm not scared of dying, I am frightened of regressing into a state of senility. We don't let our pets stay alive like that, do we? Yet our own kith and kin remain a burden to their families and feel so useless themselves. But then, everyone wants to look younger and live longer – we must be mad!

My decision to leave Hong Kong received lift-off from Lufthansa Airways. They were about to make a series of radio documentaries about the airline's training and employment facilities in Frankfurt and Hamburg for transmission on English language radio in the Far East. Would I like the job, in return for a free flight home to London and a small fee?

Would I? You bet. During my time in the Far East, the Berlin Wall had been built and I could remember catching a glimpse of President John Kennedy on his way through London in June of 1961, on his way to deliver his famous '*Ich bin ein Berliner*' speech in West Berlin. Two years later, I was reading the news of his assassination.

The deal with Lufthansa was that I would record and produce the interviews and narration for six programmes, which would be taken back to, and produced for transmission by, the head of public relations, Claus Dehio. His wife, coincidentally, had sat in front of me on the first cello desk of the Hong Kong Philharmonic Orchestra.

All flight and hotel expenses were to be met by Lufthansa and they paid 50 Deutschmarks as expenses. From the fortune I had saved after three and a half years in Hong Kong, I sent £100 back to open an account with Lloyd's on the High Street in Wimbledon. 'Have you got a rich relative in the Far East?' the bank manager asked my father. I presume he was joking, but it soon got around Wimbledon that the 'prodigal son' was returning.

Before taking off for Europe on that Saturday night in February, my friends had thrown me a lunchtime party full of Indonesian food – chicken, pork, beef and vegetables with hot, spicy sauces and a marvellous mixture of differently cooked rice. Gathered to see me off were Tony Myatt, who was always being voted Hong Kong's top DJ (who says bald isn't sexy, Tony?), John Gunstone, Barry Haigh and Darryl Patten from the small world of English-speaking radio. They were together with my musician pals Frank Fonseca, Pete O'Neill, Joe and Edna McMillan, Richard and Gwen Stuttaford, all friends who had looked after me in my darkest days. And then there was Takako Tanizaki, the lovely Japanese beautician whom I had met while recording in a local hospital. Tearful and swearing undying love, she was saying 'sayonara'. Her father had fought in the World War II and hated anything or anyone Western and, like many Japanese, never forgave America for the atomic bombing of Nagasaki and Hiroshima. She was Tani-san and I was Crazy-san. She showed me how she dressed in a kimono, which took her an hour to put on, but only took seconds to take off. There is one part of the outfit that, when pulled, allows the entire garment to fall in a heap around the lady's ankles. I only found it once – and I've not had the opportunity to look for it since!

Although she twice left notes for me at Broadcasting House when visiting London, we never met again, but she did teach me some useful phrases in Japanese, which I occasionally try out on unsuspecting Japanese golfers – the trouble is, I never understand the answers!

Imagine, then, a scene not so much from Puccini's *Madam Butterfly*, but more of one from Wagner's *Flying Englishman*, as I touched down at Frankfurt Airport in the middle of a snowstorm. Things were not working out as planned. There was a problem with my new Sony portable tape recorder, as I had dropped it on the tarmac as we were disembarking from the flight. I tested it with a quick 'One-two … one-two …' into the mic. I replayed it again and it performed perfectly. Phew, that's a relief, I thought as I walked to my first interview with the Lufthansa station boss, who then conducted me around the kitchens and catering centre. The travelling continued and, after Frankfurt, there was Bonn and then Hamburg and, eventually, I was able to give half a dozen tapes to Claus to take back to Hong Kong.

'*Danke schön*, Edward. Now, as a special treat, I will take you to the Reeperbahn to see the girls in the windows. Thank you for the job you have done. Here is a little present from me so that you can enjoy yourself, yes?'

He handed me a wad of notes and disappeared into the crowd. I was never to see him again, but after that I always thought of him as Santa Claus! So I walked up and down the Reeperbahn, ogling the girls in the windows, until I saw a blonde I really liked the look of. With my bundle of Marks in a rather sweaty palm, I went through the door and into the boudoir of Tamara, hoping that we weren't going to be performing in the window as well. It was all over in minutes – she hardly drew breath. 'Tamara never comes,' I thought idly as I was ushered out of the door, off to the airport and home to England.

The unexpected didn't stop there. On landing at Heathrow and making my way towards Customs, I could see my mother and sister waiting for me behind the swing doors. My mother was gesticulating energetically up and down her face. What on earth was she doing? Then the penny dropped – I had grown a beard while I'd been away and she had never seen it. What with that and my horn-rimmed glasses, I must have looked like a poor man's Rolf Harris.

Then there was the final hurdle to overcome. Before leaving Hong Kong, I had bought some beautiful Mikimoto pearls, the best that Japan could offer. Not wanting to pay duty on arrival in the UK, I had hidden them in one of the pouches in the carrying case for my double bass, the very same one I had lugged out to Hong Kong over three years ago. That pouch was where the spare strings for the bass were kept. Fool-proof.

Mr Customs Officer eyed me up and down suspiciously. Obviously, he'd learnt never to trust anyone with a beard.

'Anything to declare, sir?'

'No,' I lied.

'Returning from Hong Kong with nothing, are we, sir?' he asked patronisingly. 'I think we'll take a look inside that double bass, shall we, sir?'

'Help yourself,' I replied bravely. My internal turmoil was starting to show on my face.

'I'll just have a look through this,' he said, unfastening the straps of the carrying case, and he started to search one of the pouches. Now my heart was really pumping and any problems with constipation were about to be remedied far quicker than with a doctor's prescription. Just then, the swing doors out to the Arrivals hall burst open, my mother came running through and enveloped me in her arms – it had been a long time since she had seen her second-born son.

'You can't come in here, madam,' the officer said sternly.

'That's my son, and I haven't seen him for five years.'

Well done, Mum – exaggerating again. But she was a very beautiful woman and the Customs officer was quite taken aback – and smitten.

'All right, madam ... I shouldn't be doing this, but I do like happy reunions ... so go on through.' He seemed to have forgotten about the double bass and its small cargo of contraband, and finding there was nothing naughty in my hand baggage, waved us on. We were through, into the Ford Capri and down the A4 before you could say 'pearl necklace and matching earrings'.

'Thanks, Mum, you saved me from a heavy fine there!' I laughed.

'Oh, I didn't know you were doing anything suspect, you silly boy, I was just pleased to see you!'

Aren't mums wonderful?

5

MAKING WAVES AT RADIO LONDON

MAKING WAVES AT
RADIO LONDON

IN 1965, only two organisations held the monopoly for radio broadcasts in the UK – the BBC and the COI – the Central Office of Information. I had a short stint at the COI after arriving back from Hong Kong and before turning to piracy. I remember many of my colleagues at the COI well. There was the beautiful Stella who had married a Korean, and had become Stella Park. She was the chief producer in the radio section, and looked after all the different freelance journalists and news reporters. With my background in music radio, she gave me all the showbiz interviews, like Frankie Howerd, Johnny Dankworth and Cleo Laine, and the Kinks.

Then there was Don Davis, a broadcaster from the old school, who didn't like the idea of youthful competition. We were all paid per interview, so an extra man-with-a-mic meant less work in the melting pot. He told me, and anyone else who would listen, that my interviewing technique was awful, and that I shouldn't be working for such an august body as the COI. Luckily, Stella liked me, and told Don to mind his own business! Five years later, I sat next to him at a Lord's Taverners' Ball, where I was conducting my first ever charity auction. 'Well done,' he said as I sat down after my efforts. 'By the way,' he continued ingratiatingly, 'we never miss your *Junior Choice* at the weekend. Haven't we met somewhere before?' I reminded him about the COI, and how he had suggested I try another career. He hadn't realised that Stewpot had been Eddie Mainwaring at the COI, complete with beard and glasses – how I must have changed! However, his daughter made up for Daddy's gaffe with a rather pleasant long, slow dance that became longer and slower as dawn approached.

Then there was Frank Lawless, who eventually went to open a bar in Spain. In between interviewing Chief Whips and High Commissioners, he also became understudy to Frankie Howerd in *A Funny Thing Happened on the Way to the Forum!* I hoped one day I would become as versatile as him.

I stayed happily with the COI for only three months but, in that short spell, I was to have my first taste of the British pop scene and what was to become known so famously as the 'Swinging 60s'.

In the early days of the Elvis phenomenon, his manager Colonel Tom Parker was offered $100 for Elvis to appear at a rock 'n' roll concert. 'That's *my* fee,' said the Colonel, 'how much are you offering for my boy?' In Elton John's early days, he was managed by a former publicist called Ray Williams. Ray had put an advert in the *New Musical Express*: 'Looking for new talent!' A simple enough thing to do but, most importantly, one that was to produce the single most important influence on Elton John's life – a lyricist called Bernie Taupin. Elton had just left Bluesology because the lead singer, Long John Baldry, wouldn't let him sing, and Elton wanted to be more than just a pianist. With Bernie Taupin's contributions, he was soon to become what he had always wanted to be – a singer-songwriter.

Ray took Elton to Regent Sound where you could make a demo tape for £25, and sent it to Dick James, the publisher, who, in 1962, had agreed to record songs by two other songwriters, John Lennon and Paul McCartney. Elton had sung two Jim Reeves songs on the tape – 'He'll Have to Go' and 'I Love You Because' – which had convinced James that Elton was as good a singer as he was a songwriter. Years later, when Elton's original bass player Dee Murray died in Nashville, Elton went out to perform at a commemorative concert at the Grand Ole Opry, and sang those songs again in Dee's memory. They were received with more enthusiasm than Elton's own hits! In 1970, Elton had been offered $50 to appear at the Troubador in Los Angeles, so Ray tried the same approach as the Colonel had 15 years before on behalf of Elvis Presley. It worked. Elton received $250. Everyone was happy.

Ray had previously taken Elton to the Knokke TV Festival in Belgium, where he had starred in a programme called *Portrait of Elton John*. Luckily for him, the then head of Light Entertainment at the BBC, Bill Cotton, was one of the judges. Elton's career was beginning to take off, and when he sang 'Border Song' in West Berlin, everybody assumed it had been written about the East–West border crossing – but it hadn't been.

Ray was also representing the Kinks and Sonny and Cher at this time with Brian Sommerville, the Beatles' former publicist. It was Ray who had said to Brian that this chap, Eddie Mainwaring, who had just arrived from Hong Kong, was both enthusiastic and knowledgeable, to which Brian had replied, 'Then why doesn't he go and join the pirates?'

Thanks, Ray. As a fledgling entrepreneur, he was learning fast – when the Mayfair Hotel in London refused to take Sonny and Cher unless Sonny had his hair cut, Ray had the story on the front pages the next day. That story gave Sonny and Cher huge publicity, and their first Number One, 'I Got You, Babe', followed in August 1965.

It was at that time, too, that another American was headlining shows around the country. His name was PJ Proby ... and he spelt trouble! Described in the *Guinness Book of Hit Singles* as 'Controversial, pony-tail wearing, trouser-splitting teen idol,' PJ came from Texas, and wore the mutton-sleeved shirts and pony tail which had come straight out of the film *Tom Jones*; ironically, it was to be another Tom Jones who was to take over PJ's mantle. PJ, though, made a big impact on his audiences – his trouser-splitting caused near riots, and even cancellations of some performances only increased his pulling power – in more ways than one! In 1965, the manager of the ABC in Luton dropped the curtain after his velvet pants ripped open, and refunded the entire audience their money. And they called them the Swinging 60s! Even ABC television banned PJ from appearing on their programmes.

A few years later, I was to find out from my wife, Chiara, that her mother Ginetta and her sister, Pia, had tailored PJ's trousers for him. They were both qualified seamstresses in their native Italy. It was on his instructions that they had made them two sizes smaller around the crotch. But neither sister has ever admitted to being the one who used the tape measure!

PJ was great friends with Jimmy Henney, my future father-in-law, as Jimmy was publishing many of PJ's hits, such as 'Hold Me', 'Somewhere' and 'Maria'. When PJ stayed with the Henneys, Chiara had to stick a big gold star on his bedroom door. This, then, was the man who had to withdraw from his next tour due to 'ill health', giving a young and upcoming singer called Tom Jones his first opportunity to tour as part of a headlining bill which included Petula Clark, Tommy Roe, Tommy Quickly Sounds Incorporated, the Fourmost and Brian Poole and the Tremeloes. However, when PJ became too sick to rejoin the tour, it was cancelled.

In those days, Tom Jones on the bill meant very little. A year later, it would be different. Tom was still having to honour contracts he had signed before the success of 'It's Not Unusual', 'With These Hands' and 'What's New, Pussycat?' At one party, in 1965, where fellow DJ Mike Lennox and I were working under the Radio London banner (or 'Big L', as we called it), Tom told us he was working for £25, the same as us. The next night, at a different venue he was going to get £1,000!

On that early tour, Tom did sing a number on stage that has become a favourite of his, and of every karaoke singer in the world – 'Delilah'. When Les Reed and Barry Mason wrote it, it had been intended for PJ, but contractual difficulties arose, and 'Delilah' was to become Tom's seventh Top Ten hit in 1968. Poor PJ Proby missed out on that, and was not to have another worthwhile hit again.

To persuade the government that there was a demand for pop radio, it was up to people like Ronan O'Rahilly, Philip Solomon, Philip Birch and Ben Toney to create that demand. And the only way to do that was to moor a vessel, or capture a disused wartime fort outside British territorial waters, a minimum distance of three miles away, and beam the programmes into the UK via a powerful radio transmitter – there were no satellites in those days.

Fortunately, there were enough dedicated madmen to go and do just that. I was one of those who saw ourselves as pioneers, opening up the boundaries of the wireless and BBC-dominated pop radio to the millions who, up to that point, hadn't known what they were missing. And who was responsible for bringing them this new world of pop?

'Beard and glasses ... tall and skinny ... eats like a horse.'

My CV? No, just my future colleague, Duncan Johnson, describing me over the phone to the ship's captain aboard Radio London's home on the seas, the *Galaxy*. He was talking to Captain Buninga before we left Harwich for the ship, which was moored four miles off Frinton on the Essex coast. That former US minesweeper was to become my home for the next two years. It might have turned out differently if Radio Caroline had had a vacancy in that summer of 1965, but at least the advice they offered was sound – 'Try Radio London ... it's only a short walk from Chesterfield Gardens, our HQ, to their offices at number 17 Curzon Street.'

There, a pretty girl called Brenda, complete with a daring mini-skirt, offered me a cup of tea before calling through to the programme director, Ben Toney, that there was a DJ from Hong Kong looking for work.

As he emerged from his office, he was halfway through asking, 'Is he Chinese then?' He stopped in amazement at the sight of a beard and glasses sitting there, and in a slow Texan drawl said, 'You sure ain't Chinese!'

After telling him about the previous four years in Hong Kong, Ben asked me if I could go out the next day, have a look round the boat and, if I liked what I saw, start aboard the week after. I checked my empty diary, taking my time to give the impression that I was a very busy man, and then, aping Ben's Texan drawl, said, 'I sure can!' That's how, 24 hours later, I found myself chugging out to the *Galaxy*.

My starting salary was to be £25 a week paid into a bank account in Freeport, Bahamas. The date was 2 July 1965, which was exactly the same date when I had taken off for Hong Kong four years earlier, and exactly nine years to the day before I married Chiara in 1974. Now that's what I call coincidence!

But why go and sit on an old rusting former minesweeper in the first place? I remembered the words of the personnel officer at the BBC six years earlier, telling me that the only opportunity to gain broadcasting experience was to go abroad, so I had gone to Hong Kong and now, four years later, there were still no jobs available at the BBC, so the only thing for it was to join the pirates.

My companion on that first 'pirate' trip was Duncan Johnson, a six-footer from Canada whose voice was so deep it seemed to start from his ankles. His nickname was 'Shag'. Why will become clear, believe me! He had previously worked in Bermuda and, like me, his experience had landed him this job. In fact, of the original line up on Big L, only Kenny Everett had not been on air before. Paul Kaye and Earl Richmond had worked with BFBS (the British Forces Broadcasting Service), Pete Brady in Canada, Tony Windsor in Australia, and Dave Dennis on Radio Atlanta and Radio Invicta, broadcasting from Red Sands Fort in the Thames Estuary. Radio London's DJs didn't have a Londoner among them!

Duncan's account of his first week aboard did not fill me with much confidence. An oil drum had split in a winter storm, and the deck was slippery and unsteady. There was no spare bunk, so he slept on a settee with one blanket to protect him from the cold. When the ship rolled around, he would bounce off the settee and on to the metal floor, thinking all the time, 'Do I really want to do this?'

Luckily for me, that day in July was calm, there was a spare bunk, and I found I had good sea legs – in the 25 months aboard, I was never seasick. Poor old Stuart Henry lasted only a couple of weeks aboard Radio Scotland before he decided to throw up no more!

Life could be harsh, especially in the winter, when conditions could be so bad that you could spend extra days – or, on one occasion, weeks – aboard until the weather broke. The biggest hardship on board was when salt water seeped into the fresh-water tanks. Kenny Everett went on air saying he was so short of water he was slitting his wrists and drinking his own blood! Nobody could wash or shave, and the only form of liquid relief was Heineken beer and rain water, which was collected from the lifeboats. Eventually, a sausage-type water carrier was towed out to the ship before her own tanks were made good again. It was no surprise, then, that we would gaze longingly through the rain and murk at the lights of Frinton-on-Sea, and wish we were there among them, downing our pints of Worthington or Top Deck Shandy – both were advertisers on Big L, so maybe those pints would have been free. It was wishful thinking – there were no pubs in Frinton then ... it was a dry town!

Something else I had to get used to in a hurry was a name change. I have been answering to two surnames, Mainwaring and Stewart, since those early days of Radio London, when we were advised to change our names in case we were arrested for piracy on the high seas! Although broadcasts were being made from outside British territorial waters, the whole operation was viewed with great suspicion. Just in case things went against us, and we had to appear in court, we would be charged under our real names and not our new ones. That way, so the thinking went, nobody would know who we were! Some hope. If we had been arrested, the whole world would have known about it, new name or old.

Anyway, I loved my family name – it had a certain ring to it. My programmes in Hong Kong had titles like *Midday Spin with Eddie Mainwaring*, or *Mainwaring Till Midnight*. It had a certain *je ne sais quoi*. It could all have been very different, though. After my father had died in 1989, my mother told us all that we would all originally have had Mainwaring-Clapp as a surname. We were astounded. Our father Ray and his brother, Cyril, had been so embarrassed by the name that they had gone to lawyers to have it changed – officially, they got rid of the Clapp! Even in those days, the name had unavoidable connotations. There is a good West Country family by that name and there was an opening batsman, Jack Crapp, who played for Gloucestershire just after the war. He didn't take any crap from anyone. We even had one master at St Edwards who called us Smith instead of Mainwaring – he said it was easier!

Name changes on the pirates were commonplace. Maurice Cole

became Kenny Everett, taking the 'Everett' from the actor Edward Everett Horton (I've never known why!); the Australian Tony Withers, with the octave-deep 'Halloo', was renamed Tony Windsor (as he said himself, 'One queen deserves another!'); and Carl Henty Dodd made his name as Simon Dee. The only one who didn't alter a thing was Tony Blackburn, although at one time they wanted him to become Mark Roman, with his listeners, or subjects, becoming part of the Roman Empire!

Without Big L, I wouldn't have added a further name either. I have a useless – but, I've got to say, quite clever – ability to roll my stomach muscles. They can either look like waves of the sea or a miniature Buddha. That gave my Canadian colleague Dave Cash the idea of a nickname. 'When you do that, it looks like a stewpot,' he said. To this day, I don't know where the similarity came from, but the Stewpot name stuck, and with it a whole new career.

The longer Radio London continued broadcasting, the more it became obvious that there was a huge audience for non-stop pop music and regular news headlines. The BBC could not compete – the Musicians' Union made sure of that. The fact that we were transmitting from outside British territorial waters meant that we were able to cock a snook at the British government and, at that time, we were getting away with it. The fact that we were so popular was infuriating the establishment even more. The arguments and debates were incessant. The Postmaster General of the day was Anthony Wedgwood Benn, better known these days as Tony Benn. Speaking in a debate in the House of Commons in May 1965, he said, 'Whatever future there may be for local sound broadcasting in this country, the pirate radios have no part in it … as I have said time and time again in the House, the stealing of copyright, the endangering of the livelihoods of musicians, the appropriation of wavelengths, the interference with foreign stations, the danger to shipping and ship-to-shore radio, makes the pirates a menace.'

Then, conversely, Tony Benn admitted to the need for pop radio: 'It is sometimes said there is undoubted demand for light music programmes through the day – I suspect it has always existed.' The Postmaster General also admitted to listening to the pirate himself while loofahing his back in the bath!

Apart from the image of the PG and a loofah, there was one further anomaly. The Copenhagen Agreement of 1948 was an international agreement that allocated radio frequencies to European countries. While it might have been true that the pirates had pinched some frequencies on an already overcrowded waveband, others had done exactly the same thing. Did His Holiness the Pope know that Vatican Radio was not abiding by the rules? And what were President Lyndon Johnson's views? After all, Voice of America and American Forces Network were both guilty of what Radio London was being pilloried for. We never found out, even though the wife of the President, Ladybird Johnson, was one of the Texan backers behind Radio London. When it became obvious in 1967 that the British government was going to win with its Maritime Offences Bill, the financial plug was immediately pulled and over £1m profit was salted away. We got a week's severance pay and a reminder that there is little room for sentiment in big business.

Within a month of my starting in July 1965, Radio London had extended its hours of broadcasting from 6.00am until midnight. They needed an extra DJ – would I go full time? I needed no persuading, and found myself as assistant newsreader and writer as well as carrying out my DJing duties. We rewrote the BBC news bulletins from the Home Service (Radios 1, 2, 3 and 4 hadn't been invented yet) in such a way that we could read our own news half an hour later. Our newsroom was in the ship's radio and ship-to-shore telephone room, situated two decks above the studio, which was itself next to the bilge! Having recorded the BBC news, you retyped it yourself then rushed down two flights of spiral steps to arrive in the studio minutes or sometimes seconds before the half-hour. As often as not, you had run so fast you had to take one deep breath and exhale as slowly as possible to read two or three stories on the same breath. You should try it yourself – it's not easy, especially when there's a Force 7 blowing the ship around as well.

Hopefully, the DJ on at the time would have put the news jingle cartridge in the right slot and off you went: 'Wonderful Radio London ... News around the clock ...' the singing jingle rang out, and you started, 'Dateline July 31 ... London ...' then you got the pips, and you read five or six headlines until the last one, when you closed with, 'This has been Radio London News ... Ed Stewart reporting ...' followed by the final musical stab – 'dah, dah, dah, daaaaahh ...' – and you were finished. Then back on the deck for a breath of fresh air and a rub down with a wet flounder.

This form of news presentation was very American, really grabbing people's attention, and it became an essential part of the overall sound of Big L. But the BBC did get their own back. The Home Service had become highly suspicious that we were nicking and then rewriting their stories and so, on April Fool's Day 1966, they put out a spoof story which we didn't spot. We repeated it and the next day a telegram arrived saying, in as many words, 'Got you!'

So we decided that the following year, if we were still afloat, we would perpetrate our own April fool on the nation. It was a simple operation, making use of two turntables and a radio engineer whose distinct Norfolk accent suddenly broke while I was on air, '1 ... 2 ... 3 ... 4 ... 5 ... Radio East Anglia testing. This is Bob Parkin on Radio East Anglia starting transmission on 267 metres from a disused signal box on the Norwich to King's Lynn railway line ...' The engineer was sitting opposite me as he read his announcement so that I could jump straight back in again halfway through talking about the next record I was about to play, seemingly unaware that there had been any interruption. Then, about ten minutes later, we would repeat the process again, with Bob Parkin droning on about the weather, Doris Day and the sort of easy-listening music Radio East Anglia would be playing on 267 metres, one digit away from Radio London's 266! It fooled everybody, from Radio London's management team listening to their trannies at home (it was Saturday morning), to the national press and British Rail.

It was working a treat until, at 10.30am, Keith Skues started reading the news, and a couple of items gave the game away: 'Felixstowe – the famous pier that was destroyed during World War II is to be rebuilt to a distance of three miles. This is to allow offshore radio stations to come within the three-mile limit. Slough – a female zebra crossing ... oh, sorry, I'll read that again ... A female zebra, crossing the main street in Slough, was caught at nine o'clock this morning ... anybody seeing the incident is asked to call Slough 41011, that's Slough 41011. Antiques – American actress Jayne Mansfield, currently in Britain, has been interviewed on a lesser-known facet of her lifestyle ... that of collecting antiques, Grecian urns and jugs. Miss Mansfield is said to have the finest jugs in America!'

Philip Birch and programme director Alan Keen were going bananas while listening in their respective homes. It was Alan Keen's home phone number in Slough that we had given to millions of listeners, and loads of them had responded! He couldn't use his phone all weekend! He was not best pleased and had even thought of firing both Keith Skues and myself, the perpetrators of this heinous crime. What saved us was the immense publicity we received in the press, which resulted in an extra awareness of the station. The pirates, we knew, now had tens of millions of happy listeners.

A couple of them wrote to me, thanking me for showing them what a Spoonerism was! Apparently, I had said, 'Don't forget your Big L T-shirt – it comes in three sizes – small, medium and large, with 266 on the back and Big L on the front. The cost? A mere 12s 6d, which includes your pastage and poking!' Then, for good measure, I started to read the weather forecast and, quite unintentionally, finished with, 'And there'll be shattered scowers everywhere!'

In addition to mangling the English language, I was still playing my bass, and our programme director Alan Keen turned out to be a fine pianist. With fellow DJ Paul Kaye and my old friend Dick Oxlade, the very man who had persuaded me out to Hong Kong five years earlier, we had a good little quartet that usually managed to get together on Sundays. Our meeting place was invariably my family home, and there were several other 'groupies' who came along for the music and that atmosphere that Mum's cooking added to those impromtu sessions.

The party atmosphere was increased on more than one occasion by Eddie Thornton, trumpet player with Georgie Fame's Blue Flames. Coming from Jamaica, he was partial to the wacky backy. 'Not in the house, Eddie,' I pleaded, 'disappear under the weeping willow!' He did ... just as Dad returned from church, and had walked out into the garden to enjoy the sunshine, and say hello to everyone. Eddie, complete with woolly beret and dreadlocks, appeared from under the weeping willow tree, which seemed to be weeping a bit lower by then, and offered Dad a hand of welcome – with the other he also offered my father a spliff! 'Not for me, thanks, old boy, I don't smoke. But that's a nice smell, isn't it?' Eddie carried on across the lawn, giggling hysterically.

At the back of the excellent book by Chris Elliot called *The Wonderful Radio London Story*, the largest list of index entries is that for Kenny Everett. Radio London had immediately recognised that they had a creative genius aboard when Maurice Cole joined the ship in December 1964. What was to prove his undoing throughout his career was his ill discipline He could never keep the gearbox of his brain in neutral, but, being fair to his bosses at Big L, they were very forgiving – they didn't want to lose their most inventive DJ for the sake of an odd indiscretion. After one advert for a deodorant, Kenny added, 'Oooh … it's wrong to pong!' Brilliant, and luckily the advertiser thought so, too. But management didn't like his next *faux pas* – the use of the word 'orgasm'. Even though the 60s were swinging in most ways, radio was a still a bit prudish – and that wasn't just the BBC. Kenny and I were out on the deck on a balmy summer's evening twiddling our knobs. It was a sort of occupational therapy for us – we had to keep in touch with what the other stations were playing. Luckily, that evening, the reception from Radio Luxembourg was good and, as the sun was slowly dipping behind the Essex coastline, with the seagulls circling gently over the darkening sea, we continued our journey across the waveband. Then, in mid-twiddle, came the sound of Paul McCartney singing 'Yesterday'. There wasn't a murmur from either Kenny or me – we were bewitched. As the sound of the string quartet drifted away, I turned to Kenny and said, 'You know, that record is like a musical orgasm.'

'A what?' he asked.

'A musical orgasm – it comes all over you,' I explained.

Kenny looked nonplussed, but laughed all the same.

I thought I had been rather witty. The next day, Kenny opened his programme by playing 'Yesterday', and telling his audience that it gave Ed Stewart an orgasm every time he heard it! The ship-to-shore telephone nearly melted and Kenny was fired and then reinstated when he swore blind that he didn't know what an orgasm was. And we believed him. But then we didn't want to lose him either.

But we did, eventually … and then got him back again. This time, Kenny went too far. He took the mickey out of the station's biggest sponsored programme, *The World Tomorrow*. This was an American religious programme that was broadcast every evening for a quarter-of-an-hour and was worth £50,000. It was owned and introduced by Garner Ted Armstrong, who had a very distinctive and powerful voice. British audiences were used to *Prayer for Today* or *Sunday Half Hour* on the BBC, so programmes like *The World Tomorrow*, *Voice of Prophecy* and *Herald of Truth* were something of a culture shock! Kenny couldn't resist aping Garner Ted's voice. One night he introduced the programme by saying 'And now it's time for tonight's God slot, and I can see millions of you reaching for the "Off" button!'

Of course, he had to go – Garner Ted had threatened to withdraw his entire sponsorship. Kenny Everett left the ship in November 1965, and the irreverence that had cost him his job on that occasion was to prove his downfall a couple of years later on Radio 1. That was when he suggested that the wife of the Minister of Transport, Mrs Ernest Marples, had bribed the examiner to pass her driving test! That was part of his appeal, his irreverence – and don't we miss it?

But six months later, in June of 1966, Kenny was reinstated – by public demand and by the DJs themselves. Life had become dull without him. Who else, while standing out on the deck in those summer months, would have erected a large sign for the boatloads of trippers who had come out from Clacton and Felixstowe to wave at us – 'PLEASE DO NOT FEED THE DJs' it read. In celebrating Kenny's return, someone had smuggled out a bottle of champagne. Unfortunately, I was reading the news that day, and when I arrived in the studio, a paper cup of bubbly was waiting for me. The sea was rough that afternoon, the ship was rolling and I, too, was soon feeling very, very rough. As I started the first story, a finger appeared on the desk beside me, with a crisp delicately balancing on its tip. I began to laugh, took a deep breath, and started again. My composure regained, I managed to reach the final story, when I noticed a head rising from behind the desk opposite, with a piece of chalk protruding from each nostril. I convulsed again. Kenny was back!

After our Big L days together, Kenny and I never remained particularly close. We had both worked creatively aboard the boat and enjoyed some special moments, but we went our different ways, not sharing the same interests. His loss, both to his public and his friends, has been felt deeper since his death. What would he have made of *Big Brother* and the other reality TV shows of today? He would have lampooned them mercilessly, wouldn't he? And no way would he have gone into the jungle – the creepy crawlies would have done for him!

Never anyone to have done anything by half measures, even dying had to be both different and sad for Kenny. His eccentricity in life was mirrored in a tragic way in death. His great friend, the Brazilian actress and producer, Cleo Rocos, gave him a final manicure in the funeral parlour. Another great friend, Father William, who read the eulogy, said Kenny would be in Heaven, because he had such a great sense of humour; a sense of humour was a gift from God. The funeral itself included a requiem and Puccini's 'Symphonic Prelude', which had been one of his *Desert Island Discs*. Kenny had said, 'he wanted to be on the gramophone as he was hoisted aloft in a ray of God's lovely sunbeam'.

Tony Blackburn had begun his career aboard Radio Caroline in 1965, having been a band singer – or should that read 'banned'? He released a record in May 1965 called 'Don't Get Off That Train', which – far from being banned – we used to play regularly and which eventually made it to Number 19 in the Big L Fab 40, but was never a national hit. Tony was 'getting off that train' to join his shipmates aboard Radio Caroline, but kept telling those of us who were on the same tender taking us back to our respective ships that he really wished he was aboard Radio London.

One day, Tony handed a letter to programme director, Ben Toney, asking for a job. As the tender chugged away from the *Galaxy*, Ben started to read the application, which was written in an almost illegible scrawl. 'I can't read this!' said Ben Toney, promptly crumpling up the piece of paper up and throwing it overboard. Three times Tony wrote a note, and three times Ben threw them overboard. 'I'm not having a DJ aboard my ship who can't write clearly. He probably can't read either!'

Tony got his wish in 1966, but not before he had experienced the hierarchical structure on board as the newest recruit – he had to share a cabin. Unfortunately for Tony, his cabin mate was Chris Denning, a raving queen. We all took the piss – as you would. Tony wanted to take the lower bunk. 'No,' we said, 'when he climbs the ladder to the top, Chris might fall on top of you!'

'Oh, well, I'll take the top bunk then.'

'Oh, no, you shouldn't do that. Chris will climb up the ladder, and pull it up with him. Then you'll have no chance!'

Tony was panic-stricken, and spent many a sleepless night with his hands covering his crotch! He was saved when another young, gay recruit joined the ship and, as he moved into the cabin with Chris, Tony moved out, quicker than the revs on an old 78! The rest of us were nothing but heterosexual, and couldn't wait for our week's leave to enjoy the favours of the opposite sex.

It wasn't until Ben quit a year later that Tony got a job with Big L. The rest is history. Tony, always ambitious and ahead of the game, joined the BBC Light Programme a month before Big L went off the air, thereby gaining that valuable foothold which propelled him into the breakfast chair on Radio 1. And he also had another invaluable commodity – talent. He might have his knockers, but Tony has proved to be one of the great survivors, with the greatest self-motivation of us all.

Someone else who enhanced his reputation with the listening public as a Big L DJ was Tony Windsor, whose 'hal-loooow' managed to fall a full octave and soon became his trademark. Formerly a highly popular DJ with 2SM in Sydney, Australia, TW was the mother hen on Big L, and your time was made more bearable when Tony was aboard. He was very camp, and loved to give us different girl's names. For instance, Kenny became Edith Everett, Mike was changed to Leila Lennox, Tony was Bessie Blackburn and I became Sally Stewart. Then, when Cadbury's Milk Tray started to advertise with us, we made the commercial using all our names coupled to the name of the chocolate. Kenny was a Strawberry Whirl, Tony a Nut Log and I was Hazel Cluster. But for all his campness, Tony never tried it on with any of us. Well, I don't think he did. Tony nurtured and encouraged our talents, and it was a sad day when he left. He never made it on Radio 1, the mid-morning slot in which he was so popular, that having already been earmarked for Jimmy Young. But Tony's influence was apparent in the format that the Jimmy Young programmes took – the recipe, the coffee break and even the use of initials – TW now became JY. But Jimmy didn't have Tony's voice – and that deep, rich 'hal-looooow'. How unkind life can be. TW dropped out of radio completely and died a disillusioned man, a filing clerk in a London hospital. JY continued successfully and his programme became an institution.

Aside from attracting raw talent presenting the shows, Radio London was also responsible for 'discovering' new acts and giving them the much-needed leg-up towards super stardom. 'And on the Radio London Fabulous 40 this week, there's a new Number One – "It's Not Unusual" by Tom Jones ...' Big L were elated because this was 'their' Number One as well. This was the first time the station had got behind an unknown singer, and it wouldn't be the last either. In another month's time, Unit Four Plus Two would have their only Number One, 'Concrete and Clay', all because of Big L.

The growing importance of pop radio was by now becoming apparent to the music industry as well, and it seems amazing now that the endemic 'payola' system on American radio never infected the DJs in this country, unless you call lunches at Soho's Trattoria Terrazza with Jonathan King a form of mental blackmail to get your record played.

As Radio London continued its success story, it was becoming harder for us to keep pace with it all. We were having so much fun on our weeks off, we were starting to prefer life on shore. Radio London held many Big L Nights, one of the most popular being the Wimbledon Palais. Whichever group or singer was in town used to appear at these venues to play a set or plug their records. We used to compère the shows, and got paid for it too, so these dates were very popular.

About a month after introducing the Shirelles, Stevie Wonder and a local girl called Twinkle at one of these gigs, I happened to be sitting in a dentist's waiting room – not enough vegetables on the *Galaxy* had given me a problem with my gums, which wouldn't stop bleeding. And I wondered why girls weren't kissing me! I idly opened up a copy of the *Tatler*. There on the review page was the headline BIG L AT THE PALAIS, and a full page on that night's goings on. Having criticised the noise, the lighting and the screaming kids, they continued, 'There then appeared one Ed Stewart, frenetic in beard, mid-Atlantic accent, horn-rimmed glasses and wearing what appeared to be a sawn-off Chinese dressing gown ... Nobody dances much. The more orderly and clubbable members of the crowd stand in a packed mass in front of the stage and take part in various games organised by Mr Stewart, e.g. four boys sit on the chairs with bibs round their necks, while four girls force a packet of crisps and a bottle of Seven Up down each of their throats as fast as they can. The four girls then come to the front of the stage and the first to blow up a balloon until it pops wins an LP of Manfred Mann. "Shove it in, girls!" shouts one wag, and the standard of the evening has been set.' My first review – and in the *Tatler*, no less.

In the 60s, the opening times in the pubs were much shorter than they are today, especially at lunchtime. So, on our week off, we would try and find the all-day drinking clubs, which were hidden away in London. They had a special licence, which meant if you paid a small fee and joined the club, you could drink all day. One club in particular used to waive this, as they found pirate DJs something of a novelty. It was called the 142 Club, at number 142 Charing Cross Road. Occasionally, you would find yourself rubbing shoulders with some gangsters of the day, so you had to be very careful who you bought drinks for.

One day, I was chatting up a particularly pretty blonde, when I felt a tap on my shoulder, and there was this broken-nosed, cauliflower-eared six-footer wagging his finger at me, and just mouthing the word 'No!' It turned out he was a minder for one of the Richardson Gang, and the blonde was his. I was lucky not to end up with a broken nose myself – my Roman nose would have ended up roamin' all over my face.

On the way out, I recognised a face I knew – Jimmy Logie, the former Arsenal and Scotland forward. He was selling newspapers.

From one former famous face on the way down, to one very much still at the top of her profession – Ella Fitzgerald. Working for such a well-regarded radio station had its perks for those of us who really loved music, and who would grab any opportunity to see the 'greats' live. And I was quite happy to use the station's cool image to see a living legend if at all possible.

'Hello!' said the chirpy voice at the end of the phone. 'This is Harold Davidson speaking – how can I help you?'

'This is Ed Stewart from Radio London, and I'm a big fan of Ella Fitzgerald … in fact, I interviewed her when she sang in Hong Kong last year. Would you have a spare ticket so I can go and see her at the Ronnie Scott's next week?'

What a nerve, I thought, asking for a freebie from someone I'd never met. I just hoped it would be more successful than when I had phoned up the Gaumont cinema in Wimbledon, and they had asked me to spell my name, 'No, not S-t-u ... it's S-t-e-wart!' My family had rolled around the floor in laughter. But with Harold Davison, the famous agent and jazz impresario – success!

'First of all, Ed, of course you can have a ticket, but on one condition ...' (Oh no, he's going to ask me to pay!) 'I want to pick your brains about pirate radio. I think you boys are doing a great job, and Big L is on our radio sets at home and in the office.' Wow! Fame at last! 'You must come and have lunch with me at Verrey's – maybe we can talk about my representing you as well. I have a tour coming up with Georgie Fame, the New Animals, the Paul Butterfield Blues Band, Geno Washington and the Ram Jam Band, and John Mayall's Bluesbreakers. Would you be interested in being one of the compères?' Would I! 'By the way,' he went on, 'do you like fish? Verrey's is very famous for it.'

'Do I like fish? I'm bobbing about on the North Sea for two weeks at a time and you ask me whether I like fish!' There was a slight pause at the other end of the phone, and I thought I'd been a little too cheeky. 'Only the ones I catch, Harold!'

He laughed, thank goodness. A relationship was born, and Harold Davidson became my first agent. His offices were plush, his secretaries were young and pretty, and his personal assistant, Mary Titmuss, really lived up to the first syllable of her surname. Between her and Harold, they seemed to know everyone in showbusiness.

There's a line in a Ray Charles recording of 'I've Got News For You', which goes, 'I took you to a nightclub and the whole band knew your name ...' That was Mary and Harold, especially when we eventually made it to Ronnie Scott's to see Ella.

Harold was smart; he saw how big pirate radio was

becoming, and signed three of us up to his agency – Tony Blackburn, Mike Lennox and myself. He booked Mike and me to be compères for the Georgie Fame and Geno Washington tour, sending us out with £100 of his own money to Cecil Gee to buy some decent clothes.

Harold was a very likeable and honest man, in whom I had complete trust. He was astute as well, signing Terry Wogan to his agency when Terry arrived from Ireland. When Harold eventually left for America to look after the interests of Frank Sinatra, Tom Jones and Engelbert Humperdink, Terry liked the agency so much, he bought it! Strictly speaking, he set up Jo Gurnett, the lady who had taken over the day-to-day running of Harold's stable of artistes, and retained the major shareholding. And that's where many of us remain to this day. I have broken ranks a couple of times, but on both occasions found that the grass wasn't necessarily greener.

Harold Davidson was married to Marion Ryan, a lovely, bubbly vocalist, who had had a Top Ten hit in 1958 with 'Love Me For Ever'. She was also the mother of twins, Paul and Barry. Paul was a talented songwriter, with Barry being the vocalist of the team. They had hits in the mid-60s with 'Don't Bring Me Your Heartaches' and 'Have Pity on the Boy'. By signing Tony, Mike and myself to his agency, Harold cleverly swung the airplay for his stepsons on Big L. I remember vividly Harold playing an original pressing, called an acetate, of a Barry Ryan release, written by his brother Paul, to find out my opinion. A huge hit, I said, and not just because it was the Ryans, Harold's prodigies. It was a good song and performance, called 'Eloise', reaching Number Two in November 1968. It was kept off the top spot by a Western film theme, Hugo Montenegro's 'The Good, the Bad and the Ugly'. Such was the diversity of the Top Ten then.

Undaunted, Harold continued to encourage Paul Ryan's songwriting talents and was rewarded when Ol' Blue Eyes himself recorded 'I Will Drink the Wine', which reached a commendable Number 16 in 1971. Sadly, it became one of the least played of Frank Sinatra's hits, sandwiched as it was between the eight re-entries of 'My Way'!

Harold's extensive friendships helped me out of what could have been a sticky situation in 1967. Part of Radio London's activities ashore included promotions at discos and clubs such as the Starlight Ballroom, Greenford, Billy Walker's Uppercut Club in Forest Gate, and the Witchdoctor club in Catford. Mike Lennox and I had formed quite a partnership on and off stage, and were finding out how easy it was to attract the girls. A bit big headed, maybe ... but true! Imagine picking up the paper on the day we were starting another week's leave, and reading about a gangland shooting at Mr Smith's Club in Catford, next door to the Witchdoctor club, where we were booked to appear.

I rushed round to Harold's office to see if he had any connections. 'Don't worry, boys, I'll make a phone call.' With that, he picked up the phone, dialled a number and, within minutes, was in earnest conversation with someone called Eddie. We sat there transfixed. When he had eventually finished talking, he swivelled round in his chair, and said, 'Don't worry – that was the boss, and you boys will be quite safe.'

'The Boss?' we enquired nervously.

'Yes,' he went on, 'Eddie Richardson ... his gang controls that part of London. To show he's sincere in his promise of there being no trouble for you, he will be leaving a bottle of champagne for you behind the bar at Mr Smith's. I suggest you take up his invitation!'

We gulped nervously, having heard and read about the tortures and murders. But being young and foolish, we thought 'what the hell', and duly presented ourselves at the bar of Mr Smith's after our appearance at the Witchdoctor. As the champagne took effect, the girls became more attractive, and we were becoming even more flirtatious. But, once again, the strong arm of the underworld took hold, and an unsmiling character with an eye patch, broken nose and a scar down his neck politely suggested we go forth and multiply. We were getting friendly with the wrong girls – his! We took up his kind invitation to leave, and never went back. If you're going to play with fire, it's best to extinguish it yourself.

But the real fun was to be had at trendy clubs like the Cromwellian, where we were more than just novelties – we were stars. The pirates were now becoming really influential for recording artists, and so we were being fêted more and more by the singers, the groups and any recording executive who happened to be there. There was never any question of 'payola', though – that was to come later.

As you've probably guessed, the real reason we frequented the clubs on our weeks off was for the girls. My great friends at the time were Mike Lennox and Duncan Johnson on Radio London. Mike was also a male model, and I soon found myself mixing in a group of straight guys who seemed to be surrounded by beautiful girls at all times. There was Willy, a good-looking sod from Bermuda with a wicked sense of humour; and a Brummie called Softly with a chat-up line that would have made Casanova jealous – 'I suppose a fuck is out of the question ...?' He was so good-looking, it never was! Then there was Ron the Tub-King – he used to persuade girls to join him in the bath, with a promise that he would scrub their backs in a way they'd never been scrubbed before. We eventually gave him another name – the Scrubber, because most of the girls he pulled were just that! There was Mike 'the Marshall' Lennox, so called because he just rounded the girls up and took his pick! Duncan's nickname name was Shag – he was so lazy chatting up the women, he just couldn't be shagged to try.

Then came me – beard and glasses and an uncool haircut. The

models took me in hand; off came the beard, in went the contact lenses and I was a new man. So to the Cromwellian, and there, sitting at the bar, were three of the most gorgeous girls I'd ever seen. They were American air stewardesses, and it was their first trip to Swinging London. 'Hey, girls – have you met the Duke?' asked Willy.

'The Dook? A real live dook?' chorused the girls and Willy replied, 'Yes, the Duke of Wimbledon – Edward is about to inherit his father's millions!'

Before I could say anything, Willy had ordered a bottle of Moët, and told the barman to stick it on my tab! It was enough to impress the girls and, before long, I was going along with the story and, as the third bottle of bubbly arrived, wondered how I was going to pay for it. The next problem then hit me harder than the worry of the bill. If I was going to entice any of the girls into bed, where was I going to take her? I had no place of my own, and would invariably just crash out on somebody's floor. But help was at hand. 'Why don't you take her back to my pad?' asked Ron the Tub. 'The key's under the mat.'

I should have smelt a rat. Actually, I smelt mildew. When Miss Pan-Am and I arrived at what she thought was going to be the Dook's penthouse apartment, it turned out to be a basement bedsit in Bayswater. With some instant improvising of Mensa proportions, I walked over to the building opposite, which was a swanky looking block of flats, and pretended to rummage around for the key. By this time, the taxi had gone and I blurted out that I must have dropped the keys in the cab, so we couldn't get in to the penthouse. 'Oh, never mind,' said Miss Pan-Am, 'let's go back to my hotel – I've got to tell the girls I got laid by a real life dook!' And she was. And I often wonder if she ever told her grandchildren. Well, it did happen nearly 40 years ago!

Every generation moans about 'the music of today' – it's too noisy, too brash, it's unmelodic or the words don't mean anything.

When I was a teenager, the arrival of Bill Haley and Elvis Presley brought howls of indignation from the older generation. The music was too loud, the words repetitive and Elvis and his swivelling hips were too rude and suggestive. One friend of the family, who was a keen fly fisherman, exclaimed, 'There should be a close season on cacophony.' I thought that rather funny, but I'm sure he meant it! Those howls of indignation continue today at the sound of Radio 1 and many of the commercial stations – the only difference is that today's older generation includes me!

The Radio 1 of today is a sad echo of the one that opened up in 1967. Many will remember the first record to be played on Radio 1 by Tony Blackburn – 'Flowers in the Rain' by the Move. Fewer will recall Radio London's first record at 6.00am on Wednesday, 23 December 1964. Pete Brady kicked off his breakfast show with 'I Could Easily Fall' by Cliff Richard, followed by 'What Have They Done to the Rain?' by the Searchers, and 'One More Time' by the Ray Charles Singers – I don't think I've ever played that one, let alone heard it! The initial record library at Radio London was made up of no more than 50 records. These included a box given to Pete Brady by Decca Records, which included one track by a Welsh unknown called Tom Jones. That's how 'It's Not Unusual' received its first airing.

Every city in the US had its own Top 40 radio station – they were leaders in their market because they played the music everybody wanted to hear. Our American programme director, Ben Toney, decided this would be the format for Big L. The BBC chart was based entirely on record sales. The Radio London chart was more adventurous and included records that the station believed were going to become hits. It was pretty accurate, and in two and a half years only missed two Number Ones – Elvis Presley's 'Crying in the Chapel' and Ken Dodd's 'Tears' – but then who would have predicted that one! The Fab

40 was a fresher sound and anything considered past its sell-by date was dropped and replaced by something up and coming or brand new. This is how the Top Ten of the chart looked on the weekend I joined Big L on 4 July 1965:

1. 'To Know Him Is to Love Him' by Peter and Gordon
2. 'Heart Full of Soul' by The Yardbirds
3. 'Leave a Little Love' by Lulu
4. 'Help Me Rhonda' by The Beach Boys
5. 'Got Live if You Want It' (EP) by The Rolling Stones
6. 'Looking Through the Eyes of Love' by Gene Pitney
7. 'The One in the Middle' (EP) by Manfred Mann
8. 'She's About a Mover' by Sir Douglas Quintet
9. 'Mr Tambourine Man' by The Byrds
10. 'Tossing and Turning' by The Ivy League

We had to stick to a pretty rigid format, but this was what gave the station its unique sound. The hour would begin with a record from the Top Ten, followed by another from 11 to 40. Next would come a 'Revived 45', sometimes referred to as a 'Rave from the Grave', and then a Big L climber. Then you went back again to the Top Ten and 11 to 40, and then an American hit and finally an album track. That was a winning format and yet I don't know of any UK station that follows it today. We averaged 18 records an hour and a maximum of 6 minutes were allowed for commercials. That left little time for inane DJ chat and the 'Much More Music' policy was rigidly adhered to. It took a few shows to get into the discipline, but it worked. Perhaps some of today's DJs and presenters should remember the old adage – you're only as good as the music you play.

Many singers and groups were by now braving the elements and visiting the ships to plug their records. Others dropped in on 17 Curzon Street to record interviews and messages. The Beatles,

Gerry and the Pacemakers, Roger Miller, Bobby Vee and the Supremes ... they all recorded interviews and messages in London, which were then sent out to the ship. Gene Pitney, Peter and Gordon and Marianne Faithfull made the trip out to the *Galaxy*. Marianne Faithfull famously signed the visitors' book 'Marijuana Faithfull'.

Nearly 30 DJs made the good ship *Galaxy* their home over the two and a half years that it was anchored off the Essex coast.

I remember in 1967 receiving a letter from one young aspiring DJ in particular – Noel Edmonds. He wrote asking if there were any vacancies at the station, but I replied that since we were about to be scuppered, he would be better off applying to Radio Luxembourg. He did – and the rest is history.

Noel has been an astute businessman and now that he has found personal happiness as well, seems to have retired from public view. I should imagine only temporarily, as Noel took over from the unfortunate Johnnie Walker on Radio 2, when he had to take time off for his fight against cancer. What price now that Noel might slide into Terry Wogan's seat? Not very likely. Noel's interests are too wide for an early-morning show. Sitting in for a couple of months for Johnnie Walker was enough, he said. We shall see.

On Radio London one or two prosepctive DJs lasted just a couple of days, some a few months or a year or more, and some hardy souls like Paul Kaye lasted the whole course and was both the first and last voice to be heard on Big L. I joined in July 1965 and, using the language of the sea, 'went down with my ship' on 14 August 1967. In that time, the *Galaxy* foundered only once, when she slipped her anchor during a violent storm in early 1967. The first to answer the mayday call was a German tug, which happened to be in the area. The crew offered to tow us off the sandbank on which we were trapped, but Captain Buninga, Radio London's Dutch captain, told them what to do with their tow cable. 'No bloody German is getting salvage money from me!' he yelled. So we waited for an English tug from Harwich to pull us back into international waters. That was allowed.

A couple of months later, I was in the studio wishing I wasn't there, not because I was fed up with the job, but because Everton were in the Cup Final. So I persuaded Willy Walker who, by now, had turned from male modelling to life on the ocean wave, to take over while I watched the match in the Mess. By the time I had climbed the stairs, Everton were two down, and everybody was cheering for Sheffield Wednesday, just to wind me up. The second half was excitingly different, with two goals scored by an unknown Cornishman, Mike Trebilcock. As the match was nearing the end, and I was due back in the studio, Everton's winger, Derek Temple, scored a classic breakaway winner. I leapt up in ecstasy, cracking my head on the bulkhead above. I was too dazed to go back on air – but Everton had won! The afterglow of that win was not to last long, though – a Red was about to clamber aboard.

In the last few months of Radio London's life, John Ravenscroft appeared. Born on the Wirral, which is on the opposite side of the Mersey to Liverpool, John had served his two years of National Service and had left to 'seek his fortune' in America in 1960. He ended up selling insurance and falling into radio. Our lives had run similar courses. I had been offered a job in 1962 with Bernie Cornfield's Investors Overseas Services, but had turned it down. My career was to be in radio. John's start in radio coincided with the start of the Beatles' popularity in America, so he adopted a Scouse 'twang' to his voice and became an immediate authority on the Mersey sound. On KOMA in Oklahoma City and KMEN in San Bernardino, California, John had become very aware of bands such as Jefferson Airplane and Grateful Dead and, when he joined Radio London in 1967, he started to include them in his late-night programmes. John Ravenscroft had by now become John Peel and, in keeping with his laid-back style and inclusion of American flower-power music, had renamed his programme *The Perfumed Garden*. Listeners were convinced that his studio was swathed in incense and other substances that made him sound so relaxed. The foundations of his future broadcasting styles were being built.

The kind of shockwaves that swept the country when John sadly and so unexpectedly died in November 2004 had not been felt since the death of Princess Diana seven years previously. Or so it seemed. John's death didn't create the same mass hysteria, but there was a love for him that took many of who weren't his fans and listeners by complete surprise. And that included me. We had never been bosom buddies, but there had been a mutual respect there. On the few occasions that we met, we always chided each other about our respective football teams, Everton and Liverpool. He wouldn't have liked what I just wrote – putting Everton before Liverpool! John broke so many acts over the years and his contribution to British bands is incalculable. He was an inspiration to those groups and singers who hoped they would have the talent, the magic to get to the top. Even if they didn't, he'd play them anyway! John was a one-off and that's why he was never popular in the same way that a Terry Wogan, a David Jacobs or even a Johnnie Walker, who is a bit of a rebel himself, would have been. But essentially we have all shared the same talent, we 'pop-jockeys'. When John Peel died, he became a sort of deity, but it amazed many that he was offered over a million pounds to write his memoirs. What an advance. Almost as much as mine!

When John appeared on *This Is Your Life*, he was gracious enough to remember that he was given the first opportunity to play the Beatles' *Sgt Pepper* album in 1967. Radio London had been able to force Dick James, the Beatles' music publisher, to let us have one of only three copies of the original recordings. Apparently, a secretary who worked at EMI had secretly taped the session on a recorder in her coat pocket! Although the recording quality was not perfect, it had somehow found its way to our programme director, Alan Keen. Alan then told Dick James that he was going to play the poor-quality tape on the air, unless, of course, he could provide him with a proper copy. The veiled threat worked, and John Peel played the entire album eight days before the Light Programme did and three weeks before its release. This may seem unimportant today, but to be given a scoop like that actually made John Peel cry with emotion. That's how and why the last track on *Sgt Pepper*, 'A Day in the Life', became the final track to be played on Radio London. John Peel, however, was so uncertain of his future that he actually applied for a job as a keeper at London Zoo! However, he remained the longest serving DJ at Radio 1 ... and it all began in an imaginary Perfumed Garden, on board a ship.

So now, for the Big L, the end was near and we were facing the final curtain. Tony Blackburn and Kenny Everett (who said that he didn't want to be a maritime offence!) had left and were already working on the BBC Light Programme. The government was winning and soon we would be joining the rat-race of life ashore. I had been summoned to make an audition tape for the birth of Radio 1 by a BBC producer called Angela Bond. Angela had been a singer in Hong Kong and had often joined our band for a gig or session. Another case of it not always being what you know but who you know that counts!

Angela had a pile of records and a script and off I went. Angela's critique afterwards went along the lines of, 'Very good, Eddie,' – I had always been Eddie in Hong Kong, although I couldn't stand it – 'but you forgot to give me a name-check!' And with that she threw her pencil at me, hitting me on the end of my nose, point first. Welcome to the BBC! I was learning fast.

Tony Blackburn and Kenny Everett had jumped ship early and secured the prime slots on the new Radio 1. The rest of us clung on until the bitter end, and were rewarded with fan frenzy which greeted us when we arrived at Liverpool Street station on the evening of 14 August 1967, the date that had been set by the then Labour government for the outlawing of pirate radio stations. The final hour of transmission had been full of emotion, and included messages of regret, but many of hope from Cliff Richard, Dave Clark, Ray Davies, Hank Marvin, Bruce Welch and Stevie Winwood, all united in their support of Radio London. Bruce Johnston of the Beach Boys, Dusty Springfield and Ringo Starr were the last three recorded messages. Ringo said it was a bit of a pity, and radio would never be the same, and Dusty told the listeners that her mum would go potty without Radio London! Then we played the second verse of her hit 'You Don't Have to Say You Love Me', which starts 'Left alone with just a memory, life seems dead and so unreal ...' Lyrically, that was the most poignant moment of all.

The managing director of Radio London, Philip Birch, was almost Churchillian with the content and delivery of his final words: 'During the last three years, I feel Radio London has done very little harm, but an awful lot of good ... I'd like thank the 12 million listeners in the UK and the 4 million on the Continent ... if, during that time, Radio London has brought a little warmth, a little friendliness, a little happiness into your life, then it's all been worthwhile. As one listener has put it, the world will get by without Big L, but I'm not sure it will be a better place.'

Philip Birch had recorded his speech so that he could listen to the final hour on his own. He parked his car in a lay-by and cried. He was not the only one – his tears were shared with millions of listeners, and many of the Big L staff. As the climactic final chord of 'A Day in the Life' faded away, Paul Kaye made his last announcement: 'Big L time is three o'clock, and Radio London is now closing down.' Then, one last play of The Big L theme ... and Radio London disappeared for good. The memories will always remain, though, together with the pride of knowing that we had changed the face and the sound of radio in the UK.

When I think back to my time on the *Galaxy*, there are a few tracks that I will always associate with life at sea:

1. **'It's Not Unusual ' – Tom Jones**
   Tom himself was gracious enough to say that, without Big L's support, he might never have had the hit that he did. A superb song and arrangement, with Jimmy Page's guitar solo towards the end offering a taste of things to come with Led Zeppelin.

2. **'Everyone's Gone to the Moon' – Jonathan King**
   He used to take us out to lunch and made us feel really important. There was no other ulterior motive, I'm glad to say, and I loved playing this record. Very reflective of the time, and it still sounds better when heard on AM or medium wave. There was no stereo radio then!

3. **'A Walk in the Black Forest' – Horst Jankowski**
   The first record I played on joining the ship in July 1965. I'm glad we didn't have to introduce it by its original title: 'Eine Schwarzwaldt Fahrt'!

4. **'I Got You, Babe' – Sonny and Cher**
   Another song which could only have been a hit in the 60s. Cher has turned out to be one of the great survivors.

5. **'Eve of Destruction' – Barry McGuire**
   This former lead singer of the New Christy Minstrels came up with one of the decade's best protest songs. Perhaps I liked it because being a pirate DJ was the nearest I'd come to protesting about anything – in this case the lack of pop music on British radio!

6. **'Hang On Sloopy' – The McCoys**
   Another record that reminds me for ever of bobbing about on the North Sea in the middle of a Force 8 gale!

7. 'Groovin" – The Young Rascals

Being a bit of a rascal myself, to remember groovin' with a young lady on a Sunday afternoon is something of a feat. Or was it a Tuesday? Who Cares!

8. 'The Carnival Is Over' – The Seekers

When compèring a concert tour of Alpine music for Ingham's, the skiing people, I heard a song by a Tyrolean Male Voice Choir called 'Va Alpin'. It was the same, note for note and chord for chord, as 'The Carnival is Over'. I wonder which song was the original.

9. 'I've Got You Under My Skin'– the Four Seasons

Has there ever been a better version of this song than Frank Sinatra's? Not this one, but it comes a good second for originality. I've always been amazed by Frankie Valli's 'falsetto'. How did he do it in those tight trousers?

10. 'Elusive Butterfly' – Bob Lind

Only a poet could have written lyrics like these – and that's exactly what Baltimore-born Bob was. Val Doonican also recorded this, and both he and Bob reached Number Five in the charts – at the same time.

11. 'You Don't Have to Say You Love Me' – Dusty Springfield

My favourite singer of the time, she paid a moving tribute to Radio London when we closed down.

12. 'Stay With Me, Baby' – Lorraine Ellison

This was what is termed a 'turntable hit', which never charted in the UK. The most heart-wrenching performance I've ever heard from anybody on record, and she must have been feeling every word of it.

13. 'Hey, Joe' – Jimi Hendrix

The only time I was ever offered money to play a record. I never took it, of course, but the plugger who tried it on really shouldn't have bothered. This classic was to launch the career of the most charismatic figure of his generation.

14. **'A Whiter Shade of Pale' – Procul Harum**
    When I first heard this record, I cried. Like the Beatles 'Lucy in the Sky with Diamonds', the lyrics are so crazy, you wonder what the writers were on when they wrote them.
15. **'A Day in the Life' – The Beatles.**
    The last record to be played on Big L. I never could stand those loud bits in the middle and end, and still can't. But it was the end of an era – so mustn't grumble!

On leaving the *Galaxy* for the last time, the train taking us back to Liverpool Street was late. HM Customs had taken a little longer to clear us at Felixstowe, so we had missed the connection at Ipswich. But still, many fans had boarded it to make the journey to London. When we finally arrived, there was quite a shock for us. About 2,500 fans were waiting for us. The press and TV were there in force to describe the scene as the fans went wild when our train pulled in. Most of us made it to waiting cars, while one or two had to lock themselves in a ladies' loo as a temporary hideaway. The *Daily Mail* quoted a senior police officer as saying the fans were pretty well-behaved, but at the same time reminded its readers that it had to honour the conditions of the Marine Offences Act or suffer the consequences: 'The *Daily Mail* is discontinuing publication of Radio Caroline programmes because this is illegal under the new Act. Penalties range from a maximum fine of £400 to two years in jail – or both.'

Radio Caroline, unlike Radio London, had decided to continue broadcasting, and was to survive, in one form or another, for many years to come. The American backers of Radio London had thrown in the towel after making a healthy profit, reportedly to the tune of $8m, about £3m. But the closing of Radio London and the Liverpool riots were the lead story on the BBC evening news, and Alistair Burnett introduced ITN's *News at Ten* by saying, 'Good evening. Very soon, at midnight exactly, a way of life will come to an end for an awful lot of people. The government has finally produced legislation to force the pirate stations off the air … What the Act says, in effect, is that anyone who in any way helps the pirates by working for them, by taking advertisements on them or supplying them with food and equipment, is committing a crime. Already at three o' clock this afternoon, one of the best known and powerful of the pop pirates closed down. Radio London, the "mast with the most" as it called itself, surrendered and went off the air.'

Six weeks later, many of us were back – with Radio 1.

6

BBC – LICENSED
TO THRILL

IN THOSE early days at Radio 1, the BBC had to experiment. I felt we were all like decorators' glue, which had been thrown against a wall – those who stuck, stayed!

At the start of the 1960s, Radio 1 would have been unimaginable. But in 1967, BBC radio was to change for ever. It was brilliant to be part of the team that was going to make broadcasting history. From the day it opened, 30 September 1967, on 247 metres in the medium wave band, it was an instant success, with tens of millions tuning in right from the start. Famously, the first voice was that of Tony Blackburn playing the Move's 'Flowers in the Rain'. Why? No way was he going to play the Number One that week – Engelbert Humperdinck's 'The Last Waltz', and neither was he going to trumpet the start of Radio 1 with the Number 2, 'Excerpt from a Teenage Opera' by Keith West. So he 'Moved' with 'Flowers in the Rain', which was at Number Three.

Tony was one of 15 ex-pirates employed by the BBC, some of whom were rather coyly named by one of the broadsheets as

Anthony Blackburn, Edward Stewart, David Cash and Michael Pasternak, better known as Emperor Rosko. Of the established names, Pete Murray, Simon Dee, Michael Aspel, Grandaddy Jack Jackson and former pop singer Jimmy Young were also to kick off the new programmes. A highly popular Irish broadcaster was to present *Late Night Extra*. His name was misprinted as Terry Wogen and he was described as a brand-new face on British radio. Radio 1 immediately attracted huge audiences, and thousands of square feet of newspaper coverage.

'In the beginning, there was Lord Reith ...' wrote the *Daily Mail* in October 1967, 'and even the radio announcers were made to read the news wearing dinner jackets and black ties. And, in the end, there is Lord Hill with a new breed of men called disc jockeys now dressed as DJs with some of them in a paler shade of puce. They have invaded the corridors of the BBC to start a new broadcasting service called Radio 1 ... What Radio 1 is doing is to introduce a new and potentially vicious competition among the men who make up the new disc-jockey team. They have been given short contracts and a great deal of weeding out is yet to be done. The biggest failure was a much-touted American gentleman named Rosko who seems to believe that noise and raving will cover any deficiency. There was also the irritating sound of Ed Stewart babbling in the morning about how he likes his tea!'

What the *Daily Mail* failed to recall was possibly the first immortal one-liner in Radio 1's history. When the hourly news interrupted Rosko's programme, John Dunn the newsreader started with ... 'Here is the news – in English.'

The paper went on to suggest that the Top Ten would no longer consist of the most popular records but the most popular DJs. It would be less important *what* they played as opposed to *who* played it. Personally, I have always stuck by the rule that you are only as good as the music you play. If you don't enjoy the music, you shouldn't be in the job. Thirty-five years later, that rule has worked brilliantly for Radio 2 but badly for Radio 1, in listening figures, at least.

Back in 1967, the *Daily Mail* offered to print the top ten DJs voted for by the paper's readers. The paper's own favourites were Jack Jackson, Pete Murray, David Jacobs and Sean Kelly (and if you don't recognise that name he was a newsreader from New Zealand who was also one of the presenters of *Late Night Extra*).

The readers' poll looked like this:

1. Tony Blackburn
2. Kenny Everett
3. Keith Skues
4. Pete Murray
5. Ed Stewart
6. Emperor Rosko
7. John Peel
8. Simon Dee
9. David Jacobs
10. Chris Denning

Of that list, sadly, Kenny Everett, probably the most brilliant of all, and John Peel, the DJs' DJ, are no longer with us. Tony Blackburn has been working for some time with various different commercial radio stations and grabbed headlines becoming the King of the Jungle in ITV's *I'm a Celebrity – Get Me Out of Here*. Keith Skues can be heard on several local BBC stations in East Anglia; Pete Murray was with LBC for some time until he suffered another acrimonious sacking to go with the one he received from the BBC in the early 80s; Emperor Rosko is syndicating programmes to independent stations in the UK; David Jacobs and I have been with Radio 2 for what seems like an eternity, and it's a case of 'Where are you now, Simon Dee and Chris Denning?'

In response to the poll in 1967, David Lewin said he thought the result was a fair assessment of feeling about the new crew of

DJs although he still couldn't stand Mr Stewart or Mr Rosko! His final comment showed a distinct lack of foresight: 'If I had a son who wanted to become a disc jockey, I'd try and dissuade him. I don't think it is a growth industry!' There are now 6 national BBC stations, over 300 local and independent stations, as well as a plethora of stations available via satellite and digital services. I wonder if David Lewin Jr ever listened to his father's advice!

Radio 1 was twice as controversial in 1967 as it is today – and we had twice as many listeners. We were in the sights of the marksmen of Fleet Street and looking back on some of those critiques of the times, they make unkind, but amusing, reading today. Bernard Hollowood wrote in *Punch*, 'For a long time now, I have been puzzled by the identities of the people who run the radio and TV chat and record programmes. Who are Alan Freeman, Mike Raven, Ed Stewart, Simon Dee, Tony Blackburn, Jimmy Young, Terry Wogan and Pete Murray? What qualifications do they have other than appearing with sickening regularity?' Mr Hollowood then went on to suggest that these programmes should be put into the hands of real heroes such as George Best, Martin Peters, Geoff Boycott and Colin Cowdrey – 'They have good, honest faces and healthy outdoor complexions ...' (especially good for radio!) 'and they are fit and strong enough to put on records. Our sportsmen are underemployed and the likes of Simon Dee, Jimmy Young, Ed Stewart, etc. could be better employed with work of national importance, like the construction of a new airport, electrification of the London to Glasgow line, or slum clearance!'

I felt I had really 'arrived' though, when the great Patrick Campbell, who had become famous not only for his wonderful way with words, but also for stuttering, included me in one of his weekly meanderings. People found that they were not laughing at him, but more with him and the way in which he could turn his impediment into something of fun rather than ridicule. He wrote,

'We've scarcely recovered from the shock of losing Duncan Johnson, when, without warning, poor old Ed Stewart, who had been doing a really f–f–fab job with *Happening Sunday*, gets the hatchet. And no one knows why. I mean, he'd learnt his trade with Radio London and you couldn't have a finer apprenticeship than that!' I know he was taking the mickey but it was a real honour to have appeared in one of Patrick Campbell's c–c–c–columns!

Not everybody at the BBC welcomed us with outstretched arms. We were considered long-haired upstarts, though hardly any of us actually had long hair. Another description overheard by Tony Brandon went, 'Oh, look, Fortescue, over there at the bar – one of those ... what do you call them? ... pop jockeys.' Then there were the BBC commissionaires – stalwart ex-servicemen who had fought both world wars and were eking out another living in the service of another British institution. And how they looked after us, this uncouth breed of Brilliant British Broadcasters!

'Are you a member, sir?' the commissionaire asked pompously.

'No, but I've got one.'

Obviously mishearing me, he went on, 'And what is your name, sir?'

'Peter Enis.'

'Then can you sign in, sir?'

I signed in quickly – 'P. Enis' – and strode into the bar with heads turning and G and Ts spluttering as I ordered my first drink.

This line of chat got me into the BBC Club on a couple more occasions until, one evening, there, guarding the entrance to the club like a bulldog, was your very own medals-on-the-chest-shoulders-back-chin-out-regimental Sergeant Major Jobsworth. 'You can't come in here without your membership card, sir ...' They were obliged to call all males 'sir'.

'But I have been telling you I have left mine behind. But I do have a friend over there who could sign me in.'

Top left: My father, Ray, in typical pose, photographed shortly before the Second World War. My mother eventually persuaded him to lose the moustache.

Top right: Granny Ida, my father's mother. Her family, the Carters, were well-known lawyers and judges in Newfoundland.

Bottom left and right: Mum and dad on honeymoon in Monte Carlo.

Top: My mother Peggy with all her brood in 1956. (Left to right) John, Sue, mum, Mike and me. Dad was probably at work as usual.

Above: Skiffle days in 1958. Playing my bass with Tony Wall (left) and Richard Oxlade (right) who changed the course of my life by persuading me to go out to Hong Kong.

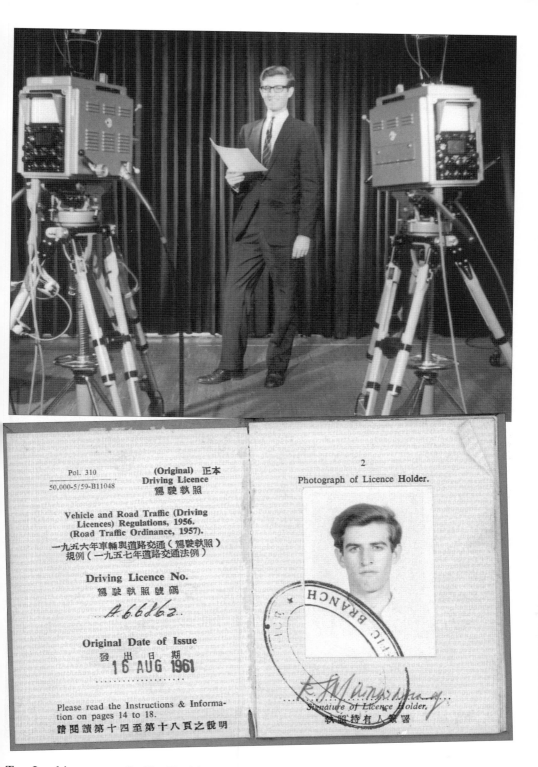

Top: Looking uncannily like Buddy Holly for my first TV appearance reading the news for Redfussion in Hong Kong, 1964. The suit cost $HK100 – about £7 – can you tell?

Above: My Hong Kong driving licence.

Top: With Louis Armstrong at a night club in Hong Kong. I was Satchmo's bass player (for one number only!). Also pictured are fellow musicians Pete o'Neil and Joe Macmillan.

Above: George Harrison answering questions as the Beatles passed through Hong Kong in 1964. Eddie Mainwaring is sitting on the right and was about to ask George the all important question, 'Do you support Everton or Liverpool?' The answer was lost in a flurry of other shouts in broken Chinese–English.

The good ship Galaxy, home to Radio London. Inset: DeeJay Ed Stewart at the helm on the cover of *Time*.

The way we were. The original Radio 1 line up – photographed on the steps of All Saints Church next to Broadcasting House, September 1967.

Back row, left to right: Tony Blackburn, Jimmy Young, Kenny Everett, Duncan Johnson, Robin Scott (Controller, Radios 1 and 2), David Ryder, Dave Cash, Pete Brady, David Symonds

Middle row, left to right: Bob Holness, Terry Wogan, Barry Alldiss, Mike Lennox, Keith Skues, Chris Denning, Johnnie Moran, Pete Myers

Front row: Pete Murray, me, Pete Drummond, Mike Raven, Mike Ahern, John Peel

The only time Ed Stewart bought Tony Blackburn a drink. He didn't like it!

Top: With George Best at his Manchester boutique, 1969. I've never seen so many girls chasing one man – and it wasn't me!

Above: Having reached the final of the TV quiz game Quiz Ball, we (that is Everton) were beaten by Celtic. Left to right: Brian Labone, Harry Catterick, me, quizmaster Stuart Hall and Joe Royle.

When the commissionaires called out anybody's name for a phone call, instead of relying on one of those newfangled microphone contraptions, they would stick out their chests and, with a near-perfect Stentorian tone, enunciate the name of the person wanted on the telephone. We delighted in phoning the reception desk and asking to speak to someone whose name was unfamiliar to them but would raise a mirthful snigger from the assembled cognoscenti. 'Calling Miss Pamela Motown – will Miss Pamela Motown please come to the phone …' No response, but a few knowing winks and a ribald laugh from Robin Richmond, the highly popular BBC organist. After Miss Truly Scrumptious, Miss Connie Lingus and Mr Ric O'Shea, it was time for the coup de grâce – tomorrow would be the night when all jobsworths would meet their employer.

The next evening, I walked up to the BBC Club desk and was about to ask for Mr Enis to sign me in, when the commissionaire turned round and – shock, horror – it was a woman! How could I ask a woman to speak to somebody with such a name? I'd probably get a slapped face or be banned from the club for life. Flustered and sheepish, I asked her if I could join the club and how much it would cost.

'How much?' my cry rang out across the room.

'Come on, Ed – cough up.' It was Robin Richmond, back for another night of propping up the bar. 'Now that you're a fully paid-up member, you can celebrate by buying me the first drink – a large gin and tonic, please!' Hoisted by my own petard! But as I was about to find out, you could claim your own copy of the *Radio Times* – free. Some stories do have a happy ending, don't they!

Well, almost. Our puerile little games of calling up the club to call out fictitious names ended when the commissionaire on duty recognised Kenny Everett's voice. He wanted to speak to a Miss Betty Swollocks. The Commissionaire had heard that one before!

There was a drinking culture that seemed to have been endemic in those early Radio 1 and 2 days in the BBC Club. If I had been working more regularly during the week, I'm sure I might have been sucked into it. One of the few announcers to have survived it is Colin Berry, still reading the news on Radio 2. Only a part-time novice then, he watched in amused horror the antics of some of the older diehards, and wondered how on earth every news story was read out with such clarity and credibility. The 'Grand Tour' would start, after the 11 o'clock shift change, at the Yorkshire Grey, the George or the Horse and Groom, which were the pubs nearest to the studios at Broadcasting House. Time for something a little more substantial? Off they would go to the Salad Bar in the club premises in the Langham, where the food was cheaper, and the lunchtime bonhomie more highly charged. At 12.55pm, Bruce Wyndham or Roger Moffatt would cry, 'Is that the time?' and rush across the road to the news studio to deliver a masterly reading of the important events of the world that lunchtime. Then it was back to the club, where another large G and T would be lined up, ready and waiting, while the hand that grasped it would be more than willing!

The Langham, when it was built in the 1860s, had been dubbed a Victorian monster, and had only become fashionable in the 1930s when Emperor Haille Selassie of Ethiopia and his entourage had decamped there for a time. During the Blitz, the Langham Hotel had received a direct hit, demolishing the very part of the building where the author JB Priestley was staying. At the moment the bomb fell, he had been in Broadcasting House, speaking on air to Canada. For JB, at least, it was a lucky day!

'And now, here's a gale warning – Gale, get out of the house, my wife is on her way home!' That was Bruce Wyndham, and one of his corny jokes – he used to present his programme in the hour before *Junior Choice* on a Saturday morning. He claimed he taught Tony Blackburn everything he knew! By the sound of that gag, he was probably right. I would listen to the last ten minutes, just in case he made a rude mention or said something silly about me to which I could retaliate. One famous morning, I had to begin 45 minutes early because Bruce hadn't shown up. Overnight announcers and newsreaders stayed in one of the many bedrooms in the Langham (it used to be a hotel), and that morning, after a particularly heavy night, Roger Moffatt had apparently wedged a table against Bruce's door, making it impossible for him to get out of his room. The dawn chorus that Saturday morning was joined by a few Wyndham expletives as Bruce tried to escape. It was funny at the time, but the question was immediately asked as to what would have happened if there had been a fire. Roger and Bruce were never allowed on the same shift again.

I soon realised that the BBC Club was not just for drinking. Many young and impressionable secretaries and producer's assistants would make it their hunting ground in order to meet and trap young, impressionabls DJs. I was easily impressed. So was Jimmy Saville, but he would never set foot on licensed premises – he would order an orange juice from the corridor, and pick up girls there!

It would have been interesting for those old newsreaders to have auditioned again for their jobs – it might have taken place in a studio called the 'Soak Shop'! One of Colin Berry's first summaries as a fully-fledged newsreader was written by a subeditor with a wicked sense of humour: 'Shares in the retail chain Soxshop have been suspended on the Stock Exchange. SoxShop recently announced a six million pound loss after a large expansion into expensive shop sites in stations and airports ...' Try reading that, unrehearsed, after an hour in the BBC Club!

The interview was going well. Penny Valentine of *Disc and Music Echo* was complimentary about the sound of Radio 1 and especially the former 'pirate' DJs. Flattery will get you everywhere, I thought, as I eyed the blonde and beautiful reporter. My hot-blooded thoughts were interrupted by the sound of the

OUT OF THE STEWPOT

telephone. 'You'd better answer that, Ed,' she said, 'it might be another contract!'

'Hello,' said the voice at the other end. 'This is James Green of the *London Evening News*. Is that Ed Stewart?'

The press. When do they ever call with good news?

'Yes, it is,' I replied, 'how can I help?'

'I've just been to a press conference with Robin Scott, the Controller of Radio 1, and he's told me he is dropping you from your *Happening Sunday* programme. How do you feel?'

Why is it that interviewers, whether from radio, TV or the press, always ask you questions you can barely answer? King Harold – 'You didn't see it coming, huh?' King Charles I – 'You want to quit while you're ahead, do you?' Adolf Hitler – 'So you're not so good out of bunkers, are you?'

Penny Valentine was very sympathetic, and assured me that this was only part of the teething troubles that Radio 1 were bound to have. I thought back to my first *Happening Sunday*. My opening record had been the Beach Boys, the same group with which I had started my Radio London career. Then we had had studio sessions on Radio 1 that first Sunday with Procul Harum, Amboy Dukes and John Walker, of Walker Brother fame, singing 'Blueberry Hill' with the Northern Dance Orchestra. The Musicians Union were certainly doing their job then! Needle time restrictions were a pain in the arse to us DJs, preventing us from playing the number of records we wanted but, at the time, there was nothing we could do about it. Most of the needle time allocation went on the most important show of the day, the breakfast show. Never once did Tony Blackburn have to play the BBC Northern Dance Orchestra's version of 'Strawberry Fields Forever'! But the rest of us did.

So – shock, horror – I was out of a job, and it wouldn't be for the first time. But as one door closed, another one opened, and the one-eyed monster was to beckon for the first time. But before that, another twist of fate was to take me in a different direction. It was not so much a slice of luck as a colour that was to help me along.

Mrs Knowles was an auralist, someone who could tell what was going to happen to you by the hue of colour that surrounded you. In my case, a light shade of green. One of my great friends of the time was, and happily still is, Tony Brandon, a product of the *Carroll Levis Talent Show*, a forerunner to Hughie Green's *Opportunity Knocks*. A couple of years before, he had been in a similar quandary about what to do next in his career. He took the advice of someone he knew well – Peter Sellers. Whenever Peter had experienced a hiatus in his life and wanted guidance as to what to do next, he went see Mrs Knowles in her basement flat in Marylebone. She seemed to have pointed him in the right direction on many occasions and she had become an oracle. So it was to be with Tony and, subsequently, myself.

Tony Brandon was a comedian and actor and, like many in the profession, out of work. On Peter Sellers's advice, he went to see Mrs Knowles, although Tony was slightly sceptical because Mrs Knowles knew that Peter Sellers was extremely famous, and she might have been telling him the things he *wanted* to hear and could, therefore, have been making things up. Of payment, Peter had said, 'All she wants is a couple of bob in the PDSA box – for her animals!'

Tony went along to Marylebone High Street. She took one look at him said he had a light-green hue, he worked in something that required creativity, and that next he would be working somewhere abroad. Two weeks later, in March 1966, Tony Brandon was the new name on 208 Radio Luxembourg!

So, I thought, I've got nothing to lose. Since my once-a-week programme on Radio 1 had gone, I was now working once a month on a programme reviewing the latest releases called *What's New*. Thinking quite rightly that the old lady had never heard of me, I was still dubious enough to go along to the appointment as Mainwaring rather than Stewart. Tony had told me by now that Mrs Knowles was the wife of a well-known surgeon. I was expecting somewhere slightly grander than the rather sparse, dimly lit room that opened in front of me. In the corner, though, was the famous PDSA box ready for my immense contribution. If the news was good, she might get both the half-crowns that were jingling in my pocket.

'You have a light-green hue, and you work in something that requires creativity ...' Then I remembered – she had said the same thing about Tony. The sod had set me up!

'Maybe,' I replied, trying to sound as non-committal as possible.

'In the next few weeks,' she went on, 'you will continue in your chosen profession, but it will take a different direction.'

'What is going to happen in my love life?' I asked.

She stared me straight in the eye. I'm sure I saw a little tear appear as she said, 'I'm sorry ... it's not going to last. By summer, it'll be all over.'

Sorry, Val.

I left one half-crown in the PDSA box. Well, it hadn't all been good news, had it? Within four weeks, I was back again – to put in a *fiver*. She had been right; the auras did send out the messages I wanted to hear. Not only had I landed the compère's job in a new TV Quiz called *Exit, The Way Out Show*, but the BBC had offered me a contract as presenter of Radio 1 and 2's *Junior Choice*. Thank you, Mrs Knowles, and I hope I put enough in the PDSA box. It's not that I'm mean – just careful.

As I've mentioned, Tony Brandon is one of my greatest friends, and the way he tells stories about me makes others, and especially myself, fall about. When he and Jill got married in 1968, I was his Best Man. He had no option really – I was living in their spare room at the time. Being a dutiful and considerate Best Man, I drove, without their knowledge, in my MGB to a local off-licence in Twickenham, having noticed that they had a special offer on champagne. I bought half a dozen bottles, and wrote a cheque for £20. That would be a real bargain today, but it was lot of money then, even to a supposedly well-paid Radio 1 DJ. After the ceremony in the register office at Mortlake, we repaired to the pub next door, where we were met by a sizeable crowd of friends and well-wishers.

'Umm, Ed ... where's the champagne?' asked Tony when the appropriate time had arrived to toast the happy couple.

'In the boot of the car – I put it there to keep it cool.'

'Good thinking, Carruthers!' and off we rushed to the car, grabbing the bottles and scurrying back into the pub with the champagne under our arms for the waiting guests. I marched purposefully up to the bar, and asked if we could have a dozen champagne flutes.

'Yes, sir,' was the reply, 'but I'll have to charge you corkage for the bottles you have brought in.'

'Oh, I didn't realise you charged corkage – after all, we have been buying lots of beer and spirits.'

'Yes, sir, but not my champagne.'

'How much will the corkage be, then?' I asked somewhat nervously.

'£1 a bottle, sir.'

'HOW MUCH?' my voice boomed out, lowering the volume of general hubbub in the pub to less than a decibel. 'How much?' I asked again, really timidly this time, hoping no one would hear.

'£6, sir ... for six bottles,' answered the landlord in a voice that everyone could hear.

'What's up, Best Man?' cried the bride and groom as one.

'I've run out of money. They want an extra six quid!'

'How much?' Tony laughed, and proceeded to peel six crisp £1 notes from his wallet. 'It's a bit much having to pay the corkage at your own wedding!'

It's innocent moments like this that have given me such a bad name. Tony Blackburn has perhaps best summed up this reputation when he said, 'What's the difference between Ed Stewart and a coconut? You can get a drink out of a coconut!'

That champagne mishap was unintentional – the next wasn't. Tony Brandon and I had been over to Belfast for a couple of Radio 1 clubs, and would be travelling back together from Aldergrove Airport. Our plane was delayed. Naturally, we made our way towards the bar, and soon fell into conversation with three businessmen waiting for the same delayed plane. When it came to my turn for a round of drinks, I suggested a game of Spoof, a little parlour game which is the fairest way I know to decide who's buying the next round. You play with three coins, and decide for yourself how many of these coins you will keep in your clenched fist. Then you have to guess the total number in everybody else's hands as well. If, say, there are six people playing, there could be a maximum total of eighteen or a minimum of zero coins. So, now it's your turn, and you have guessed a total of 12. If, when everybody opens up their hands, there are indeed 12 coins all round, then you are out of that game – you'll be getting a free drink! If not, you stay in the game until there are only two of you left. If you lose, and have had to take out a second mortgage to pay for the round, there is one consolation – you won't have to buy another one.

The businessmen weren't too experienced, and soon found themselves buying every round. Eventually, though, I lost. It had to happen that at some moment I would have to invade my wallet. As my hand rose to attract the attention of the barman, there was a loud click, and on came the tannoy: 'Would all passengers for the flight to London Heathrow make for Gate 3 immediately. The plane must take off now, while the fog has lifted.'

'Oh, I'm so sorry,' I said with a sincerity I hoped they believed, 'I'll have to buy my round on the plane!' As luck would have it, we were in the front of the plane, and the chief stewardess seemed to be a listener to Radio 1. Having made the announcement that she would be coming down the aisle with the drinks' trolley after take-off, she whispered to us that the vodka and tonics would be on the house for us. I whispered back to her that the three gentlemen sitting in row H were our colleagues and would she include them as well? Of course, she said.

At 10,000 feet, I turned round to see the three sitting in row H, and saw the stewardess pouring the drinks. She bent down towards the men and quietly said something to them while pointing in my direction. I waved back and shouted, 'Cheers, lads – that's my round then!'

They smiled back, and I'm sure I heard them saying what a generous chap I was – and it hadn't cost me a penny.

Tony Brandon just shook his head in bewilderment. 'Typical,' he muttered, 'plain bloody typical!'

When I read the charts again from the year between September 1967 and September 1968, there were a few Top Ten records that had the loudest 'ping' effect on me. Don't ask me why – it just happened that way!

'All You Need Is Love' by the Beatles
'San Francisco' by Scott McKenzie
'Excerpt from a Teenage Opera' by Keith West
'Something's Gotten Hold of My Heart' by Gene Pitney
'Walk Away Renee' by the Four Tops
'Little Green Apples' by Roger Miller
'MacArthur Park' by Richard Harris
'Honey' by Bobby Goldsboro
'Joanna' by Scott Walker
'Son of Hickory Holler's Tramp' by OC Smith

THE RIGHT
CHOICE

THE PHONE in Harry Walter's office shrilled loudly. It was February 1968, and he was just putting the finishing touches to the script for that weekend's *Junior Choice*. It had been called *Children's Favourites* in the 50s and early 60s, and millions of children, including myself and my brothers and sister, had woken up every weekend to the voice of Uncle Mac. At the other end of the phone was Derek Chinnery, the Controller of Radio 1, the station that had by now over half the population listening to its new, fresh sound.

'Harry,' Derek started, 'I want you to audition Ed Stewart as a possible new presenter of *Junior Choice*. My wife heard him reading some requests recently and she thinks he has the style we're looking for – more of an older brother than a schoolmaster.'

The audition went well; Harry had decided on a format of two pop and chart records followed by a third children's request. We started with the Beatles 'All You Need Is Love', then Dusty Springfield's 'In the Middle of Nowhere', and after that Charles Penrose and 'The Laughing Policeman'. What a mix!

The next day, I had a call – would I be ready to start on 8 February, at 8.30 in the morning on a Saturday, and 9.00 on a Sunday? The offer was a three-week contract at £50 a programme. Such excitement! Such riches!

The first record played that morning was 'Early One Morning' by Roger Whittaker, the whistler from Kenya who sang a bit – or was it the other way round? Besides the type of records we would be playing, the rest of the format was a simple one: 80 per cent would be listeners' requests, with the other 20 per cent being our own selection. This way we wouldn't be playing the same old records week after week, but could introduce new releases, and ones we thought would be suitable for the programme's audience. How else would 'Grandad' and 'Two Little Boys' have become hits if we hadn't played them first? It's all my fault!

However, I was still on trial as far as the Beeb was concerned. The name 'The Beeb' had been coined by Kenny Everett around this time, and had become part of our everyday vocabulary – he should have had it copyrighted. When, after the first three weeks, I had still not signed a new contract, I had to ask Harry Walters whether I could say, 'Join me next week at the same time!'

'Go ahead,' he said, but it went on like this for quite a few weeks until they offered me a contract for six months. My long walk across the BBC tightrope had begun. I had fallen off the first time when *Happening Sunday* had ceased to happen four months earlier. But now I had regained my balance and would retain it until the end of 1979.

It was soon after I had started my contract for *Junior Choice* that I was approached and offered a bribe to plug a record. At the time, I was being very careful to protect my image. Ed Moreno was a DJ whom I had met a couple of times when he was working for Radio 390 on one of the forts in the Thames Estuary. He wanted me to meet the current Miss Great Britain, who had just cut her first record, and would I give it a play?

Ed and I met in a pub in Shepherd's Market in London. Although there were several women hanging around (Shepherd's Market was a notorious call-girl area!) none of them resembled Miss Great Britain. 'Come back to my flat, and we'll meet her there,' Ed suggested.

At this point, I was feeling a little uneasy, and so I said to Moreno, 'I don't have any choice in the records I play – that's decided by my producer.' That was always the get-out when we were being plagued by record companies to play their records, especially the ones you didn't particularly like. We went back to Moreno's flat, but when we got there I doubted whether it was really his – it was far too grand.

'Where's the beauty queen?' I asked, my tongue out in anticipation.

'Oh, she'll be here soon.' He opened a bottle of Don Pérignon, and poured me a large glass. 'She's a real goer this girl,' Moreno went on, 'and I'm sure she'll return the favour in every way, if you play her record.' He gave me a leering wink.

'No way am I going to do this – I haven't even heard the record yet!' I laughed.

He put it on. It was less than average, and I realised I was being set up. I repeated again that I was not going to play that record, finished my glass (it would have been a shame to waste it) and, in best Sunday tabloid style, made my excuses and left.

Over the next few weeks, rumours of producers on BBC radio accepting money and favours for playing certain records were rife and what happened next came as something of a shock. The *News of the World* had started an investigation into possible payola payments to producers and disc jockeys under the banner SCANDAL AT THE BBC! In the course of the seven-week campaign, TV and radio producers, singers, record producers and pluggers were 'named and shamed' in the Sunday tabloids. Some of the typically sensational headlines included SEX-FOR-PLUGS GIRL TELLS ALL!,

FAMILY FAVOURITES FIXERS NAMED, HAS THE BBC GONE PLUG CRAZY?, and THE TRUTH ABOUT TOP OF THE POPS!

As you can imagine, those of us who had been to any vaguely 'wild' parties were first to the newsagent's on a Sunday morning. Not that we were guilty of any misdemeanour – we just didn't need the association. But I was still shocked to receive a call from Scotland Yard for a meeting with one of the officers on the case. I thought they were having me on when they told me the investigating officer's name – Inspector Penrose! The singer of that favourite children's record 'The Laughing Policeman' had the same name – Charles Penrose. But there was no laughing when I went into the Inspector's office later that week.

'Mr Stewart, I'm going to play you a recording made some time ago in a flat in Shepherd's Market. Do you remember the occasion?'

He watched my face as I wrestled with my memory. Then he let out a laugh. 'I haven't got the name Penrose for nothing,' he continued, 'and, anyway, you're quite innocent, and I would like to congratulate you on your good sense.' Then the reality dawned – the room had been bugged. He played me the tape, and I did shiver slightly as I heard my voice refusing Ed Moreno's offer of what I would get in return for playing that record. And I never knew the title of the track he'd wanted me to play. 'Love for Sale' perhaps?

This was quite an eventful time for me. The sixties were swinging and I took full advantage of the party scene. Looking back perhaps I could have been more careful.

My producer Harry Walters became concerned and took me aside one day.

'Ed, you're a children's entertainer now,' he told me, 'and all hell would break loose if the BBC found out. You'd lose your job.' He was right. I realised my responsibilities had now changed and my personal life would have to be whiter than white. I was lucky.

One BBC producer lost his job, and a fellow DJ his programme, when Fleet Street began their muck-raking.

My subsequent affairs with the actresses Ingrid Pitt and Madeleine Smith remained happy in their secrecy. It was only when I split with Eve Graham of the New Seekers and the story found its way into the gossip columns that I appreciated the meaning of the word 'privacy'. I was shattered, not only because I had lost a woman I had been in love with, but the fact that my listeners could read about it in the papers. How the end of my marriage 30 years later never made it to the gossip columns was a blessing ... and an insult. I'm obviously not that famous any more!

A cycling track that was definitely famous in its day was Herne Hill, in southeast London. And it was there that the Beacon Gymkhana DJs' Cycle Race was held on a Saturday afternoon in 1968. Radio 1 had been up and running for less than a year, and we were accepting anything that came our way. But this was different – a first prize of a Vietnamese pot-bellied pig!

The field included the usual collection of the sportier DJs like Tony Blackburn, John Peel and myself, and a couple of other recently disembarked pirates. Fraser Hines who had just become Jamie in *Dr Who* was enthusiastic, though pretty useless on the football pitch, but proved himself a more than capable racing cyclist. He left the rest of us in his wake, and was duly presented with the pot-bellied pig. I scraped into second place and received a firkin of beer. 'Firkin hell,' said Tony Blackburn, as he was presented with the third prize – a copy of *Mrs Mills' Greatest Hits*!

Fraser had arrived at the track in a car supplied by the BBC – he was filming that day, but had been given an hour off to take part in the race. Having won the pot-bellied pig, what was Fraser going to do with it? Stick it on a lead and walk it home, or return it with a 'thanks but no thanks'? No, he put it in the back of his posh chauffeur-driven limo, and drove it to his mother's house in Chiswick. He also gave it a name – Whoey. He and his mum gave Whoey so much TLC – some would say too much TLC – that Whoey became too big for the back garden. Eventually, they took him to Chessington Zoo, where he grew too big for his trotters, and they eventually had to have him put down. At least that's what Fraser told me, and he's not one for telling porkies!

One famous member of the intelligentsia in the 60s, Ludovic Kennedy, was quoted as saying that he thought all listeners to Radio 1 were morons. In that case, *Junior Choice* had 16 million morons listening by the end of 1968, and that was 4 million less than *Family Favourites*, which had an amazing 20 million. And *Junior Choice* was quoted as having the highest listening figures for Christmas Day.

Ironically, a year later it was a journalist who helped save me from extinction. Peter Dacre was a writer for the *Sunday Express*, and his column was printed next to the weekly cartoon of the incomparable Giles. He wanted to interview me about the programme, so I invited him to the BBC Club where he could mingle with the DJs and other glitterati. We got on well, possibly because I insisted on buying the first round, when the club was practically empty. When it came to his turn, I had introduced him to several of my colleagues, so his round was considerably more expensive. A journalist falling for that one – I was amazed! Anyway, we left the best of friends, and Peter assured me that the article would be in the paper the following Sunday.

The Friday before that, though, I had received a phone call which, once again, threw me into a state of utter confusion. Would I go and see Mark White, who was Derek Chinnery's deputy at Radio 1? Urbane, and with a bit of an RAF moustache, Mr White calmly told me, 'Thank you very much,' I'd made a great job of *Junior Choice*, but they would not be renewing my contract in two weeks' time. Their policy was not to create another Uncle Mac, and they would only be offering future presenters a one-year contract.

I was gobsmacked! My publicity agent, David Block, wanted to arrange a march on Broadcasting House by irate and vociferous listeners, and wanted to contact Fleet Street immediately to enlist their support. I said no – I didn't want to upset the apple cart. And that feeling didn't leave me, even 30 years later, when I was moved from the afternoon slot to make way for Steve Wright. I was offered the Sunday slot and took it. I simply didn't want to work for anyone else.

As promised, on the Sunday, Peter Dacre's article appeared in the *Sunday Express*. It was beautifully written and I felt really chuffed. Its headline was STEWPOT IS A REAL FAMILY FAVOURITE. In his opening paragraph, Peter wrote,

At nine o'clock this morning – perhaps his voice can be heard in the background while you are reading this page – about 7 million people will have switched on their radios to listen to the man with the friendly voice they call 'Stewpot' – Ed Stewart, compère of the record request programme *Junior Choice*. In 15 months, he has turned it into not so much a record show as a family gathering. He gets more than 1,500 requests a week and now, with a Saturday morning edition of the show as well, he has BBC radio's second-largest audience, second only to *Two Way Family Favourites*. For this he earns 46 guineas a programme, which in showbusiness terms is peanuts ...

And so it continued in much the same vein, with a potted history of my career to date. Lots of people had seen the piece, and were really pleased for me. Little did they know that I would soon be out of a job, but I kept the secret to myself all the same.

That following Monday morning, I had another phone call from

Mark White – would I call in and see him in his office? 'Ed, old chap,' he told me, 'we've had a rethink about future policy, and taking into consideration your undoubted popularity, we've decided to offer you another year's extension.' No mention of the article in the *Sunday Express* – just a complete U-turn in their thinking.

So I let my imagination run wild, and this is what I reckon happened. Lord Hill, the Director General, was having breakfast in bed and was perusing the Sunday papers. He reached the article and thought, 'That's good. I must phone and congratulate Robin Scott,' who was still the big chief at Radios 1 and 2. That Monday morning, Robin Scott was delighted to have received a personal phone call from no less than the DG. Finding that the man he wished to congratulate, Derek Chinnery, was on leave, he then phoned Mark White, the very man who, on the previous Friday, had given me my marching orders. That was the precise moment when Mr White found a different hue to his name – ashen. 'Just to tell you, Mark, that the DG is absolutely delighted with the piece on Ed Stewart, and to make sure we keep him on board.' I presume Mr White accepted the plaudits – and I was back in a job. No one was any the wiser – until now. That's what I call decision-making!

So, with renewed confidence from a new contract and rising listening figures, we started to add some features into the programme. When I say we, by this time I had a new producer, Don George, or Mr George as he became known. Harry Walters had moved on to produce Pete Murray's *Open House*, and went eventually to the JY programme, where he was for many years.

Radio 1, or its DJs, were always in the news but we still seemed to be walking a tightrope as far as the press were concerned. 'Hopes of a reprieve for Radio 1,' wrote a tabloid in 1970, 'rose yesterday when four top DJs signed new year-long contracts with the BBC. By signing up Jimmy Young, Terry Wogan, Tony Blackburn and Ed Stewart, the corporation clearly feels the station still has a future – despite growing speculation that it will be sold to the commercial sector. But we believe that commercial radio should be an alternative to, not a replacement for, Radio 1.'

Commercial Radio did appear in London, Manchester and Glasgow that year, but today, nearly 40 years later, there are still more people overall listening to BBC Radio than the independent stations put together.

We might have been at the end of the Swinging 60s, but there still remained a certain amount of prudishness. There was a criticism of the Ideal Home Exhibition because they had put a double bed in their Tony Blackburn Bachelor Pad feature – 'Why would a bachelor need a double bed in his flat?' asked one national paper naïvely. The reporter, with the awareness of Rip Van Winkle, had failed to appreciate that the rest of us had moved on a bit from the Middle Ages.

Then Kenny Everett appeared in a front-page item which read, 'Kenny sleepwalked to his bathroom the other night, turned on his taps, went back to bed, woke up two hours later and found his basement had flooded.' This had echoes for Kenny and myself when we rented a mews cottage off Baker Street. With fellow shipmates Mike 'Leila' Lennox and Dave 'Hermione' Hawkins (we sounded like a load of drag queens, but we had Tony Windsor to thank for that) we convinced the owner of the house that we were responsible human beings ... which we weren't!

The first night we were due to move in, we had, as usual, consumed a couple of beers, and Leila Lennox had picked up this girl who was going to christen his bed with him. Kenny had had a couple of whiskies on the train journey down and was pretty merry when we arrived at Liverpool Street, and took great delight in being wheeled to a waiting taxi on a porter's trolley! Mike helped his new girlfriend into the cab, where she promptly passed out on the floor.

Being in charge of the keys to the house, I had remained fairly sober, but nothing could have prepared me for what was to happen next. The carpet was best Wilton; the curtains were chintz and the furniture was straight from Harrods. The newly painted front door had appeared to have come directly from *Home and Beauty* and, as I unlocked it, the girl fell through, and was promptly sick all over the deluxe carpet. Chaos ensued, with mops, dishcloths, Izal and hot water making no difference at all to the smells and stains.

'Oooh!' said Kenny, 'isn't it lovely – I'm going to call it Twinkle Cottage.' We were out of there in less than a twinkle. The landlady popped round the next morning to see how we were getting on, and almost passed out before ordering us to leave. She must have claimed the carpet damage on insurance – we never did hear from her again.

While my career as a DJ and cottage destroyer was going from strength to strength, it was around this time that television appeared on the horizon, in the form of *Exit – The Way Out Show*. It was an Australian quiz show, which went out five days a week Down Under and had been brought over to this country by an independent producer called Barry Langford. My agent, Harold Davidson, had sent me along to audition for the compère's job. Barry Langford, having put many of us through our paces, concluded none of us were good enough and decided to present it himself.

After losing the *Happening Sunday* programme with Radio 1, my opportunities were now limited to *What's New* on Radio 1 and a once-a-week spot on the World Service as presenter of *Good Morning Africa*, which was a regular programme for another original Radio 1 line-up – Pete Myers.

The Monday following the failed audition for *Exit*, I was in the studio about to record an interview with a tribal leader in Ghana, when my producer, Victor Price, told me there was a very important message from Rediffusion Television. It was the director of *Exit – The Way Out Show*. Barry Langford had been taken suddenly and seriously ill and would I step into his shoes? It was very last minute, but since I had been the next best choice out of all the auditionees, would I step into the breach? Then he told me they were going through the dress rehearsal in an hour's time and recording the first show an hour after that. They would send a car for me, and not to worry about the fee – it had already been agreed with my agent – £250 a programme.

There was no choice to make. The African Service were only paying me £25 a programme, which was peanuts. Victor Price, bless him, understood the potential of the TV offer to me and let me go – the Ghanaian tribal chief wouldn't even know, let alone care who was interviewing him thousands of miles away. So off I sped to Wembley, the home of Rediffusion, magnetised by the thought of being the first 'pirate' to get his own show on TV and the fee to go with it. The marksmen and women of Fleet Street would be lining me up in their sights again – but would I care?

By the end of the ten-week run of *Exit – The Way Out Show*, I had acquired two of the attributes of a rhinoceros – a thick skin and shortsightedness. The thick skin was to ward off the arrows of scorn and criticism levelled at the programme and me. The shortsightedness came from my inability to see a shocker when it came thundering towards me! There is a third attribute connected to the rhinoceros, but that is kept in a small jar in the medicine cupboard.

To say that first recording was frightening is an understatement. The papers the next day weren't too kind, either. But they hadn't been told that I had stepped in at the very last moment – Barry Langford's name was still in the programme listings for that week. And I hadn't been able to read the quiz questions before the show, because they were different to the ones used in the dress rehearsal.

Excuses, excuses. In the *Sun*, Nancy Banks-Smith had a field day: 'This is quite the most frantic, illiterate, rock-bottom show yet. A quizmaster who hasn't heard of the word "floe",' (I had – she was Andy Capp's wife!) 'and can't pronounce the name "Titian",' (not being an art lover, I had actually said 'Titt-i-an'). 'He has, to aid and abet him, a blonde and brunette, who do not do anything in particular.'

Ms Banks-Smith could at least have said they were gorgeous, which they were. The blonde was Lesley Judd, who later took over from Valerie Singleton on *Blue Peter*. The same columnist took up the attack again a fortnight later, noticing that they had raised the standard of the competitors while the level of the show remained 'anthropoidal', being something that 'is in human form only'. What did that make her readers? I thought to myself.

My most memorable critique of the show was written by Milton Shulman of the London *Evening Standard*, saying that if Martians landed on Earth and tried to find some sort of intelligent life, they would only have to watch Ed Stewart and his contestants on *Exit – the Way Out Show* to realise there was none at all! Years later, I was to meet Mr Shulman at some reception or other, and told him that he had kindly written an article on a programme which I had compèred some time before.

'Which one was that?' he enquired.

'Oh,' I said, remembering the description for the *TV Times*, 'The new, exciting, fast-action quiz game for the way-out generation … *Exit – The Way Out Show*.'

'Oh, yes,' he blustered, 'wonderful show!'

TV has always been the icing; the cake has been radio. As the comedian George Martin once said, 'Radio is the mother of television … they're still looking for the father!'

If my early efforts with *Exit –The Way Out Show* had not been received too well by the critics, it didn't seem to have made too bad an impression on those TV companies who hadn't taken the programme for their channels. ITV was much more fragmented in those days, and not all the companies had to take all the programmes offered to them. That was a blessing in disguise for me – *Exit* had only been shown on Rediffusion, serving London and the Southeast, and HTV in Wales. It hadn't passed the public by completely, though. I found out to my great enjoyment how my appearances on *Exit* had significantly boosted my profile generally, and that fame attracted impressionable young ladies.

I was on my way back from Wales by train during the period that *Exit* was being transmitted, and sitting in the same compartment were two very pretty young girls on their way to Clacton to start a summer season as 'redcoats' with Butlins. Finding out that they had time to kill, I invited them back to my flat and we spent an afternoon reading the *Kama Sutra*. Fame certainly had its perks.

Soon, Granada stepped in with a show for children, called *Anything You Can Do*, which was a talent and quiz show. We used to have celebrity guests on the judging panel who would dutifully praise or gently criticise the acts, and everything was done very properly so as not to upset the child performers ... except when Hughie Green was on the panel. I had never been a fan of his smarmy insincerity, and could never understand how the public had been taken in by him for so long. In the studio, he was loud, demanding and completely disrespectful to the performers. His co-judge that day was Diana Dors and, between them, they upset the children, the audience – all of us, in fact – by talking and laughing during the different acts. Did he do this during *Opportunity Knocks*? I wondered.

Sadly, the series did not continue. Apparently, the local education authorities had been worried that too many children were having to take time off their studies to participate in the rehearsals and recordings. But with the '70s fast approaching, television was going to play a more prominent part in my career – like it or not!

It was probably a blessing in disguise that my TV career didn't go into overdrive at that time in my life, or I wouldn't have been able to enjoy going to see as much football as I did then. At that time in the late 60s and early 70s, I used to go with a group of friends to watch Chelsea at Stamford Bridge, and invariably ended up shouting for the other team – being a staunch Everton fan, I would never have switched my allegiance. I just enjoyed going along to the match with Peter Jones, who was then editor of *Record Mirror*, and his friends Bob and June, who were publicans. There were no private boxes then – at half-time, you queued with everybody else for your cup of Bovril. June was a fan of the dashing Chelsea winger, Charlie Cooke. She had a particularly strident voice, would wait for a lull in the cheering, and then scream, 'Come on, Charlie, set 'em alight, Charlie …' and other words of encouragement, often infuriating the other fans sitting close by.

One week, I was wearing a very fashionable rabbit-fur coat and, as usual, June was exhorting Charlie Cooke and Peter Osgood to 'set 'em alight!' Soon, I noticed the smell of burning, and I turned around to see smoke rising from my rabbit fur. The people behind were sitting there as innocently as could be but, before I could find the culprit, a flame was taking hold, so I rushed inside to the bar and doused the coat in water. 'Set 'em alight' had been taken rather too literally. It caused great mirth at the time, but with the tragic events at Bradford still to come some years later, it makes you realise how an innocent joke might have turned quickly to tragedy.

About a year after this, Chelsea were playing newly promoted Derby County, who were riding high in the First Division. The only parking space I could find meant leaving my front wheels over the metal studs that protected a zebra crossing, making it illegal to leave your car there. When I got back to where the car should have been, I found it had been towed away. The pound was over in Hammersmith and, on arriving there, not only was there a fine to pay on the spot, but I had received a summons for illegal parking as well!

Three months later, and I found myself in front of the magistrate at Marylebone Magistrates' Court – the very court where, the year before, John Lennon and Yoko Ono had been remanded on bail for obstructing the police in the execution of a search warrant, and for possession of cannabis. The Chief Magistrate was Edward Robey, the son of George Robey, the famous comedian and vaudeville performer of yesteryear. Edward Robey had a reputation for disliking anybody involved in any way with his father's profession. Allegedly, it was the personal frustration that he had not been talented enough to follow in his father's footsteps that had made Edward resentful towards anybody connected with showbusiness. So what was I, a mere disc jockey, to expect from such a person?

So frightening was the thought of losing my driving licence, I had employed the services of a barrister to represent me in court. When he asked me to explain to the Bench the circumstances of my misdemeanor, I started to explain, hardly pausing for breath, how difficult it had been to find a parking space that day, '... Chelsea were playing the newly promoted Derby County ... the match had created so much interest that all parking spaces around Stamford Bridge had been filled ... the only possible one for my car was the one I had found ... necessitating the placing of my front wheels over the metal studs ... for which I apologise profusely to the Court.'

I sat down, half expecting a round of applause for my bravura performance – and was not disappointed. 'You are quite right, Mr Mainwaring,' – my real name still appeared on my driving licence – 'The parking situation at Chelsea has become quite impossible. I myself find it difficult to park when Chelsea are at home, being a great fan of theirs myself. Case dismissed ... but remember to get there earlier next week!'

Thank you, Mr Robey. What a fine man he was!

With the arrival of the 70s, musically we kept up with the hits of the time, even making one or two of our own like Ernie, and the two I mentioned before, 'Two Little Boys' and 'Grandad'. Elvis Presley and 'The Wonder of You', Christie and 'Yellow River', Smokey Robinson and the Miracles, Simon and Garfunkel and even the England World Cup Squad with 'Back Home' were all in the mix, with the old favourites like 'My Brother', 'Three Billy Goats Gruff' and 'My Boomerang Won't Come Back'. You had to be careful with some of the words, though, in case they didn't pass the strict BBC censorship rules. 'My Brother' was full of double-entendres, such as 'My brother's only quiet when he's asleep ... but you don't know what he's dreaming about!' Terry Scott spoke and sung the words in such a way that some of the time you didn't know what you were laughing about. Danny Kaye's 'King's New Clothes' was a song jokingly written and sung about nudity, but that didn't seem to matter. However, when we played Charlie Drake's 'My Boomerang Won't Come Back', we had to fade it out before we got to the bit where he says, 'Oh, my Gawd, I've hit the Flying Doctor!' 'Oh, my Gawd' was considered blasphemous, so woe betide us if we allowed that phrase to creep through.

It was later in my career, in 1996 on Radio 2, that I managed to make the biggest blunder on the rude word front, and it was one which could have cost me my career! I should have been playing Beautiful South's 'Rotterdam', but with the CD players we were using, if you kept your finger too long on the button which selected the number of the track you wanted to play, the mechanism would revert to Track 1. Which is exactly what happened. Unfortunately, the first line of Track 1 began 'Don't marry her, fuck me!' an album track which had been changed in the single version to 'Don't marry her, *love* me.' It was the album version I had played. We only received one complaint – from a man who had nearly crashed his car because he was laughing so much! He phoned a tabloid, and we were in the papers the next day. As many in the business will tell you, there's no such thing as bad publicity!

We started to introduce guests in the Radio 1 studio, and some of the early ones were the England World Cup Squad, to promote what was to become a Number One for them in May 1970. They joined in 'live' with the record in the studio – not a pretty sound. The only passes they made that day were at the secretary in the studio – even then they were off target.

Basil Brush came to promote a new record once, and Ivan, his creator, wouldn't take Basil out of his box, so I was just talking to this human face. I found it so incongruous, I insisted he took Basil out and presented him as normal. I could only talk to that fox with someone's hand stuck up its bum!

The Monkees were very popular at the time with their zany TV series, and Davy Jones was persuaded to come into the studio to promote it. There was no morning TV at the time, so we had a bit of a scoop. Davy Jones arrived and was met outside the studios by hordes of screaming fans. He kept waving to them from the windows and they were becoming hysterical. Suddenly, one of the old diehard Light Programme executives, Anna Instone, came storming into the studios, demanding to know who had given permission for the programme to be disrupted in such a way. Luckily for Mr George, the Radio 1 Controller, Derek Chinnery, came in at that moment to congratulate him on the scoop. At the same time, he was able to tell Anna that this was how radio was now, and if she would care to go back to her desert island, she could choose her own discs!

Chiara – the woman who I was to spend nearly 30 years with – was 13 when we met in 1970, and 17 when we married. They say the quickest way to a man's heart is through his stomach. Sex might be even quicker, but food lasts longer! My wife started on my stomach (and nothing else!) when she was 13.

Chiara's father was Jimmy Henney, who presented programmes like *Housewives Choice* on radio and *Oh, Boy* on the TV. He made his living and was better known as a music publisher, mostly with Chappell's Music. Jimmy also formed the original Showbiz Football team in the 60s. Many well-known names of the day, like Jimmy Tarbuck, Ronnie Carroll, Kenny Lynch, Tommy Steele and Sean Connery were all regulars, and you didn't get many more famous than that running around a football pitch!

In 1970, Jimmy, who had by now moved to Ember records and was managing Glen Campbell, invited me to turn out for his team in a midweek match against Epsom College, where his son Adriano was a pupil. Glen would be kicking off, and the Epsom College team would be made up of masters and former pupils. Jess Conrad, who had no less than three entries in Kenny Everett's 12 worst records of all time, was in goal for Epsom College, and the Showbiz XI won easily, 9-6!

After the match, I was to meet Chiara and her mother, Ginetta, for the first time. What characters ... and what beauties! Ginetta had married Jimmy in the early 50s, with very little knowledge of the English language. Even today, she continues to fracture every syllable in the book. She took one look at me, the skinny Jack the Lad, and said, 'Eh, boy, you musta comma to my place and I cook a plate of pasta!'

I accepted with alacrity – what else could a poor boy do? The next week, Jimmy took me to his house in Wembley for what I thought was going to be a simple plate of spaghetti. No way. I arrived at 7.00pm and was greeted at the door by what I can only describe as a 13-year-old apparition. Chiara was simply stunning, and she had cooked the most beautiful roast chicken, roast potatoes, chipolatas, cauliflower and all the trimmings.

In my usual diplomatic way, I gushed, 'This is delicious ... but where's the bread sauce?'

If looks could have killed, I would have joined that chicken on the table! What a meal. 'Goodness Gracious Me' came to mind as I remembered Peter Sellers and another Italian beauty, Sophia Loren. Mother and daughter were making a lot of noise in the kitchen as Jimmy and I polished off the rest of the wine. He offered me a Senior Service, but I opened my own packet of Gauloises. He was amazed – he hadn't seen me buy my own packet before. Apparently, I was one of a trio who never seemed to have any cigarettes on them, and were for ever pinching other people's – Pete Murray and Kenny Lynch were the other two, and they're still at it, although I gave up the dreaded weed years ago. I soon found out that the paper on a Gauloise often stuck to your lip, and your fingers would slide up to the tip of the cigarette as you took a drag, giving your finger a nasty burn. Even worse, a stray bit of tobacco would get stuck on a tooth, and you'd wonder why your date wouldn't kiss you.

As I drew nonchalantly on my Gauloise, the commotion in the kitchen had produced one of Italy's most famous desserts – zabaglione, made from egg yolks, sugar and Marsala whisked together. It does not appear in the *Weight Watcher's Guide* for some reason! But what had actually gone on in the kitchen was this – the four egg yolks and the sugar had been put in a heavy bottomed pot and whipped with a wire whisk. In a slightly larger second bowl, there was some simmering water. Not boiling, just simmering. Then Chiara had placed the whipped-up egg yolks over the water in the second pot and added eight tablespoonfuls of Marsala while continuing to whisk the mixture. The foaming concoction was then poured into champagne glasses, and I was duly impressed when the dessert was served. What an introduction to my future wife, although I hadn't regarded her as that quite yet; I was still a Jack the Lad in those days, and the Henney family got to meet quite a few of my girlfriends.

So 1970 was well under way, and I had a different producer and a new flat in Harley Street. At least if this DJ lark failed again, I could always be a brain surgeon. Don George was a family man who kept in touch with musical tastes with the help of his children. By now, we were receiving over 1,000 cards and letters a week – who needed e-mails? We were also breaking Number Ones, with 'Lily the Pink', the Christmas Number One in 1968, 'Two Little Boys' the following year, and 'Ernie' in 1971.

'Football Crazy', by Robin Hall and Jimmie MacGregor, was requested weekly, but only played when there was a special match going on, like Everton v Chelsea or Everton against anybody. By now, though, I had formed my own charity football team with a former Irish international, Kevin O'Shea. We called it the Top Ten Eleven. What a name – at least it was original! The Showbiz XI, formed by my father-in-law, Jimmy Henney, had been going for over ten years, and then had come the All-Stars and the Entertainers. So we had to think of something different.

The personnel would change every week, with the vagaries of showbiz and sporting engagements, but our nucleus was strong enough to keep the thousands who came along to watch us happy, in that they had heard of us and even recognised us. There were actors like Ben Howard, Brian Marshall and Norman Rossington, while Dave Dee, Andy Fairweather Lowe, Brian Poole, Miki Anthony and Junior Campbell were the pop stars of the day; later on, Rod Stewart turned out for us as well. Not only was Rod a gifted footballer, but he was always a good sport, even when he was introduced over the tannoy system as my older brother. Actually, my real older bother, John, did play in the early days as well, until the pace of the popstar lifestyle caught up with him. He was recently a golfing executive at the Oxfordshire Golf Club and worked twice as hard as I did.

The former England international, Bobby Smith, gave us a formidable presence up front. He was what you would call a bustling centre forward and, even in his later years, when he was starting to put on some weight, he would still strike terror into the opposing defences. He went a step too far in one match, though, when somebody from the crowd shouted, 'Get a move on, Fatty!' Bobby leapt over the rails, and landed a punch which broke the man's nose. He ended up in hospital, while Bobby ended up in jail.

The same thing also nearly happened to our centre-half, the former European heavyweight boxing champion, Dick Richardson. Mind you, we were all in jail with him – at Parkhurst on the Isle of Wight, where we were playing the Prison Warders' XI. I'd like to say we had a captive audience, but they were all Category A prisoners, and I suppose it would have been pushing it a bit for the authorities to let the Krays out to watch a game of football! Bobby Smith had scored with the very first kick of the match, putting the ball over their goalie's head from the kick off. Word got around the prison grapevine and, about a minute later, a huge roar went up from inside the prison.

As well as playing in one of the most secure football grounds in Britain – Parkhurst – my efforts as a cricketer have also taken me to some memorable grounds, but it doesn't matter where you end up, there's always one thing that every cricketer wants above anything … to score a century. My brother John managed it for Wimbledon Village on a piece of Wimbledon Common specially set aside as a cricket pitch in 1960. As usual, I was determined to emulate him, but I had to wait until 1971. And it wasn't easy doing it in two hours with the opposition determined to make you earn it!

The Lord's Taverners were playing Harpenden where Eric Morecambe was President. Both teams were made up of a motley mixture of former professionals and showbiz characters, who liked to spend a Sunday in the company of their exalted heroes. Quite possibly, the feeling was mutual. I was presenting *Sunday*

Sport on Radio 1 at the time and had to be in the studio about an hour before the programme started at 5.00pm.

Sunday Sport took over from *Sports Report* once the football season had finished, and included reports on cricket's Sunday League, the motor sports, horse racing from France and cycling. That Sunday, my team captain, John Alderton, knew I had to be away at teatime and stuck me in at number three. He also knew I wouldn't want to be rushing, thereby presuming I would be out nice and early and have plenty of time for the journey back. What a cheek! But luckily for me, the Great Captain in the sky was watching over me that day, ensuring a perfect batting wicket and butter-fingered catchers in the field. The opposing captain, with a little persuasion from Eric Morecambe, reversed his bowling order, so that early runs were easy to come by, and by 3.00pm I had scored 50!

An Essex colt was the other batsman at this stage. He was hogging the bowling and I could see my century slipping slowly away, so I ran him out – or, rather, I didn't run when he called, and he sacrificed his wicket for me. I played him an ''Allo, darling' on the following Saturday's *Junior Choice*, and his fellow colts never let him get over it! The score kept rising until, with the last over before tea fast approaching, I realised I was on 89.

'Come on, lads, let me get my century!' I shouted to the opposition.

'You'll have to work for it, Ed,' they shouted back. The first ball of the last over hit my pads, plumb in front of the wicket. 'Howzat!' they screamed.

'Not out,' said Frank Lee, the Test umpire, wiping an imaginary tear from his eye.

The next ball I snicked through the hands of first slip, whose eye had been caught by the sight of two scantily clad young ladies carrying a blanket around the boundary. This was always an effective way of loosening the change in men's pockets and ladies' handbags. Four more runs and now I was on 93. The bowler was Bill Alley, a veteran Aussie medium-pacer, whose next ball, an off-cutter, completely decimated all three of my stumps.

'No ball!' shouted Frank Lee, and Bill's reply would only have been understood by a lip-reader. The next delivery was of perfect length, and I was happy to get my bat to it. Then, on the next delivery, a rush of blood to the head, I pranced down the pitch ... and missed. I should have been stumped, but Godfrey Evans juggled with the ball, dropped it, and I made it back to the crease. 'I'll expect a large scotch for that one, Ed,' he whispered, as I settled my stance for the last ball, still needing seven for my century. Last ball, and it was an easy full toss, which I smote to extra cover.

'If you want your century, you'll have to run them!' So I did. I ran ... and ran ... and ran – eight times to be exact! The fielders kept throwing the ball at the stumps and missing. They got me on my eighth run, when I was literally crawling down the pitch, completely knackered. I rushed straight to the car, but my legs were so tired, I could hardly change gear. Worse still, I had forgotten to take out my protective 'box', and being desperate for a pee ... you can imagine the rest!

Back on the football pitch, it was the Radio Team 1 of the 70s and 80s which drew the biggest crowds, the most memorable for all those who took part being a match at Wembley Stadium in 1977. Before the England v Scotland Schoolboys International, we played a five-a-side match against a team of actors, led by Dennis Waterman, who was very high-profile in *The Sweeney* at the time. The others in the team were Richard O'Sullivan, Brian Marshall, Ben Howard and Jeremy Bullock. The Radio 1 DJs were Tony Blackburn, John Peel, Bob Kilbey, Noel Edmonds and myself in goal. We won 2-1. As we were changing after the game, I said to the others, 'Do you realise we have just done what professional footballers dream about all their lives? We've played in front of over 60,000 at the home of football – Wembley Stadium. Are we blessed or just plain lucky?'

'Just knackered!' gasped John Peel. Unforgettable – that's what it was. Before that, though, the Radio 1 disc jockeys had made appearances at quite a few charity matches, and Tony Blackburn especially was beginning to realise the price of fame – and what went with it. On every pitch, he was the one to get the bucket of water from the opposition, the mis-timed tackle or the mobbing from the screaming girls when he scored a goal. And, of course, he loved it.

Tony Blackburn has been the name more synonymous with Radio 1 than anybody else, and even though he hasn't been broadcasting on a national station for nearly 20 years, his name still makes people smile – unlike his terrible jokes!

The most fascinating example of viewer reaction was when Tony was put into the Australian jungle and won *I'm a Celebrity* ... The fact that he appealed to the viewers more than anybody else showed that being a straight-down-the-middle-thoroughly-nice-chap still appeals to the public's sensitivities more than some of the 'cooler', brasher competitors on the show.

In 1972, Jimmy Henney, my future father-in-law, and I decided to drive my Triumph Stag to Italy, to the hotel owned by some of Ginetta's family in a spa town of Montegrotto Terme, just south of Padova. Some Italian members of the family, including Chiara, were going to be there as well. I had just split from Eve Graham of the New Seekers, so I was to quote the title of one of Jack Jones's records, 'Free Again'.

On arrival at the hotel, I was met by a beautiful Italian receptionist and a large Italian meal. I knew what I wanted first ... but the meal won. Their *antipasti* was followed by a bowl of spaghetti with oil, garlic, chilli pepper and chopped zucchini. There were copious amounts of wine, which hardly seemed to touch the sides. Once the coffee and grappa had gone the same way, the Andy Fairweather Lowe syndrome had kicked in – I was 'wide-eyed and legless'. So, unusually, I took a sleeping pill to relax after the long journey and the miserable sleepless nights since the break-up.

The next morning, at the usual meeting in her parents' bedroom, Chiara was laughing at what she had seen from her bedroom window. Two porters had been spotted carrying a mattress towards the secluded area where the gardening and swimming pool equipment was kept. In the middle of the mattress was a large wet patch. They all laughed, wondering who could have been so unfortunate. Little did they know that the mattress was mine. The sleeping pill had relaxed me so successfully that I had peed the bed. On waking up, and feeling myself saturated, I had tried to turn the mattress over, and had then seen the puddle on the floor. As I was on my hands and knees, looking in horror at the mess, the housekeeper, Olga, appeared in the doorway to see if the English *signore* had had a good night's sleep. I mumbled a couple of words, neither of which she understood. Olga shook her head in disbelief – she was to do that a few more times this holiday!

'*Grappa al salto*' is a great Italian pick-me-up for those with terminal hangovers – it literally means 'grappa to make you jump'! Grappa itself is a distillation of everything that is not used in the making of wine – the skins, the pips and even the stalks of the grapes. So this mixture of grappa, sugar and soda water is so revolting it literally makes your headache jump away. It was enough to make you climb back on the wagon. This I did, for at least a day, having decided that Jack the Lad was now going to become Ed the Bed. Being a sex legend in my own mind, I asked the hotel for a double bed, thinking that my success rate with girls back home was going to be matched in Italy. After my break-up, I was going to 'wash that girl right outta my hair'.

The *Radio Times* at the time had approached me about following me out to Italy to do a feature on ED STEWART ON

HOLIDAY. Writing the article was an attractive journalist called Bel, married to a famous broadcaster, and she and her team would be spending a couple of nights researching the feature. Part of the research was Italian food and wine, so off we went to Edda's, a restaurant high in the hills above Montegrotto, the Colli Euganei.

The couple who owned the restaurant were the spitting image of those couples you see on the saucy seaside postcards – the huge wife and the little hen-pecked husband. He was called Giovanino, and Edda was the larger-than-life wife with huge brawny arms, a nose and forehead that seemed to be joined as one, and the trace of a moustache on her upper lip. She would unexpectedly appear behind you and bash you accidentally around the side of your head as you were about to twirl a forkful of spaghetti into your mouth, causing everyone to scream with laughter. In this restaurant, everybody sat at long tables, with the main recipient of these blows sitting at the head. Guess who had that honour ... There was no chance to tell Edda about my fractured skull as a child, or my temporary propensity for wetting the bed – she was after me, moustache and all.

Thankfully, I was saved from further GBH to my head when her little husband appeared for what I thought was going to be an assault on our ears. Far from it; when he opened his mouth to sing, the most melodic, rapturous sounds poured out – 'Catari, Catari', 'Vicino Mare', 'O Sole Mio' and 'La Montanara' – they all flowed out of this little frame and, before long, we were all crying into our wine. Then we found out the true force of Edda's nature. Removing the hat from Giovanino's head, she went round the table with the hat in one hand, the other poised close to our heads, ready for a quick slap. Then with words *'Tui soldi o tua vita'* – 'your money or your life' – she thrust the hat into your face, her moustache glistening in the candlelight. Everybody paid up – we didn't mind being robbed. It had been a night in a million. I was rather hoping it was going to end in another way, but the *Radio Times* team, complete with the tasty Bel, had disappeared back to the hotel. I lurched back in a taxi with Jimmy and Ginetta, humming 'O Sole Mio', and poured myself into my empty double bed.

1972 was the year when *The Godfather* first appeared on our screens. Quite rightly, it has appeared in the Best Film lists ever since. It was with a great deal of excitement, therefore, that I joined the family for a wedding high up in the Euganei hills – and my feeling of excitement grew as I walked on to what appeared to be the set of *The Godfather*. The dancing, the singing, the general feeling of joy and happiness were all-encompassing as you arrived, and totally evocative of the region and its culture. Happily, there were no fleets of limousines with their suspicious-looking drivers to cloud the occasion as there had been in the film. The speeches and toasts were short, but loud. '*Viva l'esposi*' – 'Long live the married couple' – seemed to be the most popular and, as the wine and champagne took effect, so did my bravura. 'Viva leshpossums,' I stood up and cried, and was promptly told to sit down again, although everybody laughed at the mad Englishman's attempt at their language – being slightly smashed didn't seem to matter. Marriage was the last thing on my mind anyway – but the receptionist, Iris, was. She was very attractive. But once again, the demon drink let me down – would I never learn? After a wild night at the local disco, Iris came back to my room, and I thought I was going to break my duck, or even the bed. No such luck. She pushed me on to the bed – and left me there.

However, during the course of the evening, I had borrowed her red handkerchief to wipe some pasta sauce off my trouser leg. I had hoped she would do it for me, but had kept her hankie in case she changed her mind later. Which she didn't. As I was emptying my pockets the next morning, Olga the housekeeper made her now customary entrance to see what I'd been up to the night before. I'd taught her the word 'Nobody', which she could now say to perfection. 'Nobody?' she smiled, and then saw Iris's red handkerchief. 'Oooh!' she cried, running from the room and, in next to no time, the scandal of a supposed affair had hit the hotel headlines. Iris avoided me after that, so I kept the hankie as a memento. Little did they know that nothing had ever happened – it wasn't worth trying to deny it! But I did end up with somebody in my room before the end of the holiday.

Chiara's Uncle Delmo was the painter and poet who had survived the Italian Army's wartime efforts without ever cocking his pistol. We had enjoyed our usual three-hour nightcap and, being in no fit state to drive, Delmo decided to stay at the hotel. 'So sorry, Delmo, there are no rooms left,' came the answer to his request. I suggested to him that we unhinge my double bed to create two singles, and then he could sleep in my room. What a good idea, we thought. When Olga put her nose around the bedroom door the next morning, she saw a man's head and moustache poking out from the bedclothes. '*Mama mia* – he's got a man in his room!' She ran screaming down the corridor. We calmed her down, and she said she understood the circumstances. But poor Olga only looked at me out of the corner of her eye after that. What with Iris, the journalist and now Delmo, my reputation as the English lover and his big double bed was in tatters. No sex, please, we're British!

So my bachelor days continued, but I was like a rudderless ship. Girls were looking at me as an old stud, or, just as bad, an old soak. Amazingly to me, I wanted to settle down, but none of the girls I was squiring had a feel of permanency about them.

8

PULLING A CRACKER!

1974 – AND my days as a bachelor were numbered. If Willie Nelson had written the song 'To All the Girls I've Loved Before' by then, I could have recorded it as a long-player! I'd been to the parties, joined in the threesomes, and the only membership I hadn't yet taken out was that of the Mile-High Club.

At around this time, I had been making a pilot for a documentary called *Stewpot's Travels*, which we were hoping to make into a series. 'We' were David Block, a writer and publicist who had worked with me on my *Stewpot* series, and on columns I used to write in *Woman's Own* and *TV Times*. The other was Keith Beckett, a man with so much vitality and charisma that he could have made the opening of my wallet look interesting.

Unfortunately, the series was never sold, but we had an awful lot of fun making it. So I was flying back from Australia, where the girls had a completely different understanding of the phrase 'good manners'. When you showed them, their gratitude was boundless. The steward pointed to my seat, and my heart skipped a beat. There, sitting by the window, was a really attractive blonde and we started chatting immediately. We were the only passengers in that section of the Jumbo and, as the film started, I put my arm around her and drew her close. The stewardesses were handing out extra blankets and, before long, we had disappeared beneath the blanket. This being a night flight, they didn't want us to catch cold. No chance of that the way things were going!

The stewardess returned to see if we wanted anything else. She saw the contented look on my face, and the bobbing blanket below, so I mouthed the word 'honeymoon', and she smiled knowingly. 'The toilet area is free, if you want to go there!' she whispered, and wandered off whistling the song 'You Can Get It if You Really Want'. So, my new friend and I surfaced, and made off to the one place on the plane where we thought we would have some privacy. About half an hour later, we reappeared, to be greeted by two stewardesses and a large menu from the first class section, on the back of which they had scrawled 'Welcome to the Mile-High Club'! We returned, giggling, to our seats, and continued to watch the film. Its title really made me laugh – *What's up, Doc?* The only thing up on that flight was me!

I'm quite an impetuous person and still see the world through rose-coloured glasses. Chiara was now becoming like Gigi – 'growing up before my very eyes ...' She was now 17, physically very attractive, and had a mind that was mature beyond her years. She was also a fantastic cook. One Thursday, I was meeting my father for lunch in London, and asked Chiara to come along as well. She had never been to Verrey's in Regent Street, and I wanted her opinion on the menu – that's what I told her anyway! She had just finished her A-levels, so was allowed to take the day off school. The three of us had lunch together, and I was struck with her knowledge of the dishes on the menu, and even knowing how to cook them. One of the waiters was Italian, and they chatted in their Venetian dialect about the history and ingredients of the dishes. My dad was impressed too, and they talked effortlessly. I realised I was falling in love, and decided to marry her there and then. Not quite bended knee time, but it wasn't far off – that very evening, in fact.

I was meeting a good friend, Des Brown, who had organised a voiceover for me in Soho. We then arranged to meet for dinner that evening, and I took Chiara off to Lillywhite's to buy her some golf shoes. Seeing my love of golf, she wanted to learn to play as well. She reckoned that if you can't beat them, join them, and when she did join me, she beat me with sickening regularity! Off we went for dinner, Chiara, Des and myself, and it was then that I proposed – and Chiara accepted – and so did Des, as Best Man. I phoned our parents, and Jimmy and Ginetta came over almost immediately. Ginetta had always known we would get married, but didn't think it would be so soon. Jimmy hadn't been so sure – he had experienced the full glory of my bachelor lifestyle. But he was still the one who organised everything, from the registry office in Marylebone to the reception at the Dolce Notte in Jermyn Street. It all took place the following Tuesday, giving you some idea of what a master of organisation he was.

As I stood outside the registry office, I saw Chiara's car pull up, and then drive away again. Had she had a last moment change of mind? No – she was too early – no bride wants to be too early. Keep your husband on his toes from the start, Jimmy had said. At the ceremony, Chiara was so nervous she forgot her other Christian names – Francesca Marinella – but thank goodness I was able to prompt her. She was in a simple white organdie dress, while I wore the suit that many called my 'BBC suit' – small checks. In those days, my weight was around 11st – with all Chi's good cooking and the passage of time, 11st is now a distant memory – it's more like 14st now.

Off we went to the reception; the streets around the Dolce Notte seemed jammed for some reason – it was all those people coming to have a drink on Ed Stewart. As we pulled up at the door, I saw a figure I recognised – it was my brother Mike, who had been returning from South America on a steamer, and had heard the news on the radio while berthed in Dublin Harbour. After flying over, Mike had called our parents to find out where the reception was to be held, but when he eventually arrived at the right restaurant, the staff wouldn't let him in initially, because he didn't have an invitation. Mind you, neither did anybody else – but they didn't look as if they'd just got off a ship after two weeks at sea!

We dragged him inside, and were overjoyed that every member of both families was there. It was a joyous and funny occasion with friends from all walks of life: Terry Wogan, Tony Blackburn, Tony Brandon, Ronnie Carroll, Cardew Robinson and last, but not least, Jan Harding, one of the great unsung comedians of the day. I asked him to say a few words because of his wonderfully dry wit. He didn't let me down, and ended with the classic line, 'I just hope Ed and Chiara turn out to be as happy as my wife and I thought we were going to be!' Jan and Cardew had become firm friends, and besides introducing me to the world of showbusiness golf with the Vaudeville Golfing Society, they were also my proposers when I joined the famous Grand Order of Water Rats in 1976.

'Speak softly, love ...' are the first words of the beautiful love theme to *The Godfather*. That wedding night scene of Michael Corleone and Appolonia was touchingly similar to ours, except that he didn't have to leave the marital love nest at 5.00am to drive to Munich for the Final of the World Cup. I was escorting the winners of a *TV Times* competition, and the wedding had happened so quickly that I hadn't been able to rearrange the contract.

After taking a couple of days to drive there, Chiara was to fly out to meet me. I met her at the airport and drove to the hotel in Munich, to find that we were booked into a single room – I had

163

overlooked telling them I had got married. Luckily, help was at hand in the form of Billy Wright, the great England Captain, who was out there covering the World Cup for a national newspaper. Having played often for the Showbiz XI, he knew Chiara well, and hearing of the honeymooners' ultimate predicament – no bed for the night – kindly offered us his room instead. It wasn't actually a room, it was a suite, one of the perks of his job. Thanks, Billy – we could have ended up sleeping on the floor!

And something else that remains totally memorable from our honeymoon: Why did referee Jack Taylor delay the start of the 1974 World Cup Final between Germany and Holland? Answer: The groundsman had forgotten to put the corner flags in position. I sat there, on my own, waiting for the final to start; there had been no ticket for my new wife – she watched it in our room back at the hotel. Angela Ince of the London *Evening Standard* must have heard about it because, in an article a couple of weeks later, she voted me as one of the Male Chauvinists of the Year – for taking my wife on our honeymoon to the World Cup Final. But, Angela, how could you be so unromantic? A football match only lasts for 90 minutes – what about the rest of the time ...?

On our return from the honeymoon, Chiara was suddenly called to a family funeral in Italy. I had the Radio 1 roadshow to do, which presented me with a little problem – what to do with Sasha, the Afghan hound, whom I'd inherited? The answer was simple – instead of putting him in kennels, I manfully offered to take him to Devon and Cornwall in the back of my Triumph Stag. He was well trained in the house, but once you took him off the lead, then whoosh – he was off. So I tried to take every precaution.

Sasha was a completely fawn Afghan, and when he'd been buffed and puffed in the grooming parlour, he looked as if butter wouldn't melt in his mouth. It didn't actually – he used to chew it still in its silver paper. Something else he was partial to was bottoms – men's bottoms, especially if they didn't know he was there. Here a nip, there a nip, everywhere a nip-nip. He never drew blood, but he didn't half make people jump. When we first moved to West Byfleet, we creosoted the timbers, which meant the man with the brush and tin had to go up and down the ladder. Sasha couldn't resist him and, when he had reached the bottom rung, curled his lip for a quick nip. The man yelled, letting go of the tin of creosote, and the once beautiful fawn Afghan became a sticky, black mess. We had to shave him almost down to the skin and I was convinced that Sasha later became the model for Frank Muir's famous children's books about an Afghan called *What a Mess*!

On my trip with Sasha down to the Roadshow, our first stop was in Bude, and I realised to my horror that I had forgotten to buy any dog food. But the owner of the hotel took pity on us and cooked Sasha a steak – nice and rare. Meal over, it was off to the bar, where the drink of the night turned out to be Harvey Wallbangers – orange juice, vodka and Galliano. The game of the night was Spoof, which I knew well. I was on good form, fortunately, and had only had to buy one round – £9.35. For ten of us who were playing, this sounds cheap now, but it wasn't then!

The following morning, my head was clear as I looked forward to a walk with Sasha, having poured many of my Wallbangers into other people's glasses when they weren't looking. It was a perfect summer's morning. I let Sasha off the lead and started to walk along the cliffs. Whoosh – Sasha was off. In the far distance, he had spied some sheep, whose grass nibbling was about to come to an abrupt end. I vainly tried to keep up, as the Afghan (quicker than a greyhound over long distances) tore towards the sheep.

'Let's get the flock out of here,' baa-aad the ram, and they all made for the nearest point of escape – the edge of the cliff. It brought to mind the biblical story of the Gadarene swine ... except that this time they were sheep. As they disappeared over the edge, hotly pursued by Sasha, I wondered how long it would be before the farmer arrived with his gun to shoot the dog. There had already been cries from onlookers, like 'Fetch the farmer … 'e'll have 'ee!' They were looking at me, and they weren't joking.

I crept to the cliff edge, and slowly peered over, expecting to gaze out on untold carnage. Instead, I found that the cliff had fallen away to just a steep climb, and Sasha was on his way back to me, tongue out and breathing rather heavily – which reminded me a bit of our honeymoon! He slowly ambled towards me, looking rather sheepish – I hate describing him that way, but it was true. He nuzzled into my hand, looking up at me, as if to say, 'That was so much fun, Dad, but I'm sorry you're looking so puffed out!'

Luckily, the sheep were unharmed, and the farmer never materialised. The headlines could have read DJ'S DOG RUSTLES SHEEP, but they never appeared. No one recognised me, thank goodness!

On one occasion, we received an invitation from the Mayor to attend a summer barbecue at his house. He had met Sasha at a fête we had opened a few weeks before, so the dog received an invitation as well. We arrived at the party with Sasha on a tight lead – I wasn't taking any chances.

'Oh,' said the Mayor on seeing us, 'let him off – it's not fair to keep a dog on a lead.

'Don't say I didn't warn you,' I muttered to myself as I unclipped Sasha, and – whoosh – he was off into the large crowd of guests. The Mayor's wife had made this wonderful table of cold meats, chicken and shellfish, which was formed into the face of a clock. I gazed at it in admiration, before noticing that the one o'clock position had disappeared. Munching away at a side of the table was Sasha. I went to take the morsel away, but he growled at me rather too fiercely for my own safety. I looked back at the clock, and saw to my horror that three, six and seven were missing as well. And where was the little hand? Disappearing down Sasha's throat!

A couple of weeks later, a policeman friend of ours turned up at the door. In his hand was not a truncheon, a pair of handcuffs, or even a warrant; it was the skinniest, most dishevelled Afghan hound we'd ever seen. 'Can you take him on?' asked Bob, as he was moving into new quarters, and dogs were not allowed. How could we refuse?

'He's never been off the lead outside, but he's as good as gold in the house,' he assured us.

'As long as he gets on with Sasha,' I said and, at that very moment, Sasha appeared, saw the moth-eaten Kelly, and gave one short, sharp bark. Kelly cowered behind me, and the pecking order was immediately confirmed. Kelly stayed.

I thought I would walk down the towpath, take the lead off, and see how he reacted to his first taste of freedom. Whoosh – he was off. We didn't see him for two days. Apparently, he had run and run and run, revelling in the freedom he had been denied for so long. He had arrived at a canal boat, which had smelt very nicely of food, thank you, curled up and gone to sleep. A couple of days later, the owners, hearing our cries, and seeing another Afghan hound, Sasha, put two and two together, and returned the wayward Kelly to us.

However, Sasha had begun to feel his age. His back legs had gone, and the vet said we wouldn't be able to cope with him any longer. I told the kids I was taking him on an extra long 'walkies', and the vet and I shed buckets of tears as we sent him to that Great Sheep Run in the sky.

To make things worse, Kelly was much older than we thought, and met a sad end as well. Something else we hadn't realised about him was that after Sasha died, apparently the trauma he suffered had caused him to lose his bark. One day, he fell into the stream in front of the house and couldn't climb out. Having no bark, he couldn't tell us of his plight. It was bitterly cold that year, and Kelly literally froze to the side of the bridge which spanned the stream. In the spring, when the temperatures began to rise, we noticed a funny smell pervading the air – it was poor old, decomposed Kelly. So we were to lose both Afghans that same winter. We buried him facing the towpath where he had first tasted freedom.

Buster was the only dog we actually bought; the others were all rescues. Because I was going to be away a lot, Chiara said she would feel safer if she had a breed of dog with a fierce reputation. Buster was the runt of the litter and he came with an attitude to match. At £250 for a pedigree Alsatian, what did we expect? In my ignorance, I asked the breeder why they were called Alsatians and German Shepherds? Apparently, as a breed, they started as German Shepherds, but the Kennel Club were forced to change the name to Alsatian, as anything with the word 'German' in it became extremely unpopular for obvious reasons given our recent history.

Buster's pedigree was good, but his nature wasn't. The neighbourhood lived in fear of him and, when he sank his teeth into our lovely postmistress one day, I knew he had to go. He had been Chiara's dog, really, and even she couldn't stop him terrorising the children. I took him to the vet and he joined Sasha and Kelly in the great kennel in the sky.

In the meantime, though, we had acquired another rescue – a Great Dane. He arrived in the back of a 4x4 with some friends we hadn't seen for years. Uh-oh, I thought, they've got to be wanting something. They did. They wanted to get rid of Wellington, the Harlequin. He had unusual black-and-white markings, and great, doleful pink eyes. Within seconds, we had bonded. He obviously liked my pink eyes as well – a souvenir from the previous night.

Promising to be back in two weeks if we didn't like the dog, they disappeared and we never saw them again. Wellie was now with us, like it or lump it. Wellie definitely liked it – he got fed. He looked so thin, though his previous owners had warned us that he could not absorb food. It went through him – just like that. Our vet placed him on a very specific diet and eventually he put on weight, but there would still be mornings when I'd sniff the air before going downstairs to make the tea – the one domestic chore I have always thrown myself into!

Wellie and I were soulmates and we went everywhere together, but he always had an intestinal problem. Where most dog owners took a poop scoop, I took a shovel. Fortunately, he had been well trained, especially in close quarters. Where Barbara Woodhouse would say, 'Sit-t-t … and stay,' I would only have to click my fingers, or point a finger. Talk about control. It was a shame I couldn't do it with the kids.

Wellie never growled at me once – his noises would come from his other end, and he could clear a room quicker than a party political broadcast on the telly! Everybody loved him and when the old ladies, and sometimes even the younger ones, would say, 'Now, there's a big boy!' looking at Wellie, I would always say, 'You've been looking again!' They would laugh and I would think of Dick Emery and his wonderful female character saying, 'You are awful – [slap] – but I like you!'

One Sunday, we had eaten a lovely roast at my brother John's. Washing-up time came and I offered to help. It was hopeless; no matter how much I insisted, they just wouldn't let me. I have my father to thank for that. He told me that when he had got married, he had dropped all the plates on the floor … 'accidentally'. He had never been allowed to interfere in the kitchen again. My friends had remembered that, when Chiara and I were first married, I had done exactly the same during the washing-up. Like father, like son! But I did clear some plates and take them into John's kitchen.

As I took in the last load, I saw to my horror the remains of the beef bulging from Wellie's jowls. Tenderly, I removed the meat – he would even let me do that – and replaced it on the sideboard. I carved the bit of meat which was still displaying the evidence of his teeth marks and gave it to him. The unmarked bit I wrapped in silver foil and put in the fridge. John's children Bella and Nick had been quietly watching all this, trying hard not to laugh. I put my finger to my lips, mouthing 'our secret'. They kept it too. For about a day.

It broke my heart when we had to have him put down. His stomach problems had become too much for him. He was 12 when he went, a good age for a Great Dane. That's why I haven't had another dog – the pain of losing him was too much.

It's really been a dog's world; we've had four of them – but never again. No more rushing to the vet's and paying their extortionate bills, or the premiums of the insurance companies. No more leaving them in kennels, and wondering if their personality has changed ... no more guilt trips when you've had them put down. No more following around after them with a trowel and little bag. So why do we have them? Beats me. Even the little dog on my computer screen drives me mad!

We had only been married for three weeks when Chiara and I attended our first social engagement together at the Savoy in London. The occasion was the final of the Newspaper Boy and Girl Competition, sponsored by the *Daily Mail*. It was my second year as one of the judges, which included Lord Northcliffe, whose newspaper group, which included the *Daily Mail*, sponsored the event. The boys and girls had been nominated by their newsagent and the customers who relied on the morning delivery. The Gala Dinner that night was attended by royalty and leading members of the government. Since I would be compèring the proceedings, the organisers felt it appropriate that we should sit at the Top Table. At its head was the then Prime Minister, Harold Wilson. His wife Mary sat to his left, and I was next to her with Lady Northcliffe on the other side. That really was a test of conversational expertise! On the other side of the table were Princess Alexandra, Lord Northcliffe and the newly married Chiara Stewart.

Chi was scared stiff at the thought of sitting with so many prominent people (she was only 17½, after all), but I whispered to her before we sat down to talk about what she knew best – food and clothes. By the end of the meal, she had given Mary Wilson the recipe for vegetable lasagne, and had suggested to Lord Northcliffe that of course he could wear jeans. The press baron had been worried his bottom was too big!

Another bottom that looms large in the memory from November of the same year was the one that produced huge mountains of manure as I perched precariously on its owner's back. As the elephants lumbered into the ring of Chipperfield's Circus on that winter evening, the ringmaster was seated somewhat uncomfortably on the neck of the leader of the pachyderm parade. He looked like any other ringmaster in his red coat and white breeches, waving his shiny black top hat at the excited audience around him. But this ringmaster had no experience of riding elephants, and looked faintly ridiculous with his overlong hair and fixed, terrorised smile.

Chipperfield's Circus had been placed on a plot of empty British Rail land behind East Croydon Railway Station, and was in the middle of a three-week run when we went to record the TV programme. Beside the miles of cable, the galleries of lights and dozens of people attached to such an undertaking, there was also a full orchestra of musicians.

It had been decided that I would look great riding on one of the elephants as they paraded around the ring. My female charge had duly helped me up on to her back, via a toenail, then a knee and finally a gentle push with her trunk. Then, on arrival in the ring, she had dropped a huge dollop of manure, much to the delight of the laughing children. I had felt like doing something similar myself. It was scary up there on that lurching back. But I wasn't going to fall – how could I? Chiara had told me that afternoon that she was pregnant, and the baby was due in May. There would definitely not be headlines like FATHER-TO-BE TRAMPLED UNDERFOOT AT CIRCUS! I grasped the red leather straps on the elephant's head even tighter, until she suddenly stopped, raised a foreleg, and I slid down, tumbling into the sawdust. The audience thought it was all part of the act – little did they know.

As soon as rehearsals started for the orchestra, the rains came down, so much so that the ground turned into mud of such thickness that a veteran of the Somme might have felt at home. But at least Dick Chipperfield had erected a brand-new big top – this was television after all! But the ultra-deluxe material was not weathered enough for incessant rain, and it started to leak ... all over the musicians. It rained so much that an awning had to be built above the brass section, whose numbers included the famous trombonist Don Lusher. He had donned a snazzy white raincoat to keep his immaculate suit nice and dry, which had prompted a little banter from his fellow musicians. The rain poured down, the water level slowly gathering in the straining awning rose higher and higher, until the sound engineer shouted through to the director (he had had to shout, because the sound of the rain beating on the tarpaulin was louder than the drummer!), 'The trombones are a bit too muffled!' He was right – the awning had split, the water had cascaded on to the trombone section, and they couldn't play any more – their plungers were muted! Don Lusher laughed at all the others who had laughed at him in his snazzy white raincoat. At least his suit was dry!

Weeks later, when the programme was eventually seen on Thames TV, I was to receive more hate-mail than I had amassed in ten previous years of radio broadcasts. The letters came from animal lovers who resented the idea of wild animals being caged and trained for the pleasure of the watching public, both in the tent and on television. I can see now they had a point, but at that time all I had wanted to do was pursue my career as a TV performer. I believed the Chipperfield Brothers when they said

172

they bred the Siberian tigers to conserve them, otherwise they would have become extinct. Then there were complaints that the crocodiles used in one of the acts had been hypnotised, but we thought that that was stretching things a bit. I used to believe as a child you should never smile at a crocodile because they might hypnotise *you*.

The TV companies, who had never really taken any moral stand, were obliged eventually to stop showing circuses as entertainment programmes over 20 years ago – the animal conservationists had won.

There is an old saying in showbusiness: 'Never work with children and animals', the reason being that they invariably upstage you! Christopher Palmer, the same producer who had plonked me on a lumbering beast in a circus tent, obviously thought I was somebody who could escape unscathed and with my reputation intact from most tricky situations. Having booked me for the Chipperfield Circus programmes, he then approached my agent to use me as a guest presenter for the ITV travel programme *Wish You Were Here* in the summer of 1981.

'Why?' I asked him.

'Because we want to show our audience how a young family can easily journey abroad on holiday. You've got a young family. You're quite popular – and there's another thing in your favour.'

'What's that?' I enquired,

'You're cheap!' And he burst into laughter. I made a mental note: 'Must speak to my agent.'

Wish You Were Here had always been my favourite travel programme. It was less stuffy than the BBC's equivalent *Holiday*, and now that they were asking me to go to Florida, it was definitely the best! So we prepared to fly off to Miami.

However, on the night before departure, our daughter, Francesca, who was just seven then, went down with some lurgy and our GP didn't want her to fly. I explained the situation to him, so he gave us a prescription to take to America with us. In the meantime, he dosed her up with antibiotics and pronounced her well enough to travel. Poor little thing – she did as Daddy told her, as most girls do at that age. It all changed when she became a teenager.

We flew to Miami on Laker Airways. A pioneer of cheaper air travel, Freddie Laker had seen the potential of affordable holidays with cut-price air fares. Today's travellers should thank Sir Freddie for bursting the monopoly of the major airlines, and bringing foreign destinations within the reach of the majority of British holidaymakers.

When Thames TV sent the Stewart family on holiday to Florida, we flew on Laker's new service, Skytrain. Unfortunately for him, his efforts were soon scuppered by the banks, and Laker Airways went out of business in February 1982, six months after the Stewarts had flown to Miami. There was a lot of public sympathy for Sir Freddie at the time, with one businessman offering him £1m; a merchant bank was going to raise £25m, and one schoolboy even offered him 16p! The recession, high interest rates on the money Laker had borrowed to purchase his DC10s and the high value of the dollar against the pound all conspired to end his dream.

That edition of *Wish You Were Here* was scheduled for transmission the following February, on the very day, as it turned out, that Laker went under. Since the programme had been recorded and was now in the can, Judith Chalmers, as presenter, had to make an announcement 'live', before the programme went out, explaining the situation. There was sure to have been one bright spark to have noticed we were flying Laker Skytrain when it no longer existed!

When we arrived in Miami, we took Francesca's prescription to a pharmacy, or 'drugstore' as they are known there. The pharmacist didn't accept the prescription – he couldn't read the doctor's writing, so we had to visit an American doctor to obtain a second legible prescription. Soon Keka (our family name for Francesca) was back to normal, and we were enjoying the Florida hospitality, sunshine and hotspots that American families were visiting in their droves: Disneyworld, Wet and Wild and Busch Gardens. How we crammed everything and everywhere in I know not – what appeared later on the TV screen as a two-week holiday, we had recorded in five days!

The weather was very hot, and much of the time was spent around swimming pools or the sea, so much so that Francesca and Marco learnt to swim. I learnt something myself – there is a 55mph speed limit on American roads. While filming one scene, I didn't notice the flashing blue light in my rear-view mirror, and before you could say 'Gee, Officer Krupke', I had been booked for speeding. 'Have a nice day, now, and thank you for filming our wunnerful state,' the officer said with a smile as he drove away. My producer grimaced – that $60 fine would have to come off his expenses.

The next day, we were filming our breakfast in Jack's Diner in St Petersburg. Our writer, Peter Hughes, was very good at finding 'characters'. The waitress at Jack's Diner hardly drew breath when I asked her how my eggs could be cooked. 'Fried, sunnyside up, over light, over medium, poached, baked, scrambled, scrambled soft, basted, over hard or straight up!'

'How do you like yours?' I asked mischievously.

'Over hard or straight up,' she replied, not even blinking, but with a glint in her eye that spoke volumes. I bet it did. Seriously, though (and we have to be serious sometimes), I often wonder whether Americans are aware that part of the world's population is starving. If they did, then they might be more mindful of the fact that the size of some of their bodies, and the portions of food on their plates, are frankly obscene.

Thomas Edison, having invented the lightbulb in the 1880s,

moved to Fort Myers Beach in Florida to perfect his invention, using strands from the giant bamboo to make the filament in his light bulbs stronger and longer lasting. The best giant bamboos grew in Florida, where the rich and successful also liked to migrate for the winter. It was in Edison's house, we also learnt, that his other great invention, the phonograph, was perfected. When he grew deaf, he would listen to the music through his teeth – the bite marks were still visible. So thank you, Thomas Edison. Without you, a whole generation would never have enjoyed listening to their records on their Dansette phonographs.

Disneyworld in Florida was the single most popular tourist attraction in the world at that time, and the queues for the attractions looked horrendous. I say 'looked' because, by presenting a travel programme, we didn't have to stand around for hours, and wait our turn in the 90°F heat. We got a few dirty looks from people who didn't recognise us, and even worse from those who did. 'Who do you think you are?' 'I'll never listen to you again!' Charming.

The Disney music was always in our ears, but I had no complaints – I was brought up on it. *Snow White and the Seven Dwarfs* was the first film my brothers and I ever saw – Mike, the youngest, always called it *Snow and the Seven White Giraffes*. Even today, 'When You Wish upon a Star' and 'When I See an Elephant Fly' make the hairs on the back of my neck stand up on end.

My experience with the Chipperfield Brothers has put me off riding elephants for life, and I should have realised then that riding anything four-legged should be avoided at all costs. The difficulty, though, is turning down genuine charitable requests, whether large animals are involved or not.

It was around this time that Simon Bates and I entered a challenge race at Wembley Arena in aid of the Olympic Fund. I seem to remember he fell off, and I won the race but I could hardly move the next day – talk about using muscles you never knew existed!

I had barely recovered from that when Phonogram Records staged a Donkey Derby after their Charity Race Day at Kempton Park. The donkey I was given didn't need a carrot to get it going – just the sight of open country was enough – and off we shot. I got him on a short rein, pointed him in the right direction ... and we won easily. My experience at Major Walker's had paid off.

About a week later, I was standing in my local, the Blue Anchor in Byfleet, when a chap, whom I had seen in the pub a couple of times before, ordered a bottle of champagne, two glasses and then started pouring me a drink.

'That's very kind of you,' I said. 'But why?'

'Because, Stewpot, you won me a small fortune at the Donkey Derby last week, so I'm here to say thank you.'

With that, we continued to attack the bottle, while he explained that the bookies had been offering 20-1 as the odds on me and my donkey. As he finished the last glass, he took £20 out and stuck it in the charity tin on the bar. Then he peeled off a tenner, and said as he gave it to me, 'That's for winning the Donkey Derby!'

He's generous, I thought, and I wondered if 'e aw ... 'e aw ... 'e always did that.

One of the most satisfying few weeks on *Junior Choice* came after I had received a letter from a Mr Brynley Elias at the Lingfield Hospital School in Surrey. We had played a football match at the school, and had visited some of the boarders afterwards who were mostly epileptic. They insisted on showing us around the school, which was badly in need of extra facilities. The pupils had all just reached puberty, and the girls wouldn't let us out of their dormitory – we had to be rescued by the staff! Mr Elias said he had a fundraising idea, and would I be interested in helping them raise some money for the school? To raise money directly 'on air' in those days was almost impossible. Everything had to go through the Charities Division, who then gave your charity a slot on Radio 4 to beseech the millions for that week's worthy cause. Later, the BBC very successfully got around these restrictions by creating Children in Need and Comic Relief. But in 1972, the rules were very different, so Doreen Davies, who was an Executive Producer at Radio 1, decided to test these charity rules and put out an appeal that was different. If, by bending the rules, there was any complaint from the Charities Division, then the proof of the pudding would be in the eating. We ate well!

Green Shield Stamps were the market leaders at the time, employing a process whereby you swapped your collection of stamps in return for goods and gifts at Green Shield Stamp shops. So, with the petrol you bought in the first place, you received a corresponding number of stamps to stick in your book. When you had collected five books, you could redeem them for a football ... 50 books and you might get a bike!

So, for a couple of weekends, I asked my audience if they would contribute some of their books of Green Shield Stamps to help the epileptic kids at the Lingfield Hospital School. 'Look everywhere,' I said, 'down the back of the sofa, in the kitchen drawers, in the drawers where Granny keeps her drawers, in the old sweet jar, anywhere that you might think as a hiding place for some long-forgotten stamps. It'll be like a giant game of Hide and Seek!'

The response was totally unexpected. Radio 1's headquarters at Egton House, behind BH, was immersed in sacks and sacks of Green Shield Stamps. The kids had done what I had asked, and so, too, had their parents and grandparents. Little old ladies were sending their own collections, saying they would rather give them to the children than get a new hot-water bottle. Schools had created their own collection points so that the pupils and staff could leave their stamps there. We eventually weighed the stamps, and saw that the approximate number sent was nearly 20 million. I'm just glad we didn't have to count them! Lingfield Hospital School was eventually able to redeem those stamps and earn enough money for three coaches for the use of staff and pupils.

Radio 1 management approached the Variety Club of Great Britain to supply the Sunshine Coaches. That itself started an association with the Variety Club, which was to continue for many years. Anyone reading this who remembers sending their stamps to the programme should enjoy a warm glow of satisfaction knowing that they helped contribute to such a worthwhile cause. And that's what giving to charity is all about, isn't it?

One way of helping many worthy causes was to combine our love of cricket with fundraising, and one of the most extraordinary games of cricket I ever played for charity was on the Greek island of Corfu in 1978, a match that saw the clash of the Lord's Taverners and a Corfu Select XI. Cricket had been played there since the British administration of the island in the 1850s. Nicholas Parsons had holidayed there with his family and watched with some amazement as Greek men ran around what was formerly a military parade ground playing a game that had been introduced to their forefathers over a hundred years before! Being a staunch Lord's Taverner, Nicholas approached the famous cricketing charity with the idea of a match against the islanders, known as the Corfiots. At the same time, Nicholas was going to make a film of that event, and a couple of other matches in the UK, to help promote the way money was raised for the charity. The Taverners said they would be delighted to send a team out there, but who was going to pay for it? A little while later, Nicholas found himself sitting next to the Chairman of Barclaycard, who agreed to sponsor the cost of the film and volunteered his services as wicket keeper.

When Nicholas broached the idea to the cricketing authorities in Corfu, they were delighted to take up the challenge, thinking that with a name like Lord's Taverners, this would be team of some strength. Wasn't Lord's the headquarters of the MCC? As far as they were concerned, the word charity didn't come into it – this would be a meeting of great cricketers – for real!

The title of Nicholas's film – *The Lord's Taverners - Mad Dogs and Cricketers* – encapsulated the mood of the trip perfectly. The team was captained by Ken Barrington, whom the Corfiots recognised immediately as a 'famous cricketer'. There were two more professionals, the first being Jack Robertson, an immediate post-war cricketer of some renown who played for England and Middlesex. The second was John Price, also of England and Middlesex, who, although normally a number 11 batsman, managed to score a century in Corfu and help us win the match!

How about the rest then? In alphabetical order, so as not to upset anybody, there was John Alderton, together with his wife Pauline Collins as Chief Cheerleader; John Cleese; Roy Kinnear, whose left arm tweakers surprised everybody, most of all himself; Nicholas Parsons; Brian Rix; Willie Rushton; Bill Simpson; and Ed Stewart. Making up the 12 was Mr Barclaycard, who played as wicket keeper.

Having some comedians on the trip made it even more enjoyable. One morning, as he was lying on his floating lilo in the swimming pool, Roy Kinnear had asked the waiter to bring him a long, cool drink. Willie Rushton whispered an instruction to the waiter, who, having prepared the drink, walked fully clothed into the pool, presented the startled Roy Kinnear with the glass, and promptly pulled the plug on the lilo, which made a loud hissing sound that woke everybody up. We all dissolved in laughter as we saw airbed, drink and Roy disappear into the water.

Thinking we were, indeed, an unofficial Test team, the Mayor of Corfu, himself a keen cricketer, threw a party to welcome us on the evening before the match, thereby hoping that the vast amount of wine, ouzo and retsina that we consumed would render us useless the next day. Far from it. His welcoming speech went on far too long, and he gabbled away at such a speed, his poor interpreter just couldn't keep up. Each time he began his translation, the Mayor would lurch off again so fast the interpreter eventually gave up. A little was lost in the translation, and we were beginning to get the giggles: 'I am very happy to receive you in this siege [sic] in the principality of Corfu, with all the sympathy and esteem, and we are accepting your nice manifestation. Your history has taught me this marvellous game since 1850. It has been promoted by her Royal Queen Elizabeth who has developed the game in Great Britain and all Conolies. She has planted its roots in Corfu with kindest feelings and passion.'

The next day, despite the effects of the ouzo, we gathered for the grand parade. As the sun beat down from the cloudless sky, we followed the Scouts, Sea Scouts and the local marching band through the streets of Corfu Town. We were making for the old parade ground, which was to be our cricket pitch.

As so often happens with marching bands, there was one clarinet that was half a tone sharp, but nonetheless the bandsmen looked impressive in their white uniforms and tall purple-plumed hats. There were large crowds lining the streets, and even more around the pitch, swollen by large numbers of British tourists bussed in from resorts around the island. It was a truly incongruous sight, with us in our whites (I had a Radio 1 sun hat on my head as well), the Corfu team in various hues, and John Cleese at the front, making the crowds roar with one of his funny walks!

Once on the pitch, Willie Rushton observed wryly that it would be all right once they had put the heavy Hoover on it. John Cleese added that he would give it further inspection to see if he could find some grass. John Price agreed that it was not Lord's but at least it was sunny. The wicket itself was hard-baked earth, while tufts of grass made up the outfield.

Captain Ken Barrington won the toss, and put Corfu into bat. The boundaries would be signalled when the ball reached the grass verges, the edge of the car park or the tent where the VIPs were sitting. The VIPs seemed to be made up of the two teams and commentator John McKelvey, the Mayor and his party, and an assortment of military dignitaries, who sat there completely emotionless for the entire afternoon dressed in full uniform.

Putting Corfu in first, they clattered up a good score of 203 by tea. The highlight of the bowling was Roy Kinnear's almost completed hat-trick, but he was badly let down by the wicket keeper who spilled the catch. That wicket keeper was me, called to don the gloves when Mr Barclaycard suffered a nasty touch of heatstroke, and had to lie down in the shade for the remainder of the afternoon. There were one or two others who would have liked to have joined him, more from the effect of ouzo than sun!

Thanks to that century from John Price, and notable efforts from Barrington and Cleese, we eventually won the match, with our honour intact. We were less intact at the party that evening, both with our efforts at Zorba's dance, and the vocal renditions of the smash hit 'Never on a Sunday'! Nicholas Parsons and his then wife stood aghast as their daughter stripped to her bra and panties, and continued dancing on the table – everybody else whooped and cheered. The Mayor of Corfu did have a sense of humour after all, when he congratulated those who had sung, and asked them to return ... never on a Sunday, Monday or any day of the week!

The last day of the trip, and we were taken to a small island off Corfu for some private sunbathing. The more adventurous of the girls had decided to go topless, so Pauline Collins, Chiara Stewart and a couple of others who shall remain nameless to protect them from identification at the bridge club, took off their tops. So being three lads together, Parsons, Alderton and Stewart all decided to take their bottoms off, and walk out of the sea, like three

Adonises. Unfortunately, despite the baking temperature on the beach, the sea was quite cool, and if we could not have been accused of being shrinking violets before, on this occasion we most definitely were! Ken Barrington gave us some advice that evening, and we all three had to take it. If you are ever overexposed to the sun, particularly in delicate areas, run yourself a tepid bath, and add some vinegar to it. We did – and it worked for all three of us, thank goodness, or it would have been a very painful journey home!

Back at Broadcasting House, we could become quite blasé about the range of celebrities who regularly dropped in, but sometimes there were particularly special guests. Those of us lucky to be invited will never forget the day Princess Margaret came to visit BH a year after Radio 1 had opened. We were ushered into the Governors' Dining Room for tea and scones, although, under the Princess's tea cosy, there might have been something stronger. 'A royal request would be a good idea,' I thought to myself as I slurped my Darjeeling. Then, out of the corner of my eye, I noticed Pete Murray furtively sliding his way along the sofa towards the Princess. She had loads of sex appeal and all the young bloods (and a few older ones) were jockeying for position to get as close to her as possible. Before long, Pete and the Princess were in a deep and meaningful conversation. Their eye contact might have become too intense, or perhaps it was Pete's arm that moved too close to her shoulder, but this little tête-à-tête was not to be a prelude to a kiss. The Princess's mood changed abruptly as she noticed the arm along the back of the sofa. She gave Pete a look that almost turned him into a pillar of salt, rose from the sofa and beckoned to her lady-in-waiting that it was time to go.

As she gave us all one of her beautiful smiles, I blurted out, 'Your Highness, I know your daughter has her fourth birthday next weekend, and I would like to play her a request.' The room went silent ... the lady-in-waiting gave me a look, which said, 'What impudence!' but the Princess smiled and said, 'How kind of you, Mr Stewart. They've never had a record played for them before. Whatever is at the top of the charts at the moment would be perfect – what would that be?' I stumbled for just a moment, trying to remember what it was.

'Louis Armstrong ... "What a Wonderful World"!' shouted Tony Blackburn. Smart arse!

'Whatever they want, I shall let you know,' continued HRH. Suddenly, the party was over, and Robin Scott said, 'Well done, Ed. I'll send you the script tomorrow.' Poor old Pete Murray looked as though he had been jilted at the altar.

The next day, Robin Scott received a message to say that the royal children didn't want the Louis Armstrong record, but would prefer Alan Price's 'Don't Stop the Carnival'. And then came the script, which I was to read, finishing with the words '... with love from your mother and father'.

'No way am I going to say "mother and father", it's a bit old-fashioned,' I said to Robin. 'I would rather say "mum and dad".'

'No,' he replied. 'Let's compromise and say "mummy and daddy",' which I did. At the time, that was real progress!

Having only recently got married, and with a hugely popular radio show on my hands, it was naturally time for me to become even busier – and a great deal more recognisable – through a certain television programme. Shout the name of it anywhere and you'll get a response. The word itself is like a rallying call for a whole generation!

In the *Concise Oxford Dictionary*, 'crackerjack' is defined as an 'exceptionally fine or expert thing or person'. You can't argue with that, can you? The programme started in 1955 with Eamonn Andrews as the first presenter and owner of the name. In the early days, it was transmitted 'live', and beware the child who was not in front of a TV to join in with 'It's Friday, it's five to five and it's *Crack-er-jaaack ...*'

The show was meant for eight- to ten-year-olds, and was broadcast from the BBC TV Theatre in Shepherd's Bush Green in west London. The studio audience mainly consisted of Cubs and Scouts, Girl Guides and Brownies, school parties and chaperones, with the chaperones making as much noise as the rest. In the near 30 years it was on screen, many of its presenters and actors went on to become household names. I can usually tell people's ages by whom they remember on *Crackerjack* – Eamonn Andrews, Leslie Crowther, Pip Hinton, Little and Large, Don McLean, Bernie Clifton, Stu Francis, Ronnie Corbett ... and so the list goes on. Jan Hunt and The Krankies are still working today, though it must be a bit disconcerting for Jan as she is a touring actress these days and, on more than one occasion, she has walked on stage at the start of a murder mystery to the sound of 'CRACK-ER-JAAACK!' This was a children's show that had everything – corny jokes, star guests, Double or Drop and the all-singing finale, in which Eamonn Andrews mimed the words and I usually forgot them!

Double or Drop was a knockout quiz game in which, with every correct answer, you received loads of small prizes and if you dropped one you were given a cabbage. When you had dropped enough items to receive three cabbages, you were out of the game. The local greengrocer became a millionaire! For Double or Drop we always had an aspiring or out-of-work – or, often, both – young actress as hostess. Michael Aspel, who, between reading the news and compèring Miss World, was also presenter of *Crackerjack* for a couple of years, gave me some valuable advice. When he heard that I was to follow him, he advised me to ask for another hostess, as his current one had just appeared in a spread for that well-known children's magazine called *Penthouse*. Since that young girl was also an old flame of mine, I took his advice – after all, I had just got married!

Talking about that greengrocer who became a millionaire with his cabbages, if the Eamonn Andrews organisation had marketed the *Crackerjack* pencil properly they would have made an awful lot of money. It was the ultimate child's prize so maybe Eamonn had the right idea – commercialisation often degrades the aesthetic value of something and the pencil had that quality. We upgraded it to a Schaeffer pen later and then had the motif inscribed, but they were never mass-produced. A friend of mine had a Chow puppy who chewed up my pen and now he's got the bluest tongue in the country! Now isn't that straight out of *Crackerjack*?

Crackerjack was a load of fun, and we all looked forward to our daily and weekly routine. To guarantee non-stop laughter at all the scenes in the programme, the cast went out filming for a day at a zoo or holiday camp. When the results were edited, they were then speeded up, and played to the audience as a warm-up to the actual recording. The laughter which resulted was then edited in later to any part of the programme which did not have sufficient impact. The final edition of the programme was often the result of some very judicious editing.

Once again, though, despite the popularity of the show and the enjoyment we all had making it, the precarious life of the freelancer reminded me that you can't ride the crest of the wave for ever ... the wave will eventually no longer support you, and you have to swim back out there to find another one.

Picture the scene: I was in bed with my wife; Everton were on *Match of the Day* (you can tell we'd been married for a few years or 'match of the day' would have meant something completely different!). The phone rang. Typical – Everton were winning for a change, and I had to answer the phone .

'Hello ... Ed Stewart?' I could just make out a crackly and slightly inebriated voice. 'This is [his name was impossible to catch] ... of the *Sunday Mirror* here. I'm just calling to tell you that you won't be presenting *Crackerjack* any more ...' and I distinctly heard a loud cry of 'CRACK-ER-JAAACK' in the background.

'How do you know that?' I asked in a shaky voice, not wanting to believe what I was hearing. Now he had all my attention, so I thankfully didn't see Bob Latchford missing an Everton penalty on the TV.

'Robin Nash, your producer, has just told me ... we're all out here at the Montreux Film Festival. Just a moment, I'll pass him on to you.'

Robin's unmistakable voice confirmed everything. 'Yessh, darling, Ed. You're all too old and we're putting some new blood in.'

'And who is this new blood?' I shouted down the line.

'The Krankies.'

So that was it. Peter Glaze, who had been resident comic since the earliest days, Jan Hunt, Bernie Clifton, Bert Hayes, the long-serving musical director, and myself had been axed with a drunken journalist from Switzerland giving us the news.

Over the years, nothing had changed – I'd lost my job, but Fleet Street had been the first to tell me and, sure enough, under the headline in the next day's paper CRACKER SACKED, the report started with some familiar words: 'Last night, I broke the news to Ed Stewart ...'

But the saddest end to this was yet to come. Peter Glaze had been suffering from poor health for some time, and possibly the shock of his sacking was to hasten his death the following year. Many turned out for his funeral – he was well loved and respected. But did producers or management bother to show up and pay their respects? Sadly not.

So, in 1980, it was to be a new programme and radio station to begin a new decade. It all looked very exciting, and now I was working a regular five-day week instead of the two days of *Junior Choice*. Perhaps my decision to move away from the radio programme was swayed when my days of giving away pens and cabbages on *Crackerjack* came to an end. The two events happened simultaneously. My days as strictly a children's presenter were over. We all have to grow up some time!

Within weeks, though, I had made the headlines again, but this time because of my deepening relationship with the Royal Family! In August that year, it was the Queen Mum's 80th birthday, and Princess Margaret hadn't forgotten that I had performed previous royal duties on her behalf and read out her children's request on the show. Would I do the same for her mother?

We had met again at the annual Girl Guides Day at Ascot and, over a cup of tea, she had asked me whether I would play something on my afternoon show. I said, 'Of course,' thinking it would be something by Gilbert and Sullivan or Vera Lynn.

'What is your phone number?' asked HRH.

I gave her the BBC's.

'Oh, no, not them … you can never get through to the BBC. Please may I have your home number … I can then tell you directly!'

The following Tuesday, the phone went at home while I was in the garden. My mother-in-law answered and, when the voice at the other end asked to speak to me, she asked who was calling.

'Princess Margaret,' came the reply.

'Oh, yes, and I'm the Pope!' said Ginetta in her best Italian-English, and turning to the open doorway, yelled down the garden, 'Eh, boy … somebody who say she's la principessa Margaretta wants you!'

I ran to the phone and, before I could start explaining about my mother-in-law, the Princess said, 'Thank you so much for doing this for my mother. She would like to hear a record called "Car 67" … she thinks it such a touching story about real human life.'

She was right. It had been made by a Brummie DJ called Paul Phillips, and was about a minicab driver who had been asked to pick up a fare, but had refused because she had recently jilted him. This 'warm and human story' as she had described it was a one-off Top 20 hit from the previous year, but had appealed to no less a person than the Queen Mother. There certainly is no accounting for taste, and you never know who's listening. I should have known, really. Years before, the Queen Mum had told me she never missed *Junior Choice* on a Sunday, while she was taking her morning bath. The mind boggled!

While it was now time for me to move on, sometimes you are inevitably linked with one or two significant jobs or moments that come back to haunt you even after the space of many years. The power of *Crackerjack*, for example, has lasted right up to the present day. Only a few years ago, I heard 'CRACK-ER-JAAACK'! bellowed down from a building site and, looking up at the third floor of a nearby building, I saw a group of helmeted builders stripped to the waist and enjoying their lunch break. It made my day – but then it always does.

And in 1987 – a full seven years after I had finished as a presenter – there was a large concert at the Royal Albert Hall on behalf of the National Children's Homes in the presence of the Queen. After Iris Williams had performed her huge hit 'He Was Beautiful', and Mollie Sugden, Nerys Hughes and Angela Rippon had delivered their readings and performed their monologues, I was suddenly called upon to 'fill' for five minutes as another performer had failed to show up. What was 'Crackerjack Man' to do?

Dressed in my white suit and white shoes with my Royal Stewart tie for good measure, I strode into the vast amphitheatre, waited for the applause to die down and shouted out the magic word. Back came the sound of 6,000 voices in unison – 'CRACK-ER-JAAAACK!' With my pantomime experience, I then started dividing the hall up into sections, tier by tier and, as we reached the tier which included the Royal Box, I asked for complete hush so that we could hear a royal 'Crackerjack!' To this day, I won't know whether Her Majesty shouted or not, because half the audience all joined with their best soundalike Queen voices and everybody collapsed in laughter!

After the concert, when we were all to be presented to the Queen, I stood there expecting a royal brush-off at the very least, or an immediate banishment to the Tower. But, no, Her Majesty expressed wonderment that anybody could control 6,000 people with a one-word act. But before I could say that she could control TV audiences with just one look, she had moved on to Angela Rippon, expressing disappointment that we had not seen her dancing legs that evening. All this because of a dearly loved children's television programme.

By the end of 1979, Radio 2 offered me the afternoon slot, to include the long-running *Family Favourites*. My producer was to be Colin Charman, who also chose the records for Radio 2's country music programmes. I like country music, but only in small doses. Imagine my horror when I found my first *Ed Stewart Show* was made up almost entirely of country records – Colin had thought I was a fan too. We eventually compromised, and I was to stay in that slot for the next three and a half years.

Two Way Family Favourites had begun in 1946 with Cliff Michelmore in Cologne and Jean Metcalfe in London. Their burgeoning romance over the airwaves and eventual marriage kept the nation enthralled. Listening to the programme was a weekly ritual for millions. When Radios 1 and 2 took over from the Light Programme in 1967, *Family Favourites* went worldwide with Australia, New Zealand, Canada and Hong Kong joining in. When I took over the programme in 1980, after stints by Sandy Jones and Michael Aspel, the programme had lost some of its appeal with only Australia and New Zealand taking part. We recorded their contributions prior to the live afternoon transmission, and what had formerly been sacrosanct to the schedules was now considered something relatively unimportant.

In the week before Christmas 1980, Bob Hudson in Australia and Ian Thompson in New Zealand spoke across the airwaves to London for the last time. Ian, who had been the anchorman in Auckland for many years, ended his association by playing a Maori Choir singing 'Now is the Hour', and I'm sure I could actually hear the lump in his throat. Bob Hudson was presenting from Sydney – he was so slow and laid back in his presentation that I thought he was going to fall off his chair.

Our final selection of records was one of the ingredients that had made this programme so popular. Barry Manilow with 'Can't Smile Without You' was our first disc. The other records we played that day included 'Stardust' by Nat King Cole, the Beatles' 'All You Need Is Love', 'Down Under' by Men at Work, Peter Allen's Aussie Favourite 'I Still Call Australia Home', and finishing with the most requested song in all the programme's 37 years, Vera Lynn's 'We'll Meet Again'. With the closing theme of Andre Kostelanetz playing 'With a Song in My Heart', that part of broadcasting history was brought to an end. After that came the news, followed by Bobby Vee's 'How Many Tears' – quite a few, I would imagine.

By moving to Radio 2, I temporarily saved Tony Blackburn's career. He was no longer presenting the breakfast show, and Radio 1 were in a quandary as to what to do with him. By leaving *Junior Choice*, I had solved their problem – he took over! For me, it was an exciting new era – I would be on air five times a week. I had only done that during the 70s when I was sitting in for one of the regulars when they were on holiday. As well as the exposure, I would also be earning more. My original £100 fee on *Junior Choice* would now be five times that! Nowadays, we might be blinded by the purported wealth of a Chris Evans or Noel Edmonds, but they are both proven businessmen as well as broadcasters; our fees in the 60s and 70s were chicken feed in comparison. If the BBC had paid us a fee pro rata to our listening figures, I, too, would have become a millionaire by now! But as in the parable of the labourers in the vineyard in the New Testament, we had agreed our fee and had to honour it ... which I did, more than happily. Being happy in one's job is surely better than having a job just for the sake of it. The fee for *Crackerjack*, for example, with its huge audiences of millions, was also relatively small – about £150 a show. But if you weren't happy with that, there would be a queue of presenters behind you who would be.

Fortunately, I was in a position now to make the most of the limited success I'd had in my career up to this point. In May of that wonderful hot summer of 1976, we had been off to a friend's wedding party in West Byfleet, between Woking and Weybridge in Surrey. The couple were relatives of Ted and Aileen, a successful local builder and his wife. On the way to Ted's house, where the reception was being held, we had noticed a 'For Sale' sign on another impressive house down the same road. Two hours and just two glasses later, I plucked up the courage to have a closer look at the house behind the 'For Sale' sign. It was a beauty, with a long, tree-lined, gravel drive, that meandered over a stream and through a parking area up to an oak-panelled front door. I couldn't help noticing the double garage, the swimming pool and the sweeping lawns down to the Wey Navigation Canal, and I pressed the doorbell in anticipation and, for good measure, made sure the door knocker was in working order as well. The impressive door was opened.

'Good afternoon, madam ... excuse me for not making an appointment with the estate agents, but as I was passing by, I ... '

She cut me short with a hand movement that would have been a credit to a Parisian *gendarme*. 'NORMAN!' she yelled over her shoulder to a man who, I could see through the window, was quietly reading the paper. Poor Norman's privacy was about to be shattered.

Norman duly appeared. 'Well, I'm blessed!' he exclaimed 'It's the man from *Crackerjack*! Shouldn't you be on the telly?'

'Oh,' I gulped, 'it's not Friday, is it?'

We all laughed, and they invited us inside. Chiara had not got out of the car at this stage, just in case I hadn't been greeted so warmly. What a coward. Now she and I were to take our first look together at what was to become our home for the next 17 years.

Two words in Italian summed up our house in Dartnell Park: '*uno paradiso*'. My mother-in-law, Ginetta was right – it was a paradise. We eventually moved in at the end of October. At the insistence of both sets of grandparents, we immediately put up some fencing around the swimming pool and along the canal. How many times do we read of tragedies about little children falling into pools and ponds, while a grown-up wasn't paying attention? It had happened to my younger brother Mike when he was a four-year-old toddler in a garden with a lake. One moment Mike was there, the next he had disappeared, until someone noticed a trail of bubbles and grabbed him before he sank to the bottom. Once he had stopped crying, the only other thing to upset him was that they had dressed him in little girl's clothes, as they were the only dry ones that would fit him. As you can imagine, Mum became paranoid about water – hence the fences in our garden.

We also knocked down a couple of walls to make a bigger kitchen and dining room. We retiled the kitchen floor as well, but left it a bit too close to Christmas to have the job finished in time, so we had to step gingerly over the planks while the tiles were setting firm. Not the best thing for a wife who was six months' pregnant at the time with our son Marco, but since the kitchen had always been the focal part of Chiara's life, it was worth the hardship.

Dartnell Park became a perfect family home – Chiara and me,

Francesca and Marco, our dogs, friends, family, get-togethers, Christmases, holidays ... and it's our first children's party there of which we have the fondest memories. It was Francesca's fifth birthday, and her newly made chums from Miss Palmer's Nursery School and her neighbourhood friends were all invited. So, of course, was her little brother Marco, now aged three ... much to the delight of Robert, the children's entertainer whom I had booked for the day. While Francesca and her friends sat happily watching Robert go through his routine, Marco was everywhere except where he should have been. He was much too busy bursting the clusters of brightly coloured balloons, pinching little girls in the garden, and generally telling everybody the secrets of the poor conjuror's tricks. He was a bit like George in the famous Joyce Grenfell monologues on nursery schools – 'George ... don't do that.' Or like the brother in Terry Scott's famous hit, 'My Brother', 'pinching little girls up the High Street'! Poor Robert the conjuror couldn't wait to get away by the end, and tore off down the drive with Marco in hot pursuit demanding, 'Can I have another balloon, please?'

A couple of Christmases later, we gave the kids a tortoise each. Since we had two wandering Afghan hounds, we thought tortoises would be the perfect complement ... and a lot easier to look after. They were named Tammy and Tommy, and when we bought them they were still hibernating in their boxes. When spring came, we let them loose in the bottom of the garden, and put a wire fence around to stop them wandering off. Summer came and went, and the tortoises seemed happy in their new surroundings. As autumn approached, we went to find them to put them back in their boxes for winter hibernation. But they weren't in their pen. They must have escaped, but they couldn't have gone far ... they were only tortoises, for goodness sake! But they had gone – living next to a canal meant that there were any number of potential predators – a fox, a stork – whatever had happened, they were gone. The addition of a kitten to the family menagerie did something to assuage the children's sorrow, and an unexpected visit did so as well.

At the time, I had a column with *Woman's Own*, and we were all going to Chessington Zoo to look at the animals and tell the readers what they could expect to see when they visited. We played on the swings, went down the slides, and then made for the children's zoo, where I knew they had lots of tortoises. 'Maybe we'll find Tommy and Tammy there!' I whispered to the kids. I congratulated myself on my parenting skills as we approached the children's enclosure. As I'd anticipated, a thorough examination of every tortoise shell in sight ensued, until there was a cry of joy from Francesca followed by one from Marco. There were two tortoises with almost identical markings on their shells to our lost pets. Not only that, but they were also clearly in the middle of making tortoise babies ... slowly!

'It's Tommy and Tammy!' the children cried, 'But, Daddy, what are they doing?'

'Ah, yes ... they're ... er ...' I blustered, thinking hard, and wondering how to explain the full significance of the act before us to kids so young. 'Tommy is a bit tired ... so Tammy's giving him a lift home.'

'Daddy, can *we* give them a lift home?'

'No, I think it's best we leave them here now, because they've made so many new friends.'

'OK, Daddy ... good idea!'

My kids were so trusting.

Whatever our personal circumstances as a happy family unit, I had now made my decision regarding my career and, from the calm waters of the successful 1970s, I was soon to find myself in the choppier seas of the 1980s. Here's a Top Ten of those records which meant a lot to me while listening to Uncle Mac, and then when I got to play them myself:

1. 'Sparky's Magic Piano', produced by Alan Livingston, with Henry Blair as Sparky
2. 'My Brother' by Terry Scott
3. 'Gone Fishin'' by Bing Crosby and Louis Armstrong
4. 'My Boomerang Won't Come Back!' by Charlie Drake
5. 'Ugly Duckling' by Danny Kaye
6. 'Ernie' by Benny Hill
7. 'Wing Commander Hancock' by Tony Hancock and Kenneth Williams
8. 'I Wanna Be Like You' by Louis Prima from *The Jungle Book*
9. 'Banana Boat Song' by Stan Freberg
10. 'The Laughing Policeman' by Charles Penrose

9

IN THE FIRING LINE

'YOU'VE NO divine right to work for us, you know.'

I could hardly believe my ears. The recently appointed Controller of Radio 2, Bryant Marriott, sat there with his deputy Derek Mills and both were calmly telling me that I had until January 1984, and then my contract would not be renewed. 1984, when Big Brother would terminate my period of employment. I was dismayed, the news coming as a total shock. I had obviously been taking things too much for granted.

'But I've been with the BBC for 17 years and my programmes have been very popular,' I replied.

'Yes, but request programmes are old-fashioned and out of date and we must move on. You've had your day, Ed, and we will not be offering you anything else.'

Twenty years later, what do I find myself doing? Presenting out-of-date request shows!

On the day I was told that my sell-by date was up, I hadn't had any inkling of what was to come. I had just started my second year as Captain of the Variety Club Golfing Society and that day had seen the annual Pro-Invitational Day at the East Berks Club at Hanningfield near Wokingham. I had invited Euan Murray, then an up-and-coming touring pro and now a leading golf commentator, to be my playing partner. And we won! Being Captain, I presented a new golf bag, a dozen golf balls and £200 in the sweep to Euan and myself before driving back to Broadcasting House for a 3.00pm start to my afternoon programme.

I put my foot down, speeding along the A316, when another car passed me going even faster ... and there was a 30mph limit. Suddenly, another car zoomed past us, but this one had its blue light flashing and was making the noise that makes every motorist's heart skip a beat – the dreaded siren. The police car pulled us both over. Cursing my luck, and my lack of concentration, I sat there waiting for the inevitable words of custodial greeting – "Allo, 'allo, 'allo ...'

But it didn't turn out like that at all. Out jumped two likely looking traffic cops, one of whom immediately stuck his head in my window (I had already wound it down!), to see if I had been partaking rather too readily of any lunchtime liquor. I hadn't this time, but I had been on two previous occasions when the drink-drive laws weren't as stringently enforced as they are today. The first time I'd been pulled over after rounding Marble Arch on two wheels in my MGB. The tube of the breathalyser was in my mouth when a call came through for all cars in the area to proceed to Queensway where there had been an explosion.

'It's your lucky night, Mr Blackburn,' yelled the speed cop as he raced away. Not only was it a case of mistaken identity (how could he?) but the 'explosion' turned out to be nothing more than a small firework. But it just showed how sensitive everyone was becoming at that time.

The second occasion was when driving home to my flat in Clapham when the MGB had a puncture. This wasn't the best thing to happen to someone with a couple of vodka and tonics inside them. By the time I had found the jack, turned it round a couple of times and then tried to fit it, a voice broke the stillness of the midnight gloom. 'Having some trouble, sir?' The voice was undoubtedly Northern Irish and the owner undoubtedly a policeman.

'Yes,' I replied, 'I don't seem to be able to jack the fit!'

'Allow me, sir, to jack your fit and then we can wheel the change.'

A copper with a sense of humour, I thought, and promptly keeled over. I lay there for a time and heard him changing the wheel. As I staggered to my feet, he suggested very politely that he drive me home. He parked the car at the side of the road, led me to my front door, turned the key and let me into my own house! As he left, he shook me by the hand and said, 'It's a shame a man can't have a drink when he wants one. But you won't be doing that again when you're driving, will you, sir?'

And I never have. When would I meet another policeman like that again?

Back on the A316, my third encounter with a traffic cop was well under way. 'Do you realise that you were driving at 55mph in a 30mph speed limit?

'Oh, was I, officer?' I decided to go on the charm offensive. 'I'm broadcasting *Family Favourites* to Australia today and I don't want to keep them waiting, do I? It's not going to be a *Crackerjack* day, is it?' I spluttered.

Not a flicker, not a murmur from my Boy in Blue. He checked my licence, took down the particulars and started back towards his car saying, 'Now, follow me. I'll put you on the right road for the BBC.'

I never did hear from the authorities. I reckon that the Laughing Policeman read the paper that evening and felt a little sympathy when he saw the Stop Press: PETE MURRAY AND ED STEWART FIRED BY BBC.

Although there were another three months to go on the contract, working normally was impossible – it was like having the sword of Damocles dangling over you. When it finally dropped, it was to be another seven years before I would return to Auntie.

Working for the BBC has been like a long-lasting love affair, with plenty of highs and lows, tears and laughter. Just when you think it's over, a sudden spark reignites the flame again. It's been a lopsided affair with the pressure on me to keep it going. Perhaps that's been a failing on my own part – an inbred lack of confidence on one side and an ego, amounting to pride, on the other.

The BBC is the greatest broadcasting organisation in the world, and a pinnacle of any broadcaster's ambition. But how many broadcasters who have achieved success really appreciate what the BBC stands for, and what the organisation has done for them?

When you take on the challenge of a freelancer's life, with no job security, no pension and no guarantees, you have to be prepared to live by the rules of that challenge. I've always worked that way living on my own talents and self-belief. When those qualities are frustrated and sometimes ruined by the termination or non-renewal of a contract, those same beliefs are what keep you going until the next time. The other factor which helps, but is often critical, is luck. The luck of being in the right place at the right time. The luck of the face, or the voice that fits. The luck of whoever is in control, both liking and respecting your talents as a broadcaster.

In radio, nobody's indispensable – with the possible exception of Terry Wogan on Radio 2. It'll be interesting to see if Radio 2 maintains its dominance in the national ratings when Terry eventually calls it a day. The breakfast show has always been the most important for any station in the ratings war, and should always have the highest listening figures – even *Junior Choice* was top in its day. Nobody can carry on for ever, though, however much they want to – look at Jimmy Young. Capital Radio must have been desperate to keep Chris Tarrant; when he left in April 2004, the audience for his breakfast show dropped alarmingly. The wily old fox timed his departure to perfection – it was precisely when RAJAR (Radio Joint Audience Research Ltd, who compile the ratings) were measuring their listening figures. Not too many people seem to have missed Chris Evans, but then he doesn't need to work again if he doesn't want to. Mind you, as the old saying goes, money makes money, so I'm sure we haven't heard the last of him. Noel Edmonds invested wisely and took up other business interests as well – he's got to make a comeback soon.

To alter Winston Churchill's words ever so slightly – 'Never in the field of human conflict has so much been owed by so few to so many!' This sentiment could be justifiably applied to the battle for that tiny group of islands so far from our own shores, and yet so inextricably linked to them. The Falklands conflict was probably the greatest single naval and military deployment of the second half of the last century. If it hadn't been for the fortitude and single-mindedness of Margaret Thatcher, the Falklands would now be Las Malvinas, the Islanders' children would be speaking Spanish as well as English, and the Islands themselves would have been swallowed up by the Argentine Republic. I, certainly, would not have had the opportunity to travel further than anywhere I'd ever been, and to experience sights and sounds that can never be repeated.

Always liking a bit of spice in my broadcasting, I suggested to my producer of the time, Stuart Hobday, that we should go to the Falklands for Christmas. The year was 1982 and, if we flew out, we could send a couple of programmes back with requests and records for the servicemen and women and their families, thousands of miles apart. *Family Favourites* was still an integral part of my afternoon programme on Radio 2 and it seemed a natural thing to do. Once we had gained approval from the

Ministry of Defence, essential at the time, we altered our plans slightly to go out at the end of November and record the inserts, then add the records requested and put the whole package together for Christmas and New Year's Day. Most of my colleagues thought it a typically mad idea, but realised its importance. One producer thought I should receive an MBE for going at all!

The trip was exhausting with all the travelling, especially in the Hercules. It was nothing, of course, to what the troops had gone through six months earlier. But the Falklands were British so, in peacetime, we had to do our bit. That's what I thought, anyway, and so did the BBC. The Falkland Islanders were still immensely grateful to Mrs Thatcher's government that their sovereignty had been protected and that British troops had travelled so far on their behalf. The Islanders are hardy people and, even today, there are those who are prepared to sever their ties with a comfortable lifestyle back home to make a new life for themselves in an utterly alien environment thousands of miles away. They are people who relish the isolation and the unpredictable weather, where seeing all four seasons in a day is not uncommon. Where there was only the BBC World Service on the wireless, there is now BBC World and Sky on the television as well. The cruise ships ensure that tourism is a major industry, and the threat of invasion has fast receded. And they were just a whisker away from living under Argentinian rule.

At Dakar Airport, on my way out, after a nine-hour flight on a VC10, we left the plane to stretch our legs. In those days, the seats on RAF planes faced backwards so you wouldn't see the mountain coming towards you. It was hot and humid on the tarmac and, when we boarded again, the engine's self-starter would not work. They brought a ground starter ... that failed as well. After the aircrew had had no success, the Senegalese brought one that did work, from a dilapidated hangar on the edge of the airfield. I noticed a distinct blush on several RAF faces.

We landed on Ascension Island four hours later and, as all RAF planes were 'dry', I opened one of my bottles of Cabernet I had bought for this very moment back at Brize Norton. Ascension Island is about 1,500 miles from the nearest point on the West Africa coast. It is half volcanic and half tropical and, prior to the Falklands crisis, was home to some radar positions, a BBC relay station ... and a golf course!

When we arrived there, the island was swarming with troops and flotillas of ships surrounding the beaches and harbours. The island itself in daylight is a beautiful sight, with its white sandy beaches, azure sea and huge extinct volcano. It is owned by Britain but run by America. Its main importance at the time was as a satellite tracking station and refuelling stop. Ascension was halfway between the UK and the Falklands and most of the working population came from St Helena, 1,000 miles away to the south. The island also possessed a couple of drinking clubs, and it was into one of these, the Union Jack, that I was dragged screaming, later that evening. To say that I fell among thieves would be doing Ali Baba a disservice. It was when I started to sing 'Wide-Eyed and Legless' to a row of empty glasses that my producer, Stuart, dragged me off to my bunk in a Portakabin. I was in the land of Nod before my head touched the pillow.

Having been shaken awake at 4.00am for a 5.00am flight on a Hercules, I staggered into the breakfast tent and was greeted by a ribald shout of 'CRACK-ER-JAAACK!' My reply was a single word, referring to objects that are round and bouncy. I forced down fried eggs, bacon and fried bread, asked for the latrines and promptly brought it all up again. On boarding, the load master – the term used by the RAF to describe their Chief Steward and Administrator – took one look at me and suggested that I came up to the flight deck and crash out on one of the bunks.

The plane itself was slow and noisy and took 13½ hours to fly to the Falklands. If the 'loadie' hadn't been so kind, I would have spent those hours stretched out on the load ramp in the belly of the plane, or perched on the top of the luggage, which was covered by a large net. When I eventually woke up, my nostrils were tantalised by the smell of steak and onions being cooked by the 'loadie' himself. I insisted on opening the remaining bottle of Cabernet, being the hair of the dog that had bit me the night before. Now that's what I call living the high life.

As I gulped down the last mouthful, the captain handed me a pair of headphones as a large refuelling tanker flew into view. This was to be the nearest I've ever come to a mid-air collision. At 30,000ft, the two planes manoeuvred themselves into a position where the hose from the tanker could fit around the nozzle of the Hercules – 'Up a bit … down a bit … one degree left …' Down below, the Atlantic Ocean waited to welcome us if it all went pear-shaped. Scary isn't the word! Then, as we made radio contact with Falklands Control, the captain of the Hercules noticed there was an oil leak in Number Three engine, and closed it down. We landed nearly an hour behind schedule, on three engines. The captain said, 'It was a piece of piss!' I suppose that was vaguely reassuring.

It was sunny and warmer than we expected – in the 40s Fahrenheit. We were met by Peter Howard of the MOD who told us we had 'digs' at Sparrowhawk House, owned by John Smith, local historian and future curator of the Falklands Museum. But before that, he said, we had to go to the CSE (Combined Services Entertainment) Show at the Port Stanley Hall. Comedian Johnny Hackett, with whom I'd spent a hilarious six weeks in summer season at Great Yarmouth in 1968, was compèring the show. And true to fashion, Johnny came up with a line I've never forgotten: 'It's great to be in the Falklands – the Islands where the men are *men* – and the sheep are nervous!'

While I was in the Falklands, I decided to keep a diary to record the unique experiences I'd encounter during my time there. Unread and undiscovered, it lay for 20 years in the battery compartment of an old tape recorder. This was only rediscovered when my son Marco was going to flog it at a car-boot sale. I've now got a pretty accurate guide of what we got up to out there, and can remember quite clearly some of the amazing characters we met.

Since leaving Brize Norton, we'd had very little sleep – what a surprise. At Sparrowhawk a supper of Falklands prawn curry and blackcurrant trifle, eight hours' sleep and then eggs and a local Spam for breakfast prepared us for the rigours of the day ahead.

There wasn't a road that wasn't broken or potholed and we got around in either captured Argentine Mercedes Jeeps or British Army Leyland lorries. One of the stops we made was at a REME workshop where, as we were about to start recording, they presented me with an Everton mug which had come ashore with the first landings – it was still in one piece which was more than could be said about the Everton team at that time!

Then, after meeting the reinstalled Governor, Sir Rex Hunt, and hearing how the Argies had made a mess of his beautiful Government House, we went along to a real blow-up. No, not an army field rations lunch, but a couple of hours with army munitions expert John Quinn, whose nickname 'Mighty' had everything to do with Manfred Mann's Number One hit in 1968! His was a fascinating talk about the formation and strategy of the Argentinian minefields. There were still booby traps and unexploded shells around. The Argentinians had, in their retreat, mined their own minefields and, contrary to the regulations set down by the Geneva Convention, had not left any plans or positions. Ironically, if they had won the war, they would have blown their people to bits anyway. So it was the job of the Mighty Quinn and his men to locate the unexploded mines and shells and destroy them.

After the interviews, and a watery toast to Christmas and 1983, the Mighty Q invited me to press the plunger and set off the recently discovered Argy ammunition, piled high on a distant grassy hillock. I did, with great satisfaction, knowing that that was the nearest I would ever be to becoming a fighting soldier.

We gathered some more recordings that night on the accommodation ship, the *Norland*. Before leaving, though, I wanted to record the brilliant sunset that evening on my newfangled video camcorder. Huge, great things they were in those days. Inadvertently, I recorded over the mid-air refuelling sequence while coming out on the Hercules. I was so upset with my own stupidity, I hardly slept a wink that night. Later, I found another enthusiast's sequence to edit into my own little film, but it's not the same as having done it yourself. Don't give up the day job, Ed!

Our fifth day in the Islands saw another fine, cool day dawn – when were we going to get some of the famous Falklands weather, all four seasons in a day? We went to Stanley Hospital to record some civilian interviews. One of the local nurses asked me dryly why it had taken a war to get us there. I suppose she had a point; sadly, in those days before the invasion, nobody had given the place a second thought. But happily, today, more than 20 years later, the economy of the Islands is booming, and one of the reasons for this is tourism.

That Sunday in late November, over supper at our 'digs' in the Smith's family home, John and his daughter Anya talked about the Argentinian occupation. The family had built a bunker under the front porch. Besides keeping his family safe, John was able to record the sounds of the bombardments and the cries of the young conscripts for their mothers. Some of those Argentinian conscripts were as young as 14 and they were cold, miserable and always hungry. The officers looked smart and well fed, and received a miniature bottle of Black Label Johnnie Walker whisky with their more-than-sufficient rations. The regulars had good rations too, but, unlike the officers, no extras. The poor young conscripts, though, had tins of bully beef and biscuits. A good Army marches on its stomach, they say, so how could a civilised country fight a war with an Army largely made up of young, unwilling soldiers who were always hungry.

The next day, we were strapped into a Chinook helicopter to visit two of the most emotive places on the Islands – San Carlos and Goose Green. At San Carlos, we visited the Remembrance Cemetery where Colonel H Jones and his comrades lay buried. Bleak and windy, it was a hallowed place – and you could sense it. Later, we went to the actual battleground at Goose Green, where, in truth, the Argentinians should never have been beaten. They were superior in number, but their morale was low, their 'bottle' gone. And they had heard blood-curdling stories of fighting devils from the Far East called Gurkhas. British propaganda had done its work, so the victory was made possible.

Although the Argentinians had surrendered five months earlier in June 1982, the Islands were still on permanent alert, or a war footing. Everywhere you looked, you were reminded that a recent battle had been waged there, and that there was still reason to be cautious. From watching the nuclear submarine *Courageous* surfacing off San Carlos that morning to visiting a remote Rapier site for lunch, you were never away from those reminders for long.

Sheep shearing was in full swing and, as we walked from the Chinook to where the shearing was taking place, there was suddenly a huge bellow from the RSM ahead of us – 'Sir, attention, sir! You are walking towards uncharted territory. Could be a minefield, sir!' I remembered Mighty Quinn's earlier warnings and froze. We had to 'about turn', retrace our steps, and approach the sheep shearing via a safer route. I'm sorry, but I have to say it – our officer in charge did look rather sheepish.

We were then treated to a musical experience that I'll never forget. This was the day that the Queen's Own Scottish Highlanders were to be replaced by the Royal Hants Regiment. The pipes and drums of that Highland regiment put on a display that brought a lump to your throat. When they ended with the strains of 'Amazing Grace' spilling out over San Carlos Sound, there wasn't a dry eye in the house.

The next day, we were taken out on a former Argentinian patrol boat – now called the *Tiger Bay* – to visit a large repair ship, which I couldn't help referring to as the *Stenna Pod* – it was actually the *Stenna Inspector* and was one of the many back-up vessels and troop carriers which had been brought into action during the conflict and were still here five months later.

I was not going to hang around as long. We were due to take off the following day for Ascension and eventually home. I booked a telephone call to tell the family the itninerary, but when I got to the exchange at the appointed time, I found a long queue waiting to do exactly the same thing. Apparently, one of the operators was on her lunch break and the other girl could only connect one call at a time – I kid you not! Since I only had an hour before my next appointment with an old schoolfriend called John Mizen, who was now a Colonel with the Royal Engineers, I sat patiently awaiting my turn. Eventually, the operator called out, 'Mr Stewart, please.' I stood up, making my way towards the phone booth, when my path was suddenly blocked by another Mr Stewart. He was a Danish bacon salesman named Steeuart, spelt differently but pronounced the same – and he had booked his time half-an-hour before mine.

'After you, Great Dane,' I said, and he looked at me as if I was mad. They don't have dogs called that in Denmark! I never did make that call home – I was off to Colonel Mizen at the Mess, and you didn't tend to leave those places early, or in one piece.

I left as I had arrived – hungover. First, I had to settle the bill, producer Stuart having left his cheque book at home. There's crafty! Our digs at the Smith residence had cost us £18 a day each, but as I wrote the cheque for £180, John said he'd frame it and never cash it. My reputation had preceded me. Mrs Smith, though, clearly thought otherwise and my account had been debited before I arrived home. I also bought a couple of John Smith's excellent hand-drawn maps of wrecks around the Falklands to give away as Christmas presents.

I was feeling even more of a wreck as our Jeep traversed the potholes of Stanley, but felt decidedly better when watching a group of passengers climbing down from the recently arrived Hercules. Among them, I spied Alan 'Fluff' Freeman; he had also come out to record some programmes for BFBS.

'Fluff!' I cried and a couple of macho redcaps glared my way. 'Not you, lads,' I said, 'it's Alan Freeman!' Within seconds, the two macho MPs were asking for his autograph and Fluff was a happy man!

On our journey back to Ascension Island, my luck was in. I was invited on to the flight deck again for the 13-hour flight back. On arrival at Concertina City, as that huddle of Portakabins was called, I found myself not only in the same hut as a week earlier, but in the same bunk as well. Same sheets? What sheets? We thumbed a lift into the capital, Georgetown, and this time I was able to phone home via Cable and Wireless. How wonderful it was to hear Chiara's voice again and, although she couldn't say much for crying, I said I would call back in a couple of hours – it was a cheaper rate then! Some hope.

Thumbing another lift back to Concertina City, we were picked up by the headmaster of Ascension Island School, by the name of Alan Thomas – another lucky break! He offered his services as tour guide and we arranged to meet him at the now notorious Exiles Bar where I had partaken liberally the week before. This time something more important than pouring the amber nectar down the gullet appeared – the offer of a game of golf.

Ascension Island Golf Course appeared at the time in the *Guinness Book of Records* as the worst golf course in the world! It was like playing on the moon. The fairways and the rough were no different – it was a true lunar landscape, and the balls invariably bounced off the volcanic rocks at every conceivable angle. The greens (more like browns!) were formed of flattened sand. I now had an excuse for my increasingly erratic game. It was not one to add to the list of European Tour courses, but it's the nearest we'll ever get to playing on the moon.

The journey home was in the back of a Hercules, on top of the luggage. What a wreck I looked when we eventually touched down at Brize Norton – unshaven and baggy eyed. 'Welcome home, welcome ... step inside, and close the door ...' before the neighbours see you!

10

MERCURY RISING ...
AND BACK TO 2

RADIO MERCURY had approached me in 1984 and, with no prospect of any work from the BBC, it seemed a good opportunity to work in commercial radio again. They offered me a package, which, although not as much as I had been on at the Beeb, still included paid holidays and a car, into which I had to put the 40p-a-litre petrol.

Opening day of the station was Saturday, 24 October 1984. Unfortunately, I had already planned for my second Ed Stewart Golf Classic at La Manga, commencing the very day that Radio Mercury went on air, so I recorded a half-hour slot the week before I went away. My regular slot was to be 10.00am–1.00pm on weekdays.

On my return from Spain, I went into the studio for my first live programme. As the moment approached, I was all ready with the station jingle and the first record to play ... although nobody had told me about the 'Transmission On' button at the side of the console. For 20 seconds, there was no much-heralded Ed Stewart – just dead air, or silence. It could have been better named 'Dead

Stewart'. A young newsreader came in and pressed the 'Transmission On' button! How embarrassed was I? If there had been a camera there, I could have played the Buggles' 'Video Killed the Radio Star'! But from that moment on, life was good at Radio Mercury.

Pat Sharp, Peter Young and Tony Myatt were other familiar names who enjoyed life at the station. It was housed in a wonderful old Victorian mansion called Broadfield House, originally owned and built by a sea captain from his spoils of war. It was now owned by Crawley Council, with whom Radio Mercury had negotiated a peppercorn rent, as long as the building was renovated to its original state. Most of the visitors who came to be interviewed could hardly believe it was the home of a local radio station. But then, when you looked at the lake, the lawns, the oak trees, the beeches and the Douglas firs, you understood why everybody loved to work there. Nowadays, Radio Mercury transmits from an industrial estate in Crawley. I definitely saw its best days.

One lunchtime, it was around October 1985, we had just finished a wonderful meal when the doorbell rang. Our neighbours from across the road, Jan and Chris, had helped us demolish the roast lamb and mint sauce, washed down with a couple of bottles of Beaujolais for good measure. Chiara was drinking in those days, and this was her favourite red wine, especially good with the lamb. The doorbell rang again. It must be the children, I thought, coming back from walking the dogs down the Wey Navigation Canal at the bottom of the garden. But it wasn't them. Instead, there was a large, friendly man with an outstretched hand, whose first question was, 'Would you like to sell your house?'

My first reaction was to say no, and ask him politely to call again another day, and preferably not on a Sunday. 'Mr Stewart, I know that you're working for Radio Mercury these days ... I often listen myself. Then I thought you'd probably be off watching football on a Saturday, so Sunday would be the best time to find

215

you at home!' He'd certainly been doing his homework, so I gave him another chance, and calmly asked him how much he was offering. He told me.

'HOW MUCH?' I spluttered, which must have been heard the other side of West Byfleet. It brought my wife running to the door.

'What's happening?' she asked.

I told her that the gentleman standing in front of us had just offered £600,000 for the house, and were we interested?

'Tell us more,' said Mrs Stewart, as wary as ever. She was always 'Mrs Stewart' when she was in business mode; at all other times, it was 'Madam'.

'Your house is one of five my client is wanting to develop, and he has now tied up planning permission for three of them. When we have planning permission for yours, we will be in a position to go ahead.'

We went back inside the house. I made for the kitchen, while Chiara returned to our friends to tell them the news. 'Let's drink to it!' the potential buyer cried, as I popped the cork on the bottle of champagne I had just rescued from the fridge. We toasted what we expected to be our good fortune, and my mind went back to the first moment I had seen that 'For Sale' sign all those years before. It was time for a change in more ways than one.

By 1990 Radio Mercury, whom I served faithfully for six years, eventually decided it was time for me to go. They were extending each presenter's programme by one hour, without being able to offer any increase in fees. Presumably, I would not want to stay. It would have been nice to have been asked. Instead, they told me not to come back from my holiday. There was three months' severance pay, as per the contract ... and thank you very much.

As soon as I parted company with Radio Mercury, I decided there and then that there would be no more sideways moves to a local station. Whatever it took, I would try and get back on national radio. My ego demanded it! I was determined not to go through another FA Cup Final humiliation all over again. And I'm not talking about my beloved team losing – at the 1989 FA Cup Final at Wembley, the Everton fans had chanted, 'Good to see you, Ed ... we thought you were dead!'

Back at the BBC, my former producer friends had now climbed the ladder, and were in a position to offer me work again. Frances Line had become Controller of Radio 2, and Brian Stephens, Paul Walters and David Vercoe greeted me with, 'Welcome back – was it something we said?' And as well as a turning point in my career, I reached a personal milestone in 1991 – my 50th birthday! I'd also been invited to play in a tennis tournament in which Cliff Richard was playing. He had turned 50 six months before, so when I lobbed him at the net, I felt quite within my rights to call out, 'Run for it, old man!' He fell over trying to make the return, and the crowd loved it!

I had to wait until Easter 1991, when Paul Walters produced a couple of specials for me, and then a regular Saturday afternoon slot through the summer. Then there was a week of a programme they called *Star Hour*, with presenters as varied as Jimmy Tarbuck and Daniel O'Donnell. Thankfully, I'd kept my nose clean and had never knocked the BBC, so was being welcomed back. It could have been different if I had accepted an offer from the *News of the World* in 1984 to 'tell all' – but I hadn't been interested, and that had been proved to be the right decision!

The work was gradually increasing, but it wasn't paying all the bills, so whatever was offered to me, I was taking. One opportunity to earn some money suited me down to the ground – karaoke. It was a form of entertainment which had started in the restaurants and clubs in Japan, where the word literally means 'empty orchestra'. Perfectly ordinary people would stand up and sing a song in front of their friends and other customers. The idea took hold and, as it became more Westernised, changed in style and content so that people could sing almost any song they liked with the words in front of them on a screen. The backing track was copied with the arrangement almost note for note to mimic the original. So it was that Rocky's opened in Cobham in Surrey, with Ed Stewart as compère twice a week, and it was to become the most popular karaoke club in the area.

Rocky Taylor was a highly successful stuntman, who had nearly lost his life in a horrific accident in 1985. It had taken him six years to receive any compensation for the injuries he received. His career had begun much earlier, when as a black belt in judo, he had been asked to teach Cliff Richard some moves on the set of *The Young Ones*. Following his success on that film, Rocky had decided to become a stuntman.

It was on one of Michael Winner's films, *Death Wish III*, that Rocky almost lost his life. His stunt had been to jump from a burning building on to a pile of cardboard boxes 40ft below. As he was pacing out his moves on the top of the building, a kerosene drum exploded prematurely, throwing flames and black smoke high into the air. Rocky now found himself unable to see the boxes below, so ran to the back of the building to see if there was an escape route there. There was a metal stairway but the thick smoke hid it from view. By this time, the entire building was ablaze and Rocky knew he had to jump to where he thought the boxes would break his fall. He missed by a foot, and landed on concrete, breaking his back and his pelvis, and severely damaging his internal organs. He thought he was going to die.

He was transferred to St Thomas's Hospital, and lay there for weeks, barely able to move. The whole episode was caught on video, and shown on the news – millions watched it in horror.

Rocky did sue, but it took a long time for him to receive any compensation – five years to be exact. Mr Winner had disclaimed any responsibility but eventually settled out of court for £250,000. As you can imagine, Winner is not one of his favourite people.

But with his compensation, Rocky turned the Old Turk's Head pub into Rocky's Karaoke Bar, and Ed Stewart fulfilled another ambition, singing Sinatra songs with Nelson Riddle arrangements, just for fun – along with the many thousands of others who used to like the sound of their own voices, until they stood on the stage and put their money where their mouths were! Karaoke is often derided, but usually by the people who've never got up there in the first place.

In October 1991, I received the news I'd been hoping for, and was offered the Radio 2 afternoon slot in 1992 between 3.30pm and 5.00pm. The line-up then looked like this: Sarah Kennedy had her Dawn Patrol, which she still has today; Brian Hayes was in the breakfast slot (Terry Wogan wasn't to reappear until the following year); and Ken Bruce occupied the mid-morning slot, which he still does today. Then there were two and a half hours of Jimmy Young, until Gloria Hunniford at 2.00pm, I took over at 3.30pm, followed by John Dunn at 5.00pm.

Apart from Ken, Sarah and myself on Sundays, the presenters have totally changed since then. Brian Hayes is still on air, practically everywhere! He is one of the unsung greats to my mind. Jimmy Young has retired, screaming and kicking all the way to the bank. Gloria Hunniford seems to have semi-retired to advertising orthopaedic beds – obviously the next step will be chairlifts! John Dunn, after fighting the spread of cancer for many years, sadly died in 2004. What a loss his voice is to radio. His dry sense of humour gave us so many wonderful moments. It was he that announced after Rosko's first programme for Radio 1 in 1967, 'And now here is the news – in English!' He never sought the limelight and succeeded in retaining his privacy. He possessed one of the most distinctive voices of his generation, with his command of the language delivered in a tone that was essentially the 'Queen's English'. There are but a few left on radio today. John was one of only two presenters on Radio 2 (guess the other one. Answers on a postcard, please!) who could be guaranteed to be sent anywhere Club Class. The reason being that at 6ft 6in he couldn't fit into Economy!

But back in 1992, there was an immediate problem, which, thank goodness, was not seen as a great one. I had already signed to perform in pantomime at Croydon with Windsor Davies, June Brown (Dot in *EastEnders*) and Andrew O'Connor, for which there were to be matinées on Wednesday and Friday for two weeks in January, just as I was starting my new *Ed Stewart Show*.

Luckily, common sense and a bit of understanding took over – and thanks are due to the then Controller of Radio 2, Frances Line – and for those two weeks of matinées, Radio 2 let me record my hour and a half in the morning. Traffic updates were not a feature on Radio 2 at that time, or I wouldn't have been there for them!

It was on my new show that I started my Accumulator Quiz, which was to become so popular. Forty seconds of quick-fire questions made for very exciting listening, and soon caught on. That year also saw the introduction of Chay Blyth's Round the World Yacht Race. We wanted to cover it by taking satellite phone calls from the boats, wherever they were around the world. This involved a lot of technology but, again, made an exciting listen. My producer at the time, Alan Roberts, and I even spent a weekend in very cramped conditions aboard one of the yachts off the Isle of Wight, just to get a feeling of how life would be for the sailors. I was relieved to get out of my bunk in the morning – it was like being in a torpedo tube. The only way out was head first. One night was enough for me, but they were going to have months of it, and were either mad or brave – or both!

Soon 1992 became 1993, with a change of producer. Phil Hughes took over and this was the start of a working relationship that, for me anyway, was never bettered. Behind every successful producer was an equally good, sometimes even better, broadcast assistant. (They weren't called 'secretaries' any more.) Sara was no

220

exception. All three of us shared the same sense of humour – Phil was 'the Prod', Sara 'the Bakewell', and I was 'the Turn'. When we went to Roros in Norway in the winter of 1998, I became the Arctic Turn. See what I mean about the humour?

When we started together, we were working from Studio SB3; the new continuity studios had not yet been completed. SB3 was directly over the Bakerloo Line and, sometimes, the vibrations from two trains passing each other could set off some gremlin somewhere and the studio would just break down.

And it wasn't only the Underground system that had caused the architects of Broadcasting House so many headaches when building work began in 1928. In the early 1800s, a deep sewer had been built diagonally across the site to drain surface water away from the hills of north London, such as Parliament Hill and Highgate. In Colin Reid's excellent history of the BBC called *Action Stations*, he points out that the original civil engineer, Marmaduke Tudsbery, had had to sink an artesian well more than 600ft below the foundations, avoiding both the Bakerloo Line and the sewer, to provide fresh water to the new building, which was eventually finished in 1931. The freehold was transferred to the BBC in 1936 for £650,000, with certain provisos which make fascinating reading today:

There shall not be used, exercised or carried on in or upon any part of the premises hereby transferred, the trade, business or calling of a Butcher Purveyor, Meat Slaughterman or Fishmonger ... Farrier, Blacksmith or Common Brewer ... Tripe Seller, Fried Fish Shop, Vintner or Tavern Keeper ... Coal Shed Keeper, Railway Parcel Booking Office or Brothel Keeper ...

There wasn't much else that anyone could have been permitted to do in Broadcasting House, other than broadcast!

And from one grand old building to another. How bitter-sweet the 90s were! I was working regularly and my personal flag was being hoisted ever higher – a five-day-a-week programme, growing popularity and a great feeling of belonging to what was becoming the nation's most popular radio station. 'Pride comes before a fall' goes the saying, and maybe that deadly sin had been to blame in some way. When, to the outside world, you seem to have it all, it's very difficult to admit that you're actually losing it. The bitter part of the early 90s was about to happen and, even now, I have a lump in my throat when I think of it; it made me shudder as I began to commit to paper the events of the day we moved house. Anybody who has gone through the same situation will appreciate my feelings.

To the outside world, we were living in a large house with a swimming pool and a large car, with two lovely children and a couple of dogs. Our property was one of several earmarked by developers, and six-figure sums were being talked about, which inevitably made you think of early retirement. Then the developers went bankrupt, just as our house was the next in line. I had remortgaged when Radio Mercury had let me go, and my subsequent unemployment left it very difficult to meet the repayments. Selling the house to the developers would have solved those problems. Now they were gone, and we had to wait until the next ones appeared on the horizon.

Money was extremely tight for us at this point, and it reminded me of some of the sacrifices my parents had made on our behalf, and the sense of responsibility regarding money that had been instilled in me from an early age. Growing up, we were never well off, but our parents scrimped and saved to be able to send us to boarding school, and it was, ironically, some misfortune that turned things our way.

Having qualified as a solicitor, Dad decided that, rather than go into a partnership and private practice, he would join the Civil Service, attracted by the pension he would have on retirement.

Then, when the Second World War broke out, he was very patriotic, and invested the money left to him by his late father in War Loan Bonds. By the end of the war, they had lost a lot in value, and the bank manager, feeling rather guilty about having given him such poor advice, offered Dad an overdraft facility to see us through our years of education. Lloyds had a heart – I only wish the Nat West had felt the same 50 years later.

So making money has never been one of my strengths – losing it has come a lot more naturally.

By the mid-70s, I was well into my BBC career and doing my best to educate the children at the best schools. By this time, there was another worry. The M25 was being built 200 yards away from the bottom of the garden, and it looked as if the value of our house in Dartnell Park, West Byfleet, along with all our neighbours', was going to plummet. Solicitors were offering to fight for compensation on our behalf. We took one firm on, and they came up trumps. I was offered £28,000 by one of the government ministries and, lo and behold, the cheque duly arrived. Just as I was about to bank it, the demand notice from the taxman flopped through our letterbox – the fates had conspired on my behalf, and I found myself in yet another financial disappointment. But as I was consoling Chiara on the one hand, I was also saying on the other, 'Thank goodness for the compensation cheque ... what would we have done without that?'

There was no compensation cheque to save us now, though, as we faced losing Dartnell Park for good. The mortgage company and the bank were getting fidgety. How long could this continue? I had no agent at the time – the 15 per cent they would take would have eaten into my income even further. The fee from the Beeb was low compared to what the other established presenters were receiving, but I was so relieved to be working again that I hadn't driven any sort of hard bargain. In retrospect, it was crazy not to have had an agent – but you can solve all your problems in retrospect, can't you?

Finally, in 1993, the 'We cannot afford this situation to continue ...' letters arrived from the bank and the mortgage company, demanding that I sell the house. There was to be no more borrowing. Despite my optimistic assurances that another developer was around the corner (one did appear about 18 months later, building over a dozen country houses across Dartnell Park), the financial institutions weren't prepared to take the risk and wait – so our house had to go. It was either that, or bankruptcy. Neither of our families were in a position to help and, anyway, I didn't want the stigma of that word 'bankruptcy' attaching itself to me or anyone else.

At this point, somebody running the shopping channel, QVC, entered my life. His name was Peter Ridsdale, the very man who later became the free-spending Chairman of Leeds United FC, with the well-documented results of overspending and the subsequent near catastrophic repercussions for the club. He paid me a five-figure sum that would possibly have spared me from having to sell the house. Ironically, that offer wasn't made until a month later – just too late to save me.

Sixteen years in one house will naturally create a wealth of memories, but the abiding one was always of a full and happy home. Chiara's parents, Jimmy and Ginetta, were there most weekends and, if any of her family came to visit from Italy, they would always come to stay with us. Birthday parties abounded, and we even had a 21st reunion, in 1988, of the closing down of Radio London. Keith Skues, Tony Brandon and Duncan Johnson were there, with Mike Lennox and Willy Walker arriving unexpectedly from Canada and Bermuda – that was the real reason we had the party!

In the run-up to our departure from the house, Chiara was still recovering from the effects of her third back operation, so all the arrangements, which she would usually have organised in her own efficient way, had now been taken over by me with all my usual inefficiency. And this extended to not getting large enough removal lorries for all our possessions.

On the day of our departure from the house, we'd managed to shift quite a bit of stuff, but I had returned to the house to apologise that the removal men had not been able to fit all the furniture and other bits and pieces on the lorry. Thinking that there would not be a problem, I walked into the drive and saw to my horror that all the remaining items of furniture had been dumped unceremoniously outside. I then saw a group of very unhappy looking people including the owner and his wife coming towards me. We had an angry exchange of words and I wondered whether the noise and commotion would raise any concern among our neighbours, but no one came to see what the cause of all the noise was.

Eventually, I carried the sofa and a couple of leather chairs out of my old house and into my neighbours' Chris and Jan's back garden without anyone lifting a finger to help me. I was totally exhausted and had to leave a couple of things in the house. Our rowing boat and outboard were still berthed at the bottom of the garden, on the canal. The new people didn't want them, and claimed I was abandoning them. Then I staggered towards the station to catch the train to Waterloo, and thence to the BBC, with the sound of the new owners disgruntlement still ringing in my ears.

I reflected on my position, and decided to stop off at the estate agent's and call my solicitor. When I arrived there, the events of the previous half-hour suddenly overwhelmed me, and I burst into tears. I had never done that before, and the poor estate agent was as shocked as I was. Years of never showing my emotions had suddenly caught up with me.

After a strong cup of tea which the bewildered young man had made for me – there was no one else in the office – I made my way to the station and caught the train. I still had a programme to do, after all. I got to the Beeb and worked away as if nothing had happened.

When in doubt, call in a solicitor. You never meet a poor one but, in this case, they were worth every penny. 'You suggested that our clients had in some way abandoned their possessions even though Mr Mainwaring [I still use my real surname on official business] arrived at the property before 1.00pm to collect them,' the letter from my solicitor stated. 'Clearly, there was never any intention by our clients to abandon their property. So far as we are aware, there is no rule in law which permits your clients to retain our clients' possessions in that way. In the circumstances, we take the view that your clients are wrongfully retaining these goods. Thus, unless within 24 hours we have agreement from your clients that the possessions will be released to our clients or their agents, then the matter will be reported to local police forthwith. Our clients will also be reporting your clients' threatening behaviour throughout the incident.'

The letter did the trick, and all was resolved. Our *'paradiso'* slowly faded in the memory ... until I decided, ten years later, to return and see what had happened to the place.

They say you should never go back. Well, I thought, what harm could it possibly do?

Down I went along the towpath to where the old house still stood. Our house and land where we had lived for so long had sold for nearly half a million pounds, we had heard. The garden was a posh estate now with houses built and sound proofed against the ravages of the M25. They had filled up the swimming pool and built a road over it. I could still hear the shouts and cries of the children, their cousins and friends, as they swam and played in the clear-blue water. Now all I could hear was the continuous rumble of the most crowded motorway in Europe. The greenhouse and the sunken pond, which we had cleared and made into a barbecue and outdoor eating place, had gone too. But the giant willow was still there, weeping. And so was I.

But the work was relentless, and thoroughly enjoyable, which meant that my tears were not allowed to flow for very long. In 1993, while our home was being wrenched from our grasp, Radio 2 was helping to celebrate the RAF's 75th anniversary by sending some of their presenters to bases around the UK and even further afield. John Dunn's early-evening programme came from RAF Cranwell, home of the famous college; Ken Bruce was sent to Cyprus; Jimmy Young to Germany; Gloria Hunniford was winched aboard a helicopter from the sea by a crew from RAF Lossiemouth; and I was sent back to the Falklands for the second time – 11 years after my first visit.

I could see the whites of the Harrier pilot's eyes. Our RAF Tri-Star jet was barely 30ft away as the Harrier escorted us into British airspace as we prepared to land at Port Stanley Airport. Eleven years after the conflict, British troops were on a permanent war footing; the Argentinians have never given up their claim on the islands. As we taxied to a halt, the ever-ready fire crews held up their voting cards as if we had been taking part in an Olympic plane-landing competition – 5.9 … 5.9 … 5.9 … 6.0 – a near-perfect landing, good enough for a gold medal!

On arrival at Port Stanley, we were driven to the new complex that housed most of the 2,000 troops, the inappropriately named Mount Pleasant. This was to be our home for the next week and we were made more than welcome. The sole purpose of the trip was to record a special programme for RAF Day, 7 April 1993. Broadcasting 'live', though, would prove to be an impossibility. ISDN circuits were not yet in operation and BFBS could not provide us with a satellite link. There was one from London to Stanley, but not the other way round. So the production team sent to record this epic *Ed Stewart Show* consisted solely of my producer Phil Hughes and me.

In 1993, the civilian population of the Falklands was about 2,000 people – it's about the same today. But that was paltry compared to the number of sheep – there were around three quarters of a million of them! The islanders were well protected; with 2,000 military personnel, they enjoyed a one-to-one ratio. The cost to the British government – and, naturally, the taxpayer – was £60 million a year then, probably more today. Let's hope that the current and future governments continue to protect the independence and way of life of these and other British islands around the world.

Minefields and no-go areas were still plentiful on the Islands that year and, as ever, there were 'Stills'. And they weren't the ones with which you make illegal hooch.

During the conflict, many of the troops noticed that the locals were wearing woollen hats as protection against the inclement weather. The hats were rather like the ones worn by Benny from the soap *Crossroads*. So the Islanders became Bennies, which, naturally, they didn't like very much. So, after a complaint was made to the commander of the armed forces that this was something of an insult, an edict went out to all ranks that islanders were no longer to be referred to as 'Bennies'. With typical service humour, an alternative name was coined – 'Stills', short for 'still Bennies'!

Even if we weren't going to be going live on the day, we had to record the programmes as if we were doing a live broadcast for real, and at the same time that the actual programme would eventually be transmitted. It meant leaving spaces for where the news, weather and traffic updates would be inserted. Because of this, the timing of my chat and the records I played had to be precise.

We started at the same time that the programme would be transmitted, two minutes past four; if I inadvertently gave a time check, at least it would be the correct one! Although I would have preferred the excitement of broadcasting live from 8,000 miles away, at least I'd be able to hear the finished product.

It had been very different in years gone by. During the period of the conflict and for months afterwards, we would be in the studio in Broadcasting House in London, with special twice-weekly editions of *Family Favourites* to the Falklands. The mailbag was huge and some records became especially popular, because 'the message was in the words'. Two unknowns became hits – 'Seven Tears' by the Goombay Dance Band and 'Hurry Home' by Wavelength. The shows were then boxed up and sent out to Port Stanley, to be played locally on British Forces Radio or FIBS – Falkland Islands Broadcasting Services.

One of the first things I had done on landing in the Islands again was to visit the FIBS studios and meet the Controller who was then, and still is, Patrick Watts. 'Welcome, Ed,' he said, 'I expect you've come to find out how your programmes have been received,' and before I could get a word in, he added, 'BFBS wouldn't let us transmit anything that had not originated from them, so you're literally on the shelf!' I looked up and there, indeed, were two piles of neatly stacked and unopened programme boxes. I thought of all those families and friends who had carefully written their messages and chosen their records not knowing that all their efforts were sitting on a shelf in the South Atlantic. All because of red tape and petty jealousy. Sorry, folks … we tried our best.

Now, in 1993, the RAF in the Falklands were celebrating their anniversary in as spirited a way as any proud organisation around the world – and we were part of that. We could look forward to dinner with wine in full Mess dress with the officers, a night of unparalleled drinking and snooker in the Sergeants' Mess and a right old piss-up and disco in a huge hangar with all personnel, which would bring our visit to a close.

The evening in the Officers' Mess had started quite normally with everybody standing around sipping their pre-dinner drinks; there were three or four female officers as well, which brought a welcome tastiness to the evening. Phil and I had packed our jackets and ties to wear at such an occasion, but we did look a bit ordinary compared to the superbly cut suits of the officers. Then, into dinner. But as much as we wanted to talk to them about life in the RAF and out there in the Falklands, they wanted to hear about Radio 2, *Top of the Pops* and *Crackerjack*. After a meal of fish soup, Roast 365 (a local term for lamb or mutton, which you ate 365 times a year!) and a sherry trifle, the CO rose to say there would be no speeches tonight but those of us who felt like it could tell a joke. He added that when he felt he had heard one so awful that it might offend the ears of the ladies present, that person would pay for the first round of drinks at the bar!

The third bottle of Fonseca Special Vintage Port was the one that did the damage. It made me brave. 'Mr Stewart,' beamed the CO, 'perhaps you would like to start the proceedings?'

I turned to Phil. 'What are our expenses like?'

'Spent!' he lied.

Oh, well, I thought, in for a penny in for a pound. I told the one about two sailors on shore leave looking for a couple of tarts. You'll have to imagine how the joke pans out, but it ends with the line 'Please ... be a teabag!' Howls of laughter from everybody except the WRAF Wing Commander sitting opposite me, who turned ashen with horror and promptly left the table.

'Well,' said the CO, 'I think Mr Stewart has set a wonderfully abysmal standard for the evening and we shall now retire to the bar. The first round is on the BBC!'

'Oh, no it's not ... it's on him!' laughed Phil with glee. I believe my IOU is still framed there.

The next day, Phil and I were well and truly shedded. This is part of RAF parlance, which I described to the millions listening to the programme. Feeling 'shabby' is when you are a bit tired and emotional, 'shedded' is when things are a bit worse than that and 'gubbed' is when the morning after feels like the end of the world. Shedded I most definitely was after the Officers' Mess, and gubbed took on its full meaning after the evening in the Sergeants' Mess.

Top: Enjoying a blind date with Cilla Black in 1970 – she seems to be having second thoughts …

Above: How young we look. Me with David Cassidy and my Junior Choice producer at the time, Don George, 1973.

If a Hepworths made-to-measure suit can satisfy this lot, think what it could do for you.

You won't be surprised to learn that the five gentlemen below are quite vocal when it comes to picking their clothes.

They know what they want and they know why.

By way of a demonstration we made them a suit each. A Hepworths made-to-measure suit.

If you'd like to turn the page you'll see how we managed to give them suits that not only fitted, but also fitted in with their own fashion ideas.

And that's what a Hepworths made-to-measure suit is all about.

Look-in
The Junior TVTimes No 2 16 Jan 1971 Every Friday 1s. (5p)

Stewpot in Morocco
colour feature

FREE GIFT
Complete your
Magpie Studio

The new Freewheelers

see pages 8–9

Top: Oh dear! This must have been that fashion desert somewhere in the 1970s. Terry Wogan, Emporer Roscoe, Tony Blackburn, me and Noel Edmunds.

Right: Getting the hump for *Look-in*.

Top: Chiara and me on our wedding day with my brother Mike, who nearly wasn't allowed in because he was 'improperly dressed'. 2 July 1974.

Above: Chiara with our kids Francesca and Marco and their grandparents who were always called by their first names, with the Italian word for grand parent in front of it: Nonno Ray, Nonna Peg, Nonna Ginetta and Nonno Jimmy.

Top: On the Radio 1 Roadshow with Simon Bates, Tony Blackburn, DLT, Peter Powell, me and The Kid (Dave Jensen).

Above: The Crackerjack pantomime, Robinson Crusoe. From left, Jan Hunt, me, John 'I'm Free' Inman, Peter Glaze, Don MacLean.

Some of my sporting adventures.

Top: At the speedway. *Left to right*: me, David Hamilton, Leapy Lee, Troy Dante.

Inset: With (*left to right*) Greg Norman and Sandy Lyle at Moor Park for the Bob Hope Classic. I was secretly terrified of playing in such august company.

Above: Spot the real cricketers! This was a benefit match for Middlesex profesional Norman Featherstone at Lords, 1972. Back row, left to right: Brian Rix, Elton John, Michael Parkinson, Peter Cook, me (in need of a haircut), Nicholas Parsons, Ray Barrett. Front row, left to right: Gerald Harper, Malcolm McFee, a friend of Vic Lewis, Wes Hall, David Frost.

In the presence of royalty.

Top: Shaking hands with the Queen at a packed Albert Hall after a charity concert in aid of the National Children's Homes. She assured me she had shouted, 'Crackerjack!' as loudly as everyone else.

Above: With Diana Princess of Wales, Earls Court, 1991. Note the lustful eyes. Well mine, anyway!

Top: My beloved Wellington.

Above: Francesca, Marco and me in 1980.

Top left: Me and my gorgeous daughter Francesca.

Top right: Chiara and I with Francesca and Marco, photographed in 1982 at the Surrey Golf and Country Club, Foxhills which was like a second home to us.

Above: At Marco's 18th Birthday party, 23 March 1995. Marco and I are clearly enjoying our karaoke moment, but is Chiara trying to sneak away?

We arrived there at the appointed time of 6.30pm. And within half an hour there were two columns of lager in front of us.

Then the Irish Rangers arrived. 'It'll be a pint for you then, will it, Stewpot?' And before I could say a half would do, a pint of Guinness was staring up at me. 'And what's your chaser – whisky?'

Not wanting to look a wimp, which I probably did anyway with three untouched pints in front of me, I said, 'Vodka'. I looked at Phil. 'What are we going to do? We've that ride on an Eric tomorrow'. For those who might be a little confused, the people who make helicopters are called Bristow ... Eric Bristow is the famous darts player ... Eric. Simple!

Just then, in walked our saviour – senior aircraftsman Smith complete with a snooker cue. 'Fancy a game of snooker, Stewpot?'

Looking at what were now six pints and vodkas in front of me, I immediately realised that here was our great escape. Armed with two pints of lager in one hand and two vodkas in the other, we followed our leader to the snooker room, returning to the bar again only when we had lost the snooker match – which didn't take long! I noticed the pints we had left behind earlier were still there. Carrying four of them back to some waiting onlookers, I said jokingly, 'Here's a drink from ABBA – the winner takes it all!' Sometimes, I don't know how I get away with it!

We weren't laughing the following morning, though. No one had prepared us for gale-force winds, which howled around our hangovers and helicopter as we flew off to a remote listening station in the mountains of West Falkland. But the men at the listening station had that typical RAF humour which we were rapidly getting used to. As the Eric landed to great waves and cheers, I noticed a large banner outside their hut which read 'Welcome, Noel'!

No socialising that night, thank goodness. Tomorrow was to be the big recording day, so I would have to have a clear head. Something did wake me up once, though – the sound of bonking in the next room. Girls serving in the Falklands were outnumbered about ten to one. They could take their pick ... and they did.

We hoped the programme had recorded well. Phil had chosen the music to fit the place, the occasion and the mood, including everything from the 'RAF March', '633 Squadron', Patsy Cline and 'Crazy' (she was very popular there), Frank Sinatra and 'It All Depends on You' ... or 'ewe', considering the local woolly population! We also included 'The Long and Winding Road' by the Beatles and Mark Knopfler's 'The Road', which we played to commemorate the building of the new tarmac road from Mount Pleasant to Stanley, about 30 miles long. But we ended with a tribute record by two local musicians, Terry and Amelia Betts. Theirs was a song written after the liberation in 1982 as a tribute to the men of the Combined Services who gave their lives to free the islands. It was called simply 'Two Five Five' – the number who had died.

So to the final venue on the last night – the Hangar Disco. I was up on stage, and the ones who came and joined me were from my *Crackerjack* generation. The noise was deafening – it would have terrified the Argentinians! We instigated an adult game of Double or Drop called 'Double or Drop 'Em' – instead of a cabbage for every wrong answer, you had to take off a piece of clothing. Not a good idea, especially when two of the contestants were well-endowed and rather inebriated WRAFs. I seem to remember leaving through the back of the hangar as the Red Caps came running in the front. Off to the airport ... sharpish.

I was never born to be rich and, among my peers, you have probably gathered by now that I am mercilessly ribbed for being tight. Someone else at the BBC at this time was also being extremely careful with money, but on this occasion it was on behalf of every licence-fee payer in the UK. One of John Birt's first assignments when he became Director-General was to secure the licence fee, and then make the BBC a more streamlined, efficient organisation. Radio 2's old habits of long lunches and extended foreign trips for executive producers would become a thing of the past.

One of those wonderfully lavish institutions which has been saved from the chop is the annual Presenters' Dinner at Broadcasting House. There was a special pecking order at these occasions: Terry Wogan would start the evening next to the Controller, Frances Line, but after the main course – and I do want to assure you that your licence fee is being well spent, the food being delicious – Frances would ask us to turn the place cards over, and move around the table to a different chair. It was a cunning way of making sure that someone else was sitting at the Controller's right hand – and that someone was always Jimmy Young! Frances had to be very careful that nobody's noses were put out of joint. We were all one big, happy family after all!

My card now revealed that my companions were to be Ellen Jamieson, who had just climbed on the wagon, and Ken Bruce, who had most definitely fallen off it! The port was being passed around the table in ever-decreasing circles, until it stopped in front of Ken and me. The limousine drivers, whom Frances had supplied for such an eventuality, took us to our different homes about two hours later, and we were both grateful that, being a Friday night, which by now had become Saturday morning, neither of us had a programme that day.

Several years later, the annual bash came round again, but this time it was held at the Reform Club in Pall Mall. In previous years, we had sat at the Long Table in the Governors' Dining Room in Broadcasting House. James Moir, who had taken over from Frances Line as the Controller of Radio 2, and who proved to be a great success, had instigated the change of venue for the annual jamboree, although it was debatable whether the Reform Club was the best choice for such an event. There's something strangely staid and antiquated about those old clubs, which almost makes it a sin to enjoy yourself too much! I suggested a lap-dancing club for the following year.

The invitations always stipulated black tie, and you could just catch a whiff of mothballs from one or two of the dinner jackets. But the dress code was strictly adhered to. Not this year, though – despite the traditional surroundings, rebellion was in the air.

Phil Jupitus and Mark Lamarr were in lounge suits – or I think that's what they were. Either they were making statements or they couldn't read! Phil Jupitus sat at Terry Wogan's table, looking decidedly uncomfortable – Mrs Wogan didn't even know who he was!

Chiara and I were at the loudest table with Ken Bruce. Ken and I seem to have known each other for ages, although rarely socialising, except when I've bought the drinks. As I said, we rarely socialise. This time, though, we were on rare form, and sitting opposite me was Steve Harley. His 'Come Up and See Me, Make Me Smile' is one of my all-time favourites, and I felt like a naïve fan as I complimented him. Then he told me that he never missed my Sunday show, with its 'great variety of music'. 'Why don't they play those sort of records during the weekday programmes?' he asked.

I looked at Ken. He was squirming. I laughed, 'Hearing a Frank Sinatra record on *The Ken Bruce Show* is about as common as rocking-horse manure!' It was that sort of evening.

There were three notable absentees from that dinner – Steve Wright, Sarah Kennedy and Jimmy Young. Steve had taken his son Christmas shopping in New York.

Now, Steve was no stranger to New York, as he had made another visit there for an Independence Day Special one year. He was to be there for four days, and the PA noticed he didn't have any luggage. So she dutifully went out and bought him some underpants and hankies. She gave them to him, and said that they would be put on his BBC expenses for the trip.

Later that week, they were checking in for the journey home, when the PA noticed that Steve was still carrying the same bag with the new pants in it – unopened! On mentioning this to him, Steve told her he had washed his pants every night, and dried them by hanging them next to the open window of his hotel. His crew couldn't stop laughing at this – the windows of the hotel were all hermitically sealed. Moral of this story? Tell the truth about your dirty washing!

So Steve – with washed or unwashed pants – was unable to attend the Reform Club bash that year, and no Sarah Kennedy meant that it was a much quieter room. Sarah is delightful company and loves to party, and I can remember a couple of occasions when I received a call in the middle of the night to go in and present her programme, as she was feeling 'unwell'. Undoubtedly, Sarah is one the presenters that makes Radio 2 unique.

The third absentee was Jimmy Young. Jim had only returned to his show after a lengthy lay-off with post-operative problems, and so a late night was out of the question. He was a 'Sir' now and had to look after himself. Added to that, he had been told that he was no longer going to present a programme that had been his for 30 years. Rejection is never easy to accept, and Sir Jim had found it very difficult. But change is inevitable, as I have found to my chagrin, and the best way to accept it is to be graceful. And grateful. To know that you have contributed to other people's enjoyment of life is a gift with which some of us are lucky to have been blessed. It will never be taken away from us and, for that alone, we should be grateful. Johnny Walker almost abused that gift when he was exposed by the *News of the World* in a drugs scam. He was lucky enough to be given a second chance by Radio 2. Let's pray that that chance has not been for nothing, as Johnny continues his fight against cancer.

As the swingeing cuts began to take effect in the early to mid-90s, even the number of bands and orchestras was starting to dwindle and, eventually, even one of the most popular events for listener and presenter, certainly as far as I was concerned, the Outside Broadcast, was to become less frequent. But there are three or four which have stuck in the memory.

I have always loved meeting my listeners. It's not just for the fascination of seeing what they look like, but hearing their stories of what radio, the medium, has meant to them. Radio is a friend to countless millions, and I love to meet the people to whom that friendship has meant so much. 1995 and 1996 were years when, in the words of the old Heineken commercial, we reached places other programmes never reached! First, there was the Eiffel Tower. Nothing different about that. But how many people have walked all the way up?

Everyone is allowed up to the first level, but nobody – *nobody* – gets to the top of the tower without special permission. How we got it I shall never know. The French authorities said nobody had asked them before. To say it was scary is an understatement. As you climbed higher, the wind became stronger, and the railings you held on to for balance seemed dangerously low. On the bottom tier there was a wire mesh to prevent any attempted suicide, but further up there was nothing. We made frequent stops for the odd bit of broadcasting, but otherwise you kept your gaze fixed firmly on the bottom in front, and prayed you wouldn't be blown over the edge. We had some prize-winners from the accumulator quiz with us, but they wisely refrained from the long part of the climb. Now every time I see the Eiffel Tower on the television, I tell anyone who is in earshot, 'I've climbed all the way up there!'

I am a man of limited technical ability (my comment about bouncing radio waves at my first interview just about sums it up), but I have always had the utmost regard for those whose knowledge is greater than mine. Who better to explain the technicalities of an Outside Broadcast than my old Superprod, Phil Hughes? Those wanderings up and down mountain sides, yomping over the Falklands or merely struggling up the 2,000 steps of the Eiffel Tower, always meant that someone had to hump the equipment in the famous backpack. Thank goodness it was never me.

The day we climbed the Eiffel Tower it was an unfortunate soul called Kevin Long who had trained for this unenviable task for many weeks at the bar of the BBC Club. Kevin carried not only the backpack, which weighed about 30lbs, but also a small mixer which connected the microphones into the output of the transmitter. The transmitter, incidentally, had a long 'whip' aerial so Kevin had to be careful going under doorways. This meant he could not enter a French *'pissoir'*, usually built for Parisian midgets. As I talked into the microphone, the signal went through the little mixer and then from the transmitter off into the French airwaves. Down on the bank of the River Seine, and within an easy line of sight from the Eiffel Tower, was the main BBC OB vehicle. The signal from Kevin's backpack was picked up there and fed to the mixing desk in the van.

Earlier that week, the French Telecoms company (the equivalent of BT) had installed some connection points next to the van which ran through to the road and then off to the local telephone exchange. So once the engineers had jacked into those connections, a circuit could be established, via the local exchange, then to the main Paris international exchange, back to BT in London and on to the BBC back at Broadcasting House.

In order for me to hear the news and the records, which were being played in London (Kevin had actually refused to carry the turntables as well), we had to have a reverse circuit back from London. So all the time we were in two-way contact with the studio. All this meant we had no wires to trip over, meaning that Kevin did not fall off the Eiffel Tower. This really was 'the wireless'!

Later that summer, we decided to join the Cystic Fybrosis Twin Peaks Challenge, in promoting awareness of the charity and its work funding research into this debilitating and sometimes fatal disease. The twin peaks were Snowdon and Ben Nevis, with broadcasts coming from the middle of Lake Windermere and Wythenshaw Hospital as well. Everything went well until we got to Fort William and Ben Nevis. It had been a real team effort, with Chiara coming along for moral support and to help with the driving. We had kippers for breakfast every morning – somebody had told me they were very good for energy. But I've always loved kippers for breakfast, especially with a glass of champagne. They keep repeating on you all day, and you don't have to eat again for hours! The tastiest ones of the week were in Fort William.

The Thursday that we arrived in Fort William was the day of the Great Parade, and Radio 2 would be leading it. Unbeknown to me, the tourist authority had kitted me out in full Scottish regalia – the kilt, jacket and sporran ... the lot! The next day was the culmination of the week's challenge. We had been joined en route by all sorts of people, but it wasn't a long walk Botham-style – we were driving ourselves up the motorways. But at Ben Nevis it was different.

Rebecca Stephens, the first woman to reach the top of Everest, joined us to help us succeed in the challenge. An assorted bunch of climbers, listeners and those who wanted to show their support of the charity also made up the motley bunch endeavouring to walk up Britain's highest mountain. The BBC team included producer Phil Hughes, our BA Sara Clifford, engineer John Wilson and myself. And I mustn't forget Mrs Stewart, who was to find herself involved in an adventure that only happens to those who least expect it!

The programme was due to be broadcast at 3.30pm that afternoon. We began our climb at 10.00am. When I say 'climb', it sounds as if we were all roped together with picks and crampons and mountaineering boots. But it was nothing like that. There is an established path from the bottom of Ben Nevis which winds its way in zigzag fashion all the way to the top. It's been hewn and trampled by thousands of feet, and is far easier to negotiate going up than it is coming down.

At lunchtime, we stopped for a break. The August sun was very hot, and we all needed a rest for water and food. The effect of the kippers was definitely wearing off. We were about 1,000ft from the top, and I could see a large patch of snow, and wondered whether we would have to cross it, or would Rebecca know of a way around it. Just then, we heard the sound of a boot sliding on the shale, and looked up to see the producer, Phil Hughes, lying on the path, clutching his left leg and crying with pain. He had suffered what we learnt later was a fracture of his tibia and fibia, and would need immediate help.

Ironically, the record we would be playing while all this was going on was 'Pick Yourself Up' by Frank Sinatra. As our mountain guide, Wayne Naylor, quickly bound Phil's legs together, we made a quick 999 call, were transferred to Mountain Rescue and, within 15 minutes, we could hear the whirr of rotor blades, as a helicopter appeared over the top of the mountain. Our two main priorities at this stage were to get Phil to hospital and to get the programme on air. My BA, Sara, took over as producer, and my wife Chiara took over as Mrs Hughes to accompany Phil to the hospital. She vividly recalls the moment they were winched up into the helicopter, saying, 'They strapped me in, told me to close my eyes, and we took off. Of course, I couldn't resist opening them, but found I was swaying around so much I quickly shut them again. The next thing I knew, my feet hit the ground again and I was on the mountainside. A strong cross wind had sprung up, so they told me to unharness myself, and they would come back for me. The second time I was hoisted was no easier than the first, but eventually I found myself in the 'copter sitting next to Phil ... I don't know who looked greener, Phil with pain or me with fear! The helicopter soon landed on the helipad next to the hospital, and

Phil was stretchered off to a ward. I felt so sorry for him – he was meant to be taking the family on summer holiday that weekend!'

Meanwhile, back on the mountainside, we're about to start the OB, to the sound of the helicopter in the background, a situation which you would want to describe in detail. Back in London they had been unable to contact Phil's wife, Judy, to tell her the news, so I was told not to tell the listeners what was happening. It would have been awful for her if she'd heard about Phil's accident on the radio while picking her children up from school. I was also told not to mention why the helicopter was hovering overhead in case it frightened the listeners as well – one of them might have had a friend or relative walking on Ben Nevis that day.

The rest of the OB went smoothly; we walked over the snow without incident, and the views from the top of Ben Nevis to the Isle of Skye were stunning. Poor old Phil – his leg is still not fully recovered. He reminds me of the old Tommy Cooper joke, where this guy walks into the doctor's and says (using a really good Tommy Cooper voice), 'Doctor, I've got a bad leg. What shall I do?' And the doctor says, 'Limp!'

Actually, Phil went to the BBC Medical Officer for a check-up before embarking on that fairly arduous trip. He was given a clean bill of health, apart from a slight weakness in the muscles of his left leg, but he'd been told that that should not prohibit him from taking part in the walk.

My 'travels with my Auntie' continued with a flight to Naples; before long, they would be calling me Sherpa Stewart. This time we were going up Mount Vesuvius. The main differences between Vesuvius and Ben Nevis are that one is a volcano and you don't start climbing it until you are two-thirds of the way up, and the other is Ben Nevis. This adventure was to be the prize for winning that previous week's accumulator quiz. I can think of more appropriate rewards for mental alacrity, but Radio 2 listeners are a hardy lot, and indeed it was two pensioners who joined us on the walk – and they participated fully in the experience. Once again, Chiara was on the trip, this time as an interpreter. And, boy, did we need her. The further south in Italy you get, the less anybody seems to speak English.

We landed in Naples during a thunderstorm. If that was unnerving, so, too, was our next stop at RAI Uno, the Italian TV and radio station, where I would be broadcasting that Thursday, before climbing Vesuvius on the Friday. When we arrived at their studios, I couldn't help noticing that the RAI Uno commissionaire looked slightly different to his BBC equivalent – he was holding a gun, and in his belt was a revolver. On approaching the reception desk, we were met with one of those smiles which display a lot of teeth, but the lips have hardly moved.

'ID, please.' Those were the only two words of English we were to hear over the next few minutes. She examined my BBC pass, in the name of Ed Stewart, and then my passport, in the name of Edward Stewart Mainwaring.

'*Soni differenti, questi.*'

'Ah, you see, that's my professional name, and this is my real one.'

Claudia was unimpressed (I had seen the name on her badge) and was equally unimpressed when I tried explaining in my own Italian way. 'Chiara,' I called, 'you'd better take over!'

By this time, producer Brian Stephens was getting a little anxious, as we were now due on air in less than half an hour, and we had not even contacted the BBC in London to tell them that we had arrived. There followed a harangue in Italian at which Chiara politely smiled, and we were eventually escorted through to the studio.

What dear Claudia had pointed out was that nobody went around Naples without the correct identification, and that it was only out of the goodness of her own heart, as well as the fact that La Signora spoke such good Italian for an English girl, that she was letting me through. The others were all right – they didn't have two names, as I had!

When we appeared in the studio, with just ten minutes to spare, we were greeted by the engineer, with 'Where have you been? I thought you'd been arrested!' He had worked for the World Service at Bush House for five years, and spoke perfect English. If only we had known!

Children in Need is one of the BBC's greatest fundraising efforts. The bulk of the money is raised via television, but every year Radio 2 and its listeners contribute at least £1 million. One way of persuading listeners to part with their cash was by offering trips that money can't buy, and more often than not I would be part of the package. Not that I needed much persuasion – a journey to the Bahamas to go swimming with dolphins sounded very tempting. The Kingdom of Fife offered a weeks' golf, the culmination being a round on the Old Course at St Andrew's. Most importantly, the people who gave in their tens of thousands for these holidays were a delight in themselves, which made the whole experience that much more enjoyable. That was the only risk – what if we hadn't got on? But we did, very happily.

Another memorable trip was, once again, Radio 2's unique auction for *Children in Need* – meeting Father Christmas in his own underground grotto in northern Norway. We called it 'Ed's Winter Wonderland Christmas Cracker' – a bit of a mouthful, but a great prize deserved a show-stopping title. Sara and William Briggs had a more than generous father who paid over £12,000 to *Children in Need* for the trip. His daughter had cystic fibrosis, and so his generosity would go a long way to improving Sara's treatment, and the research into it. This was a very special Christmas present.

Roros, one of the highest places in Norway, had been for many years the centre of the copper-mining industry, and several shafts had been preserved. One such fell to a depth of 200ft and, at the bottom, the old workings had been turned into an auditorium. An ideal place for a rock concert.

That evening, the brass band from the local school accompanied our singing of Christmas carols and, as the last notes of 'Silent Night' drifted away up the mine shaft, it was replaced by the sound of sleigh bells, and there was Santa Claus on a sleigh pulled by two reindeer – it was magical. There were tears in the eyes of the Briggs family as the children received their presents from Santa Claus's huge sack. There were tears in our eyes, too, because we didn't get anything! But it was a very touching moment, the memory of it helping us to climb the hundreds of steps back up the mine shaft. As we reached the top, we saw the twinkling lights from a cluster of cottages across the border in Sweden – I hadn't realised we were that close. The temperature was -15°C, and we hoped vainly that there might have been a brandy or schnapps to warm us up. Sadly, there was none – my little flask was in my golf bag at home. Mind you, alcohol is extremely expensive in Norway, but can be prescribed on medical grounds. One doctor is said to have written out 48,000 prescriptions in one year. I wonder if he's retired yet!

Now, I love my food, but I found myself gagging at the sight of the Norwegian delicacy, *lutefiske*, which literally means 'rotten fish' ... and it is. It is described in the tourist manuals as an 'acquired taste'. But did I use the word 'delicacy'? Definitely the wrong word; it was more like a disaster – it had to be the most evil-tasting mouthful I had ever tried.

Do you remember those imaginary books we laughed at as children – *A Mess in the Road*, by GG Dunnit, and *Return of the Swallow* by Eileen Over? The only thing that stopped me from returning my swallow was a large draught of lager, but that mouthful of *lutefiske* stayed in my stomach for the rest of the day, and every time I burped ... well, the smell of the stuff was enough to put you off in the first place, but the Norwegians have survived on it for ages. Before the advent of fridges and freezers, they would preserve the fish in the ice and snow. As spring came, and the temperature rose, so did the pungent smell of the fish. I must add, though, that all was not lost on the Norwegian culinary front – the reindeer steak which followed was delicious.

After the meal, it was suggested that we went for a *canny fahrt*. I explained that I hadn't eaten enough of the *lutefiske* for nature to have taken its course so quickly, but it was then explained that *canny fahrt* is a horse and sleigh ride. We piled on to a sleigh with fur blankets to keep us warm, and off we sped through the narrow streets of Roros. The *canny fahrt* was well named. I don't know what they fed the horses there, but the one pulling our sleigh blessed us with several highly pungent aromas! The same went for the sleigh drawn by huskies that we experienced the next day – the dogs didn't stop to answer the call of nature and, if you didn't keep your eyes open, some airborne projectiles might close them for you.

There was one further event which made Roros unforgettable – apart from the programme and the *lutefiske*, that is. We took over the downstairs of the hotel where we were staying, and it was the only time I have presented a programme with a log fire burning throughout. Sara, our assistant, wasn't too pleased when I sent her out in her T-shirt to check the temperature. It was -10°C! After our farewell dinner, at which they tactfully did not include the *lutefiske*, we had a bit of a knees-up before we caught the midnight train to Oslo. As always, when a rock 'n' roll record is played, I was up on the floor, ready to jive with the nearest victim. Unfortunately, the woman I had grabbed had, without my knowing it, brittle bone disease. I had flung her around the floor a couple of times, when our hands slipped as we turned on the final chord of 'Rock Around the Clock' and, before I knew it, she had rocked on to the floor, breaking her arm in the process. Before I could say 'Save the Last Dance for Me', her husband appeared and shouted, 'Go Now!'

While thinking to myself, 'Should I go or should I stay?' my producer, Phil, said, 'Get out of here with boom-de-de-boom. Before they call the cops!'

With a quickly mumbled, 'I apologise,' I made my way to the waiting coach, humming 'Softly As I Leave You'.

I'm sorry, Unknown Roros Woman. I know now that your arm did eventually mend, and please excuse my 'Careless Hands'.

From my earliest days as a DJ, the music has been my passion. I've looked forward to every record I've played. Much of today's music leaves me cold so I'm happy not to have to play what I don't like. In 1999, I must have been going through a musical menopause, but I was still completely unprepared for the summons I received from the Controller's office one cold afternoon in February. Big avuncular Jim Moir seemed a bit nervous, and his usual pleasantries did little to disguise the bombshell he was about to drop.

'You're a fine broadcaster, Ed, and we're indebted to you for the excellence of your programme, but the station has to move on. We will not be renewing your contract when it ends at the end of June.'

I was dumbfounded. Figures and reaction had been very favourable, but now it was happening again. I was being shown the door ... or so I thought.

'We don't want to lose you completely, though, so I would like to offer you a two-hour time slot on Sunday afternoons, and the breakfast show when Terry is on leave.'

I could sense that he wasn't enjoying this – we were good mates, after all, and I was the first presenter he had had to confront since he had taken over a couple of years before. I learnt later that Jim had been aiming to replace me with Steve Wright before this, but because my father-in-law, Jimmy Henney, was very ill with cancer, he felt uneasy about the timing of such a move.

Eventually, we agreed on a story that I was retiring to pursue other interests. Radio 2 didn't want a furore if the papers got hold of the story that I'd been sacked.

'And if I don't go along with this story, what will happen?' I asked.

'We won't be able to offer you the Sunday programme.'

Decisions, decisions. Radio 2 was by now the most listened to of all the national stations, and I could still be a part of it. I had to decide between sticking two fingers up at the BBC, or staying. I've stayed and, in so doing, have learnt more about rail timetables than I knew existed.

A third of Radio 2's output originates from Birmingham, including all the overnight programmes – *The Organist Entertains*, *Listen to the Band* and so on. I travel there every weekend by train. Much criticism has been levelled at the rail industry, the price of tickets, the poor quality of the rolling stock and the plight of the traveller. A lot of it is justified, but I would still travel by train for the very good reason that I'm an obsessive listener to CDs, cassettes and the radio itself. Armed with my CD/radio player, I'm as happy as a comedian with a new joke. I wonder how many of the critical pieces are written by journalists who travel regularly on the train.

Sunday remains a day on Radio 2 that means everything to the listener who likes the 'old' music. From Michael Parkinson in the mornings through to Malcolm Laycock and David Jacobs, the music appeals to those whose radio listening began in the 30s, 40s and 50s. Long may it continue, if only to keep ageing broadcasters in employment – and I count myself in that category! There are hundreds of thousands of young people who like the simplicity and melodic nature of yesterday's music – listen to Jamie Cullum, Jacqui Dankworth, Clare Teal, Katie Melua, Amici Forever and the other youth bands that are playing jazz for a start. May Radio 2 continue to champion their causes!

Apart from Radio 2, only Saga Radio has a really wide variety of music, but its stations are only licensed in the Midlands and in

Glasgow. The Gold stations rarely play anything before 1960. Am I sounding like a sad old git? Probably! But there are millions of us around who have to fight the spectre of ageism – at least leave our music alone, please.

I understand now why Lesley Douglas was appointed Controller of Radio 2, following Jim Moir. She understands that the reason for Radio 2's continuing success is the breadth of the music played on the network. Most important of all, as far as I'm concerned, is that Sundays seem to be safe from the erosion of show, film and standard music which seems to be happening elsewhere through the radio dial.

The one thing that remained constant throughout all the ups and downs of the 90s was the love of the music. And it just goes round and round. I really enjoyed playing the following tracks from this period, some of which are by singers who were new to me at the time, while others were already established:

1. **'Over the Rainbow' – Eva Cassidy**
   How sad that Eva never lived to know her immense popularity. To my mind, hers is the most beautiful and emotive rendition of this classic song.
2. **'Unbreak My Heart' – Toni Braxton**
   Such an original title, 'Mend My Heart' wouldn't have felt the same. One of five singing sisters from Maryland, despite several other hits in the 90s, this one Toni's really hits the spot for me.
3. **'Hero' – Enrique Iglesias**
   Who said sons can't match their father's success? Enrique has and he's been out with Anna Kournikova as well!
4. **'Seven Seconds' – Youssou N'Dour and Neneh Cherry**
   Senegal's greatest musical export together with the winner of the Best New Female Singer award in 1990, combined to produce a recording that has always hit me right there!

5. **'Angels' – Robbie Williams**

   The lad has the bravado and the talent to continue being a superstar. This recording is what first established him internationally.

6. **'The Earth Song' – Michael Jackson**

   However controversial his image has become, he still comes out with classics. One of my favourites.

7. **'If Tomorrow Never Comes' – Ronan Keating**

   A song in which the lyrics compel you to listen to more than just the melody.

8. **'Days of Pearly Spencer' – Marc Almond**

   I'm so glad that somebody chose to revive this song, originally written and recorded by David McWilliams in the late 60s. I never understood why it wasn't a hit in the first place.

9. **'Perfect Day' – Lou Reed and Various Artists**

   There were over a hundred artists featured if you include all the orchestral players. A brilliant idea to have recorded this for BBC's Children in Need. It's as much fun today trying to match the voices to the singers as it was when it first appeared in 1997.

10. **'Tears in Heaven' – Eric Clapton**

    The most poignant lyric he ever wrote, understandably. Even if you have not been affected by the loss of a child, this is emotional in the extreme.

11

BALLS!

WHO SAID, 'Charity begins at home'? I've always thought it started on the football and cricket pitches, golf courses, the Variety Club Sunshine Coaches or the PHAB (Physically Handicapped Able-Bodied) clubs. Any way that you can support charities by having fun when raising money should be an important part of everybody's life. These days, a large part of my life is taken up playing charity golf events – and I love it. Golf is my physical pension for old age.

The Mayor of Epsom was 52, and about 5ft 2in – jovial and friendly, he made us welcome at his ball. Part of that evening's proceeds would be going to PHAB. I am President of PHAB, having taken over from Rolf Harris, who himself had followed Sir Jimmy Savile. PHAB was established in 1957 in response to the belief that disabled people want 'opportunity, not pity'. There are now some 235 PHAB clubs spread around the UK. Membership is in the region of 15,000 and is made up of almost equal numbers of able-bodied and disabled people, which properly reflects PHAB's unique mission. That mission can be summed up in its commitment to 'look at the ability, not the disability, by making more of life together'.

My function that evening was to accept a cheque on the charity's behalf, and to draw the raffle. The tickets for the raffle had been selling well over the past couple of months, so the prize winners might not necessarily have been in the function room in the grandstand of Epsom racecourse, a new but excellent venue for such an occasion. The first prize winner, a Mr Jones, was not there, but he had left a barely distinguishable phone number. I asked if anybody had a mobile phone, so that I could tell the winner his good news. Unfortunately, the organisers of the raffle had forgotten their list of prizes, so everything was going to be a mystery!

I held the phone to the mic and dialled what I thought was the number in front of me. 'Hello, may I speak to Mr Jones?'

'There's no Mr Jones here,' said a woman's voice, and she promptly cut me off.

The diners roared. 'Redraw!' they cried. The lady who was lending me the mobile phone looked a bit dubious – she was imagining her next phone bill. I got her to draw the next ticket and dial the number – she graciously went along with it! A child's voice answered.

'May I speak to your mummy or daddy, please?'

'You can't ... they're busy.'

The crowd roared with laughter again, and even more when the little girl put the phone down.

We drew another ticket . The crowd hooted – it was the Mayor's. I called him up to the stage, all 5ft 2in of him. His face was beaming. 'What do you think you've won then, Mr Mayor?'

'Since I arranged the prizes, I know I've won the Aston Martin!' he exclaimed, to more roars from the excited crowd.

'You have. Unfortunately ...' I called after him, as he skipped back to his table like a little boy, '... it's only a Dinky!'

He beamed back at me and, as quick as a flash from a speed camera, shouted back, 'Well, at least you've got the driver for it!'

We all fell about – it was that sort of evening. A woman at the next table cried, 'A raffle with cabaret … wonderful!' Not only was it an evening with a lot of laughs, but we had found a mayor with a real sense of humour!

Balls have played a large part in my life … and most of them I've kicked, headed, driven, bowled, square cut or putted for the sake of charity, and the love of the game. Be it football, cricket or golf, I have always tried to make myself available whenever I can. Charity is a word that has come to mean a lot to me over the years. Not as a beneficiary (yet!), nor as a philanthropist, with millions of pounds to give away like John Paul Getty. As a participator, I have fulfilled many of my boyhood dreams. Being blessed with enough ability to take part in just about any sport, I have had the opportunity to play with many of the greatest names at some of the most famous and beautiful places in the world. One moment you're reading about Brian Close's averages in *Wisden*, the next you're standing next to him in the slips! And the same is true of all the sports I've been privileged to be a part of.

One typical Sunday in the life of this charity footballer consisted of waking nice and early to nurse a raging hangover, until, gradually, the realisation kicked in that I should have been at Tino's Café in Victoria to catch the coach to Billericay.

I hadn't told the others yet, but I'd invited the very pretty and very fast athlete Lillian Board to kick the match off for us. I'd met her at a fundraiser in aid of the 1968 Olympics, and invited her along. She seemed very interested. In my usual gallant way, I had asked her to meet us at Tino's, near to the Victoria Palace Theatre, so perhaps she wouldn't turn up at all. On the contrary – she was there before me, and David Hamilton and Dave Dee were immediately taking the mickey. 'Too fast for you, is she, Ed?' and 'You'll have to be quicker than this, Stewpot!'

She turned out to be a real charmer. When I apologised to her for not being there to meet her, she displayed a quick wit. 'Don't worry, Ed ... you can run me home later!'

There were over 7,000 people there, and half of them had to come to see Lillian. She was dearly loved at the time, and the whole country was devastated a few years later when she died of cancer. She was a very attractive girl, but her father didn't allow any full-blown relationships in case it affected her training. I got no further than a gin and tonic and a quick smooch.

It was a close match – we won 8-7! After that game, I went on another of my hospital visits, and recorded an interview that was to give me one the most famous catchphrases on radio – ''Allo, darling!' I've never managed to trace the boy who recorded that for us. He must be in his early 40s now. A listener sent me a copy of the original tape a couple of years ago, which they said was recorded in Billericay Hospital. By way of proving that it really was him, I asked for the original, which unfortunately they said they had lost.

There were two boys in the interview, one of whom was called Andrew, who had a girlfriend called Tracy, the other being a little giggler who eventually came out with ''Allo, darling'. I was asking them and the other children there to send a message to their girlfriends and boyfriends, but they became tongue-tied. Not so the giggler – he had a girlfriend called Heidi who lived at 8 Kensington Gardens. That was the main clue. No mention is made of the hospital's name or in which town 8 Kensington Gardens was. Presumably, it was Billericay, since I was recording in the hospital there. Maybe you know who ''Allo, darling' is and, if so, please tell me!

It's a sobering thought, but many people who have led a successful and fulfilling life will be remembered for one blemish, one human error that condemns them to a life of ridicule. How could that have happened to Dick Rowe, the man that signed up the fledgling Rolling Stones to Decca records? Because he failed to sign the Beatles, and he is remembered for that. England goalkeeper David Seaman has served club and country well for years, yet he is now remembered for misjudging a 40-yard shot in the match against Brazil and conceding a soft goal.

And what about Doug Sanders who, at St Andrews in 1970, missed a 3ft putt to win the Open and then lost the play-off to Jack Nicklaus? Or the man who became more famous for losing the Open at Carnoustie than for nearly winning it – Jean van de Velde. He gained notoriety by trying to play out of water and failing miserably.

Added to all of these triumphant failures must be the Wembley Stadium fiasco. The old stadium had become a centre point of my life on several occasions and, although it was past its sell-by date, to have just bulldozed it to the ground was nothing short of a sin. Now, at least, after all the wheeling and dealing is over, we can look forward to a brand new national stadium.

It wasn't until 1968 that I first went to Wembley, to see the Cup Final between Everton and West Bromwich Albion. My agent, Harold Davison, had bought me the ticket, knowing my love for the team, but it was a sad day for Evertonians. We lost 1-0 to a headed goal by Jeff Astle, who, 35 years later, was to die tragically from the effects on his brain of all those headed goals. Two years on, and I was off to Wembley again, but this time in a professional capacity at what seemed at the time to be quite a bizarre event. Speedway was coming back to Wembley!

Bernard Cottrell was a local businessman who found the money to persuade such household names as Ove Fundin, Reider Eide, Ole Olsen, Dave Jessup and Barry Briggs to reinvent the Wembley Lions and bring speedway back to north London. He also booked me to be race announcer and on-course interviewer. One minor drawback – I knew next to nothing about the sport, but was soon to find out that it was the second-largest spectator sport in the country, after football. I had only ever been to one meeting as a kid, at Wimbledon Stadium, where one of the famous names was Split Waterman, a relative of my mate Dennis.

Undaunted, I relied on one of the stronger features of my career – my adaptability. Within a couple of weeks, I was conversant with the terminology, the riders' names and little bits of trivia – did you know there are no brakes on a speedway bike? Nor did I! You govern your speed on your throttle and boot. It was a brilliant experience, culminating in a one-lap race against David Hamilton, Troy Dante and Leapy Lee. We were squeezed into our leathers, waited for the tapes to lift, and then … zoom! Actually, it was more like 'phut'! It was the slowest race the fans had ever seen. We were all terrified and poor old Leapy, forgetting he didn't have any brakes, went straight into the railings. The rest of us crawled around the track and, at the finish, I could only marvel at the bravery and expertise of the professionals. We'd only been going 15mph – they go around at about 65mph and up to 85mph on the final straight!

If I couldn't get the crowd whipped up into a frenzy with my speedway prowess, then my agent had another idea.

'How would you like 70,000 girls screaming at you?' Harold asked me.

Very much, I thought. 'What's the gig then?'

'Conducting the singing at the Schoolgirls Hockey International at Wembley.'

'I'm there already!' Though nothing could have prepared me for what confronted me a couple of Saturdays later. You've heard of St Trinian's? This was like St Trillions with an ear-splitting, screaming roar of excitement that made your ears bleed. These girls were going to enjoy themselves whatever happened.

The singing never stopped from start to finish. The most popular song was 'I've Got a Lovely Bunch of Coconuts', included as part of a Cockney medley. I was asked to drop that from the song sheet for the following year. Apparently, some of the Women's Hockey Committee didn't like the hand movements the girls were making as they sang the song. The mind boggles – I couldn't see from my position right in the centre of the pitch.

The schoolboys' internationals followed a couple of months later, and they were loud as well. Not as vociferous as the girls, but they still sang as if their lives depended on it. They were more impatient for the game to start, and I would get a little more stick from them. But these meetings in the middle went on right through the 70s, and never became a bore.

On one occasion, it was decided to hold a five-a-side before the start of the match against West Germany. I've told you the story in an earlier chapter. The Radio 1 team would take on a select team, playing across the pitch for ten minutes each way. I remember thinking as I led the team out, 'There are pro footballers around the country who've never played before a crowd this size, and might possibly never have the opportunity that we have today. We're lucky sods.' The attendance that afternoon was 65,000. We'd changed in the England team dressing room, and we had walked down the tunnel on to the famous Wembley pitch. It was kids in the sweet shop time all over again!

Apart from the girls at the hockey matches, the best singers by far were the thousands who came to the Wembley Rugby League Final. It was a day with a real family feel, and everybody was so well behaved. They joined in the songs without a boo in earshot – if I'd asked them to sing 'Humpty Dumpty', they would have obliged without a second thought!

One track that they would all have known was 'Football Crazy', that old *Junior Choice* favourite. It was used as the theme to an ITV programme on the Cup Final morning in May of 1974, and the match that year was between Newcastle United and Liverpool. An OB team had taken me to the two cities, to record some interviews with fans at different schools. We wanted their opinions on who was going to win, who the most influential players might be, and I was told a couple of jokes as well. But, uniquely, there were two guests on the programme who were already superstar fans – Rod Stewart and Elton John.

Rod was a very good footballer, having had a trial with Brentford, but had wisely decided on a singing career, with kick-arounds and charity matches satisfying his ambitions. Elton, on the other hand, had had no such footballing aspirations, explaining that his short-sightedness prevented him from seeing much of the pitch, let alone the ball! No way was a football going to damage the diamond-encrusted frames of his glasses. But Elton, whose real name was Reg Dwight, was part of a famous footballing family. His cousin Roy had played in the 1959 final for Luton Town against Nottingham Forest, and had been carried off with a broken leg. Elton, continuing the family tradition, had become a director at Watford.

The footballing fans at the schools we went to record in Anfield, Liverpool and Wideopen in Newcastle were like any fan in true footballing environments – partisan but astute. Liverpool won 2-0 on the day, but perhaps more memorable was this joke from one of the kids: Name three footballers you can eat. Tony Currie, Pat Rice and Malcolm Macdonald. Malcolm Macdonald? Yes – he's a pudding! The strange thing was, he did actually play like one that day! The use of 'Macdonald' as an answer these days would be obvious but, in May 1974, McDonald's had not yet started their chain of restaurants. Their first one opened a month later, in Woolwich, southeast London, with the opening ceremony being performed by ... me!

One musical phenomenon which began in the 70s was the football record. Football teams and individuals decided they wanted to sing. This progressed from the footballers themselves to supporters as well. Not every footballer was blessed with a good voice, except for Julio Iglesias. He had been a goalkeeper with Real Madrid but, after an injury ended his footballing career, took up singing and playing the guitar. Wisely, he never made a football record. Paul Gascoigne and Kevin Keegan did, although few people today will actually admit to owning a copy! By far the most successful club team has been Manchester United, with eight entries in the Top 50, and 6 of those in the Top 20. England and Scotland's World Cup squads both recorded massive hits, with or without Skinner and Baddiel or Rod Stewart respectively!

The team to beat more recently has been Arsenal, although they only had partial success with a Top Ten record called 'Hot Stuff' in 1998. One Manager of the day was known to play Max Bygraves records on the coach to their away matches, with the assurance that, if they lost, he would play them on the way back again. No wonder they were unbeatable for so long!

The first World Cup song ever recorded was by Lonnie Donegan in 1966, called 'World Cup Willie'. It never charted. I've calculated the charts for countries, players and clubs by putting their chart positions in my own Footballers' Top Ten. The figure in parentheses is the highest chart position the track reached in that year.

NATIONAL TEAM CHART – ENGLAND AND SCOTLAND

(Nothing from Wales, Ireland and Northern Ireland has ever been in the charts)

1.	'Three Lions' by Baddiel and Skinner and the Lightning Seeds	1996, 1998 (1, 1)
2.=	'Back Home' by the England World Cup Squad	1970 (1)
2.=	'World in Motion' by New Order	1990 (1)
4.	'This Time We'll Get it Right' by the England World Cup Squad	1982 (2)
5.	'Ole, Ola (Mulher Brasileira)' by the Scottish World Cup Squad/Rod Stewart	1978 (4)

6. 'We Have a Dream' by the Scottish
   World Cup Squad   1982 (5)
7. 'How Does it Feel to be Top of the
   World?' by England United   1998 (9)
8. 'Purple Heather' by the Scottish World
   Cup Squad/Rod Stewart   1996 (16)
9. 'The Great Escape' by The England
   Supporters' Band   2000 (26)
10. 'Say It with Pride' by the Scottish World
    Cup Squad   1990 (45)

CLUB AND PLAYER CHART

1. 'Come on You Reds' by Manchester
   United   1994 (1)
2. 'Fog on the Tyne' by Paul Gascoigne
   with Lindisfarne   1990 (2)
3. 'Anfield Rap' by Liverpool   1988 (3)
4. 'Pass and Move' by Liverpool   1996 (4)
5.= 'Blue Is the Colour' by Chelsea   1972 (5)
5.= 'Ossie's Dream' by Tottenham Hotspur   1981 (5)
7.= 'We're Gonna Do it Again' by
    Manchester United   1995 (6)
7.= 'Move the Red Tribe' by Manchester
    United   1996 (6)
9. 'Hot Stuff' by Arsenal   1998 (9)
10. 'Leeds United' by Leeds United   1972 (10)

A real toe-tapping list, I'm sure you'll agree! Other clubs 'bubbling under' as they to say in the *NME* were Everton, Rangers, West Ham United and Brighton and Hove Albion – and that well-known crooner, Kevin Keegan.

My association with Wembley had taken a bizarre enough turn with the speedway, but more strangeness was to follow with Evel

Knievel in 1975. The world's greatest daredevil came to Wembley to jump a row of double-decker buses, to beat his world record. As I stood there with my microphone in my hand, waiting to announce the Great Evel (real name – Robert Craig) I thought to myself, 'Thank God for an easy life!' Earlier in the afternoon, there had been a chap balancing on a 40ft pole, swaying to the music in the breeze. He was followed by quite an elderly man who dived into a small pool of water from 50ft up. After that, tearing down a ramp at a million miles an hour came Evel Knievel, hoping to jump over a row of buses and land safely the other side.

Well, he didn't. Later, he would say that the wind had got up as he took off, and blew him off course. He landed on the side of the ramp, amid whirring wheels and cries of horror from the 50,000 crowd. Fellow commentator David Hemmings, myself and the St John Ambulance volunteers rushed towards him. Evel had suffered a broken collar bone, but was still able to thank everyone for coming. That almost included our first child, Francesca, who was a couple of weeks overdue. When Evel crashed, the shock which hit Chiara must have travelled to the womb and got her moving – Francesca appeared the next morning!

Until the late 70s, Wembley had not realised its full potential as a venue for events other than sport. Up until then, the Wembley Arena had been used for concerts and other gatherings. Live Aid made its immense presence felt there for the first time, and major bands and singers subsequently filled the huge auditorium with their noise and glitter over the years. The Beach Boys, Celine Dion and Michael Jackson all packed the great arena out, with special flooring laid to protect the hallowed Wembley turf. As a family, we went to the Cliff Richard event in June 1989 – Chiara's father had been the first person to introduce Cliff on TV in *Oh, Boy* in 1958, so Cliff had invited him back to do it all over again, 31 years later. We got through a box of tissues before the end of the set!

When the Three Tenors came to Wembley, Mother Nature decided to play her seasonal tricks – we got drenched. The anomaly was that those in the expensive seats in the middle of the stadium (I had wangled freebies, naturally) had no cover from the rain. They had paid the extra to be closer to the singers. Those in the less expensive areas, where you didn't get such a good view, had seats which remained bone dry. I found the performances of the singers somewhat disappointing. It was the final concert in a series around Europe, and you had the feeling they couldn't wait to get off the stage. And they didn't like it when you joined in.

The last Cup Final I saw was when Everton beat Manchester United in 1995. I was a guest of the Controller of BBC Radio, who had never been to a football match in her life and, since we were sitting next to each other, she came down firmly on Everton's side. To return to our hospitality suite after the match and see the smug smiles wiped off the faces of the United supporters, especially Angus Deayton's, was one of the outstanding memories of 1995. Everton, the underdogs, had won 1-0!

And from large round balls to those of the small white, dimpled variety. The fear of failure can be a serious handicap in many walks of life – those of us who perform or present have to overcome it on almost a daily basis – but for any golfer, be they amateur or professional, for charity or in a tournament, the four most terrifying words in the English language are, 'And on the tee ...'

This will mean very little to those who think, as Mark Twain did, that 'golf ruins a good walk'. It is more than just carting a couple of sticks around and trying to hit a little ball into a small hole. Why is it then that so many people love the game so much? Because it's a challenge. Not the challenge of controlling a ball that's kicked at you, thrown at you or bowled at you – you don't even have to catch it. This is a ball that doesn't move – it waits for you to hit it! Sometimes you want to hit it as far, as high, as low or as gently as possible, just to see it disappear down that little hole in the ground. It's a game in which you have to use your own wit, your own judgement. Golf is a physical game in as much as you have to walk anything between four and fourteen miles, depending on how straight you can hit the ball! It's as much a game of temperament and how successfully you can withstand the mental pressure the game demands of you. Above all, it's meant to be enjoyable – so why do we put ourselves through so much torture so often, and risk looking like plonkers time and time again? The most frustrating part for me is that I've rarely been able to master golf in the same way I have managed some success at football and cricket.

My first ever Pro-Am, and a perfect opportunity to make a fool of myself in a good cause. It was the day of the Harry Secombe Classic at Effingham Golf Course in Surrey. I hadn't slept a wink the night before and, in the rush to get to the course, had left my golf shoes in the flat. On arrival, I went straight to the pro's shop, explained the situation and wondered if they could lend me a pair. Having tried unsuccessfully to sell me a new pair (who did they think I was – Paul Getty?) the young assistant pro offered me pair of his – two sizes too large and a bit turned up at the toes. Well, this was the 70s, when everybody wore much more colourful clothes than they do today, and that Sunday was no exception. My yellow-and-black check trousers looked good in the sunshine and my bright scarlet shirt lent me an uncanny resemblance to Rupert the Bear!

'And on the tee … Ed Stewart,' announced Johnny Blyth, the starter. Up I stepped, placed my ball on the tee-peg … and promptly knocked it off with my shaking fingers. Polite sniggers. I tried again. This time the ball stayed there – it was a new one, and had only just been presented to me as a token 'thank you' for turning up on the day.

'Swoosh' – my first shot missed the ball completely and I almost lost my balance on the follow through. Lots of laughter.

'I'll get it next time,' I joked.

'Swoosh ...' This time I took a divot, which knocked the ball of the tee, and again produced gales of laughter. Then Johnny the starter took over.

'Nice trousers, Ed ... are they from the BBC?'

I looked down at my Rupert Bear trousers. 'What do you mean, BBC trousers?' I yelled back.

'Small checks!' The crowd fell about again, and I've used that line ever since. It never fails to get a laugh. 'Come on, Ed ... third time lucky.'

'Swoosh ...' This time good contact but with a large slice, which took the ball towards the car park where a policeman was directing the cars into their spaces. Like manna from heaven, a line came to me which gave me my third laugh in a minute. 'Fore,' I cried, as the ball zoomed towards the unsuspecting copper who turned his head towards the sound of my voice. 'Oh dear ... now he's going to book me for dangerous driving!'

The professional in the team, Dave Snell from Worksop, shook me by the hand and said, 'That's a great act you have there, Ed.'

'That's no act ... that's the real thing,' I replied, and we went off down the fairway for what was to become a memorable afternoon. Dave won the pro's prize and I was given a white scarf to go with my Rupert Bear outfit. Johnny the starter also gave me an old ball he had found in the rough – for giving the best impersonation of a bad golfer he had seen all year!

The Licensed Victuallers Christmas Golf Day at Burhill in Surrey was notable in that no one went home without a prize – some people had brought (and in some cases bought) a present, my contribution being an Ed Stewart radio and a CD of Christmas hits. The 'Nearest the Pin in Two' competition looked inviting as we approached the tee and my first shot landed in the middle of the fairway. There, in front of me, was a virgin green. Nobody else had landed on it. Ten yards away was the white marker to denote the best shot so far.

The standard of golf that day wasn't that high, not being helped by the incessant rain. As I stood over my second shot, I realised that this was an opportunity for possible glory. The ball flew low but true with a slight fade, until it hit the white marker and bounced on to the green, a mere 6ft from the flag. 'You lucky bastard,' groaned the others – no mention of the brilliant execution of the shot. My caddy, known occasionally as my wife, proudly printed my name on the marker fully expecting to see her husband on the prize-giving platform later that evening. Those others who had been so mocking just moments earlier were Gareth Hunt, Robin Sculthorpe and Alan Bowes. They were struggling. Robin had the severest case of putting 'yips' I had ever encountered. The poor man hardly dared reach the green in case he had to putt. He was now reduced to using a two-iron instead of a putter, and three-putting every green was a sad normality. When I suggested he used a broom handle like I did, he told me where I could stick it. Since I'd already done that with my driver, it would have been too tight a fit anyway.

Alan, who had made his fortune by buying and selling hotels and pubs, lived under the misapprehension that he could escape from the rough using his driver. He spent so much time there that he found more balls than he could ever use. He was nowhere near the green in five. Apart from that, he had an almost terminal case of the shanks, a shot which can ruin your card, and bring you to near suicide.

It has been said that to mention Shakespeare's play *Macbeth* by name, is unlucky for actors – they would rather refer to it as the 'Scottish Play'. There is a similarity in golf. When you play a certain shot – moving your body prematurely, thereby hitting the ball off the heel of the club, it is known as a 'shank'. If you are unfortunate enough to have played such a shot, it is deemed very unlucky to mention it by name, as in, 'Oh, bother, I've played a shank.' Invariably, your next shot will be another shank.

Alan had them, and it showed. Back in the bar, his conversation was minimal. He escaped to the loo and, on his return, I asked him what the matter was. 'Even the toilets have Shanks,' he sighed.

Then there was Gareth Hunt, who addressed everybody as 'My Lord' and received a similar rejoinder as 'My Liege'. It had been raining heavily that morning, and Gareth was for ever drying the grips on his clubs in a way that invited vulgar ripostes. Some were of his own invention – 'I must stop rubbing this handle so much – it's starting to enjoy it!' or 'If I keep rubbing this handle and a genie doesn't appear, I'm in trouble!'

Prize-giving time and only one of us received something on merit – the nearest the pin on the ninth. Alan, who had forgotten what a green looked like, had hit one straight for a change, and won a case of wine. A great prize for a man who bought and sold pubs and hotels. So, as a gesture towards Mrs Stewart's helpful caddying, he presented the wine to her. I didn't tell him she was a teetotaller until I had the case safely locked in the boot of the car. And what happened to the Nearest the Pin in Two prize? Sadly, the last team in the field had a plus-one handicapper in their midst – a 'Very Good Golfer'. He was six inches from the hole and so won easily. His prize? The Ed Stewart radio and CD of Christmas hits. And I'm sorry, Mr 'Very Good Golfer' – I forgot to include the batteries!

'M– A– R– C– O! *Marco*,' our son said pointedly to the Greek waiter who had kept calling him Michael. He was six, too young for anyone to realise that he was dyslexic, and well before we knew what the word 'dyslexic' meant. But he was enjoying his unofficial spelling lesson, as were the other golfers sitting around the swimming pool.

We were on the island of Rhodes and this was to be my first

Golf Classic. Some of my friends who were club professionals had organised groups of their members to come out and play. The course was at Afandou on the eastern side of the island and Olympic Holidays were arranging the flights and hotel. All I had to do was invite some celebrities, who would help draw the paying golfers. I had also invited Malcolm Campbell of *Golf Monthly* and Tom Scott, the venerable golf correspondent for BBC Radio, to come and give the golf course an assessment. Malcolm wrote a feature on where he thought the 18 most exciting holes in Europe were. One of them was the tenth at Afandou, a par three where you had to hit your shot straight and true on to the green, or you would be looking for your ball in the small valleys which surrounded it.

This was the first time there had been a golf competition like this on the island, and it was an immediate attraction. Before I knew it, many names had accepted – Bobby Charlton, Dickie Henderson, Tim Brooke Taylor, Mick McManus, Kenneth Wolstenhome, Richard O'Sullivan, Roger Kitter and Noel Murphy. Noel, the Irish folk singer, was the best golfer on our circuit, then playing off a handicap of one. As part of the cabaret, we had Roger Kitter using me as the umpire for his popular hit of the day, 'Chalk Dust', a clever satire on the histrionics of John McEnroe. The highlight, though, was Dickie Henderson, whose hilarious cabaret spot went down as well with the Greeks as the British in the audience. But with due respect to everyone else, the biggest coup was getting Telly Savalas to play. I had met him at the Bob Hope Classic, and there and then asked him along. He said yes immediately – he had never visited Rhodes before. He added a bit of serious star status to the line-up of celebrities, and the Greek Tourist Board and Olympic Holidays were delighted. But then, two problems arose.

The original choice of hotel, the Faliraki Beach, found they had overbooked and suggested putting the celebrities up at another one further down the beach. I said no way was I splitting the golfers up – they had booked these trips to meet, rub shoulders and play with the celebrities; the tourist board duly found a magnificent hotel, the Capsis, and we were all booked in there. Then my wife Chiara had to switch the rooms around, so that couples were getting the doubles, and single players were not ending up in suites on their own, however much they wanted to. It was just as well, since Bobby Charlton had been allocated a twin over the kitchens, while Noel Murphy, an unknown in comparison, had been allocated a suite with a balcony overlooking the sea!

The second problem was one over which we had no control. Telly Savalas was bringing not only his wife and son, but two of his brothers and their families as well, and they were all flying over from America. On top of this, he only ever travelled first class and stayed in five-star hotels. But it seemed that the huge publicity and goodwill derived from the visit of Telly Savalas would offset the extra expense to Olympic Holidays. How wrong I was! I think it almost broke them, and personally I never received any expenses. So, a drink with Ed Stewart meant a drink with Ed Stewart, and nobody else. All the expenses went to pay for Telly Savalas, and he never once put his hand in his pocket – he didn't have any! But having said that, Telly gave as much as he received in other ways. He was kind and polite, never turned down a request for an autograph and was good company wherever he went.

Afandou Golf Course was built in the 70s when the generals had come to power in Greece. They ordered that no further building work at the course was to continue. Instead, an enterprising restauranteur had built a taverna opposite the entrance to the golf course, and that's where you went for a drink after your round of golf.

One day, we were all sitting there, Telly included, sipping our retsina (it's definitely an acquired taste, but then, when in Greece …) when a woman stalled her car while trying to reverse into a space in the car park. No surprises there, then! Then she kept turning the engine over until her battery gave out. Who was first out of his chair to help push-start the poor lady's motor? Why, Telly Savalas of course. Wide-eyed, and even wider-mouthed, she couldn't believe that Kojak had his shoulder against the boot of her car. With one extended push, the car burst into life again and, blowing kisses to all and sundry, but especially to Telly, she careered off down the road again. 'Who loves ya', baby?', shouted Telly at the disappearing vehicle.

On the final night, after the superb cabaret, it was time for prize giving. Telly Savalas had not had a good week on the golf course, but had promised to present the prizes … on one condition. He had seen those bronze statuettes glistening away on their marble plinths, already being engraved with the names of the prizewinners by a local craftsman. 'Eddie,' said the rich bass voice behind me, 'I'd love one of those statuettes for the mantelpiece in my New York apartment – how about it?'

'But, Telly, you haven't won one!'

Then a broad grin, a knowing wink at my wife … how could we refuse the most famous cop in the world? 'Who loves me, baby?' At that moment, I was thinking that Kojak did. And just for a simple statuette.

And if I'd come up trumps with Telly Savalas in Rhodes, how about this for a line-up at the Bob Hope Classic in 1983: Greg Norman, Sandy Lyle, Ed Stewart and Bill Mullins, who was to organise the following year's event. Together, we were the Four Stars. You stand there on the first tee, waiting for your name to be called, and wondering why you put yourself through this year after year, month after month, week after week – and you can't even play the game properly. It can't be just for the prezzies, although the ones at the Bob Hope Classic are very good –

cashmere sweaters, a golf bag with your name on it, golf balls, tees and even a putter make the pain of standing on the first tee almost bearable. Almost.

Just as I was wondering which swing to use, everything was put into perspective when I was introduced to Greg Norman. 'I hear you do something on radio and TV, Stew?' he asked.

'I'm working for BBC Radio 2 at the moment. Yes, I used to present a programme called *Crackerjack* and, even though I'm not presenting it now, it still has a huge following. Just a mention of the word and the crowd will shout it back at you. Try it!'

Greg tried it. Immediately, the crowd shouted it back at him: 'CRACK-ER-JAAACK!' He laughed as he walked up to his ball and, in one fluid movement, whacked it 300 yards down the fairway. Always the showman! Greg's partner, Bill Mullins, refrained from anything more than a look of disbelief, and hit his ball hard and true into the trees.

The slightly less demonstrative Sandy Lyle was my partner and he hit one out of sight. 'Further than I go on holiday,' as Jimmy Tarbuck might have said.

'Follow that, Stew,' cried Greg and, as I stood trembling over the ball, shouted 'CRACK-ER-JAAACK!' As the crowd responded, I hit what is sometimes called a Bing Crosby – 'straight down the middle'! It took me another two shots to reach Greg and Sandy's balls, we were laughing so much. After that, whenever there was a large crowd, Greg would shout the magic word – he was enjoying the thrill of the instant reaction.

By the time we had reached the 18th green, I had almost run out of balls. The last one in my bag was a freebie, presented to the celebrity golfers on the first tee where the manufacturer was promoting a ball of differently coloured halves – bright yellow and red. Obviously, they would be easier to see in the dark, or in the rough. In those circumstances, it would be a useful addition to the rear light on my trolley. Greg waited until we reached the green, and raised his arms to quieten the crowds of people in the hospitality tents and in the stand. I had played into a bunker and the commentator, who thought he was a comedian, whispered over the microphone, 'Watch Ed's swing ... it's like the way he walks ... funny!'

I blasted out of the sand, 3ft from the pin – the crowd went wild! Greg Norman had the last word, though. As I was settling down for my birdie putt, he pointed at my half-yellow and half-red ball and, turning to the crowds, said, 'Look at Ed's ball ... half blood and half sick!'

The crowd convulsed – and I missed the putt. But it was all for fun and, supposedly, all for charity. There had been a lot of criticism that the classic had not raised that much – apparently, Bob Hope charged so much for the use of his name that there was not an awful lot to give back. That's all so different to the magnificent work of the Variety Club Golfing Society, which year after year raises up to £1m through golf tournaments around the country. The generosity of sponsors and supporters, both celebrity and golfing, never ceases to amaze me.

Although Bob Hope could not possibly attend every event held in his name, there were many occasions which he attended personally. While the band played 'Thanks for the Memory', Bob Hope made his way through the standing ovation he was receiving at the Grosvenor House. In fact, the band seemed to play his signature tune 100 a hundred as Bob shook hands with just about everybody, and acknowledged the warm applause he was receiving.

Bob Hope was a legend in just about everybody's lifetime. In 1983, he had reached his 80th birthday, and was still travelling the world on behalf of the US government and Bob Hope Enterprises. He brought the glitz, the razzmatazz and a calibre of showbusiness stars that had never been seen in the UK before. From former President Gerald Ford, Howard Keel, Johnny

Mathis, Vic Damone, James Garner, Telly Savalas, through the British homespun talent of Bruce Forsyth, Jimmy Tarbuck and Ronnie Corbett, to the professionals like Nick Faldo, Tony Jacklin and Sandy Lyle, the Bob Hope Classic attracted anybody who was anyone – like Terry Wogan and me! What with being partnered by a professional and the huge crowds who packed every tee, fairway and green, it was like playing in a major tournament.

That summer of 1983, there was a prize for anybody who could play the eighteenth in two shots. The prize was a house worth £35,000 for any professional who accomplished that magical feat – no one thought an amateur, let alone a celebrity, would be that good. But Jerry Stevens was – he played his second shot on to the green and into the hole for a two! Later, he was presented with a specially inscribed plaque by no less a person than President Gerald Ford. With typical style, the main organiser of the tournament, John Spurling, contacted the manager of Garrard's, the famous jewellers in London, and purchased a Waterford crystal vase. Garrard's then found an engraver on that following Sunday morning, in time for the official prize-giving that night. The vase was engraved with Jerry's name, and a description of what the prize was for. The top value of what an amateur could win in those days was £100 – it looks to be worth far more than that on Jerry's mantelpiece today. Jerry didn't win the house – the value of it went to charity.

Perhaps John Spurling had an inkling of what was to come on Bob Hope's arrival at his hotel, the Grosvenor House. John was awoken in the middle of the night by the hotel manager, urging him to get out of bed and come over to the hotel – Mr and Mrs Hope were not happy, and wanted to check out. John got dressed and went to find two American pensioners wandering the streets of Knightsbridge. When he caught up with them, Dolores confronted him, rasping, 'Who chose this hotel?'

'I did,' said John.

'Why's that?' she barked.

'Because I got it for nothing!' came John's reply.

'There's no better reason than that,' quipped Bob, and there were no further complaints.

Playing in the Bob Hope Classic was undoubtedly a great privilege. Besides various other goodies which were presented to you every day, there was the thrill of meeting and playing with some of the great names of the showbusiness and recording worlds. And I even found I had something in common with ex-President Ford. We both hit a spectator and, for our and the unfortunate's pains, were both rewarded with a couple of funny one-liners. The ex-President's inability to play the game was a distinct lack of timing – he couldn't even fart and chew gum at the same time. Gary Player, at one of the prize-giving dinners – I was not a recipient myself, I hasten to add – commented that he had seen my swing across the fairway, and it reminded him of watching Roy Rogers unsaddling Trigger. I blushed, while others around me fell about. But then if you are going to be the butt of a joke from one of the world's greatest-ever golfers, who cares? It was a compliment he even noticed!

Back to that night at the Grosvenor it was really star-studded, with Princess Margaret and just about everybody I've already mentioned enjoying themselves. Iris Williams had sung 'I Will Survive' and 'He Was Beautiful'. An unknown American comedian was introduced as the President of the American Golf Society, and proceeded to give an inebriated speech which brought the house down. Nobody knew he was actually a teetotaller. His name was Foster Brooks, and the memory of his act has stayed with me for ever, although I've never seen him since.

Bob Hope closed what was an unforgettable evening, but the press were already making waves about the classic, and how much it was going to make for charity. Margaret Forwood wrote in the *Sun* about the extravagance of the evening, and commented the following morning '... and what was Ed Stewart doing there? Had he paid for his ticket?' No more than you had, Margaret.

Handling a star of such magnitude had become something of a challenge for John Spurling. First of all, Bob Hope did not allow his name to be used cheaply – he charged. This is why the event ran for only three years. If Bob had waived his fee, a lot more would have gone to charity and, who knows, the event might even be running today.

Stories abounded about some of the celebrities overcharged on their hotel and airline expenses, but however true the stories were, the Bob Hope Classic left a sour taste in the mouth for some of those who took part, as players and as sponsors. Jerry Stevens now runs the Variety Club Golfing Society in a highly professional and successful way, raising huge amounts every a year towards the purchase of Sunshine Coaches for schools and homes that look after disabled children. There's never been anything untoward there. I should know – I've twice been Captain.

At another memorable Pro-Am event on the beautiful San Lorenzo golf course in the Algarve, I couldn't help singing, 'I know you're out there somewhere ...' as I retraced the path of my slice and searched in vain for my ball. It was a pleasure, though, to be playing for the first time on the Algarve, that superb stretch of southern Portugal, which has become a golfers' paradise. The reason I was singing those particular words that day was because my partner in 1990 was John Lodge of the Moody Blues. They had recorded a song of that title in 1988 and, although not a huge hit, it was one of my favourites, and suited perfectly the erratic golf we were playing that day.

John Lodge and I were two of several guests on Jimmy Tarbuck's annual jaunt to the region. This was to be my first visit and, unfortunately, coincided with a Portugese air-traffic controllers' strike, which meant we couldn't land at either Lisbon or Faro. After a six-hour delay at Gatwick, we eventually took off for Seville. From there, a coach was supposed to take us across the river Guadiana. The plane was packed with golfers and celebrities, many of whom were then the cream of sport and showbiz – Henry Cooper, John Conteh, Lawrie McMenemy, Mike England, Jasper Carrott and Robert Powell, to name just a few.

Eventually, our flight was allocated a take-off time at 9.30pm. We had been at the airport since 3.00 that afternoon, and were glad to get away from the sandwiches and beers which the airline had plied us with during the delay. We boarded expectantly – and sat on the runway for another quarter of an hour until we got clearance for take-off. Up in the air, the cabin crew opened the wine and champagne, and everybody began to relax again.

One of the golfers aboard was a bookmaker who had worked his way up the plane with a list of the possible times that we, as a party, would be arriving at our hotel on the Algarve. Times started at midnight and finished at 6.30am the next morning. You were allowed one entry each, at £10 a time. The slots were at ten-minute intervals, which meant that the person guessing the time nearest the actual moment we arrived at our hotel would receive around £300. Chiara and I were sitting right at the front of the plane, and when Reg the bookie got to us, there were only two slots left – 6.20am and 6.30am. We bought them both, but secretly hoping that we wouldn't be the winners, because that would have meant this was going to be a very long journey. We settled down eventually, happy in the knowledge that it wouldn't be too long now before we'd be in our luxury coach making for San Lorenzo.

We landed at Seville just before midnight, and there was a large coach waiting to transport us, our luggage and golf clubs to our hotel on the Algarve. Unfortunately, the ferry which would take us across the river into Portugal, which was still a long drive away, was not running, and would not be until 7.00am. So we would have to drive north to the first bridge. This, we worked out, would take about two and a half hours. Not ideal, but as the fates seemed to be against us, we had no option but to settle down in our seats and try and sleep, however fitfully.

Before we moved off, there was another commotion outside the coach, with arm and hand movements becoming ever more desperate, and we thought there was going to be a fight. There was a language problem. Luckily, the Italian dialect which Chiara spoke was similar in many ways to Portuguese, and so she was roped in as the interpreter. Apparently, the coach's luggage compartment was not big enough to take all the golf clubs. But there was no way the golfers would leave their clubs lying on the pavement until the following morning, when another coach would pick them up and take them to San Lorenzo. Chiara asked the coach driver if he knew anybody with a truck or lorry who would transport them for us.

Yes, he replied, his brother would do that for us, but he would have to phone to get him out of bed. Forty-five minutes later, a battered old transit van arrived and, at 1.00am, we were away. Most of us had dozed off when we felt the coach come to a sudden stop. The driver was talking to man on a donkey who was pointing in a different direction to the one in which we had been driving. Chiara managed to make sense of things, by telling us that our driver had missed a turn-off for Faro and the Algarve, and we were now 40 miles from Lisbon. There were no motorways in Portugal then, so the driver did a three-point turn, carefully missing the ditches either side of the road, and off we sped south, towards Faro, and an increasingly worried Jimmy Tarbuck. Jimmy doesn't like flying, and had driven to Portugal from his house in Spain.

When we eventually arrived at San Lorenzo at 10.00am that morning, Jimmy was out playing golf! The happy twist to the story was that Stewpot had won the pot for guessing the nearest time to our arrival at the club, 12 hours after departure from

London, and Chiara hid the money so that no one, including me, could find it. To this day, I've never found out where that was – but since I was 'resting' at the time, it was probably just as well … I might have spent it!

Jimmy Tarbuck has been one of the stalwarts of charity and celebrity golf for years and I wonder who can fill his shoes when he decides to hang up his bag … or his balls. Jimmy is also a personal friend and, in 1991, there was one occasion which started promisingly, but almost ended in disaster.

Chiara and I were enjoying a meal in our local Chinese restaurant one evening, when we heard a familiar laugh. Unmistakably, it was Jimmy Tarbuck's. There he was with his wife, Pauline, and a group of friends. After the meal, I asked them back to the house for a drink. After the usual cracks about 'Should we bring our own?' or 'Have you got a corkscrew?', we drove back. Seated comfortably, and with a glass of Chateauneuf de Tesco's in our hands, we began watching a video of my first Captain's Day at Walton Heath in 1983, as Captain of the Variety Club Golfing Society. It was a great privilege for me to have been asked, and I was determined to make it a day to remember. I had asked Michael Samuelson, the famous film producer who was on the Crew of the Variety Club, whether he would sponsor one of his camera team to make a film of the day. He obliged, and the result was a 20-minute masterpiece, featuring many entertainment stars of the day like Eddie Large, Dickie Henderson, Mike Reid, Frank Carson, Jonnie More, Roger de Courcy … and Jimmy Tarbuck.

We had one camera at one of the largest bunkers, filming everybody trying to play out, and then later edited Bach's 'Air on a G String', which was the music for the Hamlet ad, to the pictures. Then there were jokes, missed putts and wild swings, and the result was pretty hilarious.

Chiara, being young and beautiful, always attracted the

attentions of the Jack the Lads among the players. Mike Reid (my Vice-Captain) was no exception, asking why she was married to an old fart like me – which was a bit rich, as we're the same age – and commenting on her attractive 'arris'. (Aristotle ... bottle ... bottle and glass ... arse!)

Somebody else who possibly wished he hadn't appeared on this film was Jimmy Tarbuck. I had inveigled the Badger Brewery in Blandford to supply some liquid refreshment for the day. This they had done, from the side of a wonderful 1920s-style lorry. They also supplied a wonderful blonde in her 20s to be a serving wench. Say no more. Jimmy, for the sake of the film-makers' art, was all over her like a rash, so much so that his fellow team members were calling impatiently on the tee, and the rest of us were waiting impatiently at the side of the 1920s lorry, enjoying that wait slightly more than the golfers! It was all a bit of a laugh, and little quips like 'That's the nearest you've been to a birdie all day!' and 'She's a lateral hazard!' abounded.

I hadn't looked at the film again for some time and had forgotten all about its dubious content. Unfortunately, Jim had appeared fleetingly over a couple of pages in a previous week's edition of a Sunday paper, and I noticed a slight frostiness between him and Pauline. When we reached the point in the film where Jimmy and the blonde were getting to know each other a little bit better, we all froze. There was a long pause, until Pauline rose from her seat and calmly said, 'Home, James,' and he quietly followed. To this day, I don't know whether he's ever forgiven me. But it's not often that a consummate professional like Jimmy is lost for words!

Back in Portugal, ten years later, and having had no air-traffic controllers' strike to contend with this time, a bloke walked past our group in a pair of Union Jack swimming trunks. 'Nice pair of trunks!' shouted Gareth. 'Can't see the flagpole, though!'

Quick as a flash, the owner of the trunks replied, 'Nothing's running up that this week!' It was Stan Boardman, and it was going to be one of those weeks.

We were back on the Algarve courtesy of an invitation to the Henry Cooper/Mike Reid Classic at Penina, which was the course Henry Cotton made famous as much for his caddy as anything else – it was a donkey called Pacifico. Penina had also played host to the Portuguese Open seven times. Now that Meridien have updated both the hotel and golf courses, it is a true paradise.

Besides the two hosts, the celebrities included sportsmen Alan Wells, David Lloyd, Dave Jessup, Phil Parkes and John Virgo, while Bernie Flint, Stan Boardman and Duggie Brown were among those providing the entertainment, while Robert Powell, Derek Martin, Michael Greco and Gareth Hunt represented the luvvies.

In a tribute to those Morecambe and Wise sketches in the 70s, Gareth and I decided to share our room. There was a bit of light-hearted banter, of course – we were known as the Odd Couple. We had our reasons, though. The room hadn't cost us anything – it was part of our package – and it wasn't that we were being mean, just careful! While everybody else paid £150 extra for the privilege of being alone, they found themselves in a smaller room than Gareth and me – we had a suite!

The week had taken us around some breathtaking courses – Penina, Boa Vista, Palmares, San Lorenzo and back to Penina again for the final round. I had been drawn with a team of three Portuguese players, two of whom hardly spoke English. Since my Portuguese never ventured beyond '*Bom dia*' ('good day') and '*obrigada*' ('thank you'), they were three of my quietest rounds of golf – except when I was cursing my wayward shots! It must have helped – we were in fourth place going into the final day, 11 Stableford points behind the leaders (this system meant that we were awarded extra points for bogeys, eagles, etc.), but, despite a jaw-dropping Bing Crosby from me on the final round, we still only managed to come fourth. Not bad for a team that couldn't communicate with each other!

And finally, a parting shot from a two day-event called the Celebrity Masters. There's nothing like a two-day event to bring out the real golfer in you – and I was nothing like a real golfer! But the 'goodie bag' made up for any disappointment in my performance. The goodies this time were a Burberry holdall, a Ping putter and a dozen golf balls. A week later, at a golf day in Wiltshire, the plastic goodie bag contained 4 ballpoint pens, 2 keyrings, 1 can of hairspray, a 160W bulb, 1 golf ball and £30 for your petrol money. That was a rarity, and a pleasant surprise. Many of us travel thousands of miles to play charity golf, so every little helps.

One slightly worrying trait I've noticed is the dearth of younger players coming through from the world of showbusiness. Today's golfing celebrities more often come from the world of sport. How long before Bruce Forsyth, Jimmy Tarbuck, Ronnie Corbett and the rest of us have to hand over to the up-and-coming singers and comedians? It's a sobering thought, but those 'same old faces' have had a marvellous time playing a sport we all love, and have known that our efforts, together with those who organise and sponsor, help to make the lives of those who were not born with the same advantages a little more pleasurable. We are blessed with many young sportsmen and women who makes us 'ooh' and 'aah' at their achievements – but where are the ones who will make us laugh at their inadequacies? Let's hope they are out there somewhere, so that the good efforts of the Variety Club Golfing Society especially can continue to offer hope to thousands of beneficiaries. We are raising up to £1m a year, but the performers of today and tomorrow are needed to sustain those amazing efforts. No one's panicking at the moment, but in 20 years' time ... who will be representing the world of entertainment?

And if you're ever in need of something to sing on a golf course, here are some suggestions:

1. Bing Crosby – 'Straight Down the Middle'
2. Johnny Tillotson – 'Poetry in Motion' (*your swing*)
3. Andy Williams – 'Almost There' (*your opponent's swing*)
4. Moody Blues – 'I Know You're Out There Somewhere' (*when you've lost your ball*)
5. 'Goodbyee, goodbyee, hit your ball in the rough, goodbyee ...'
6. Theme from *Lawrence of Arabia* (*when your opponent's ball lands in a bunker*)
7. 'Air on a G string' by Johann Sebastian Bach (*made famous in the Hamlet cigar ad.*
   Try singing that to your opponent and see what reaction you get!)
8. Frankie Laine – 'Rawhide' as in 'Rolling, rolling, rolling ... keep that golf ball rolling ...' (*when your opponent overhits his putt*)

It may also be handy to bear in mind some really useful phrases to cover all eventualities during your next game:

A *blondie* – a fair crack up the middle.
The clubhouse bore is a *thrush* – an irritating c**t.
A *district nurse* – a missed putt that just shaved the hole.
Son-in-law – not quite what you'd hoped for.
Fat shot – gouging out too much earth.
Army golf – when you're playing in a somewhat erratic way – left, right, left, right ...
Red Arrows Golfing Society – whoosh to the left, whoosh to the right.

No round-up of my sporting endeavours on behalf of good causes would be complete if I didn't include the other ball that has given me so much pleasure over the years, and has enabled me to meet and worship the great and the good, accompanied by the sound of willow on leather. I'm talking about the hard, red leather missile that can cause so much pain and damage, as well as offering so much satisfaction as it's stroked away effortlessly for four. In my case, the pleasure of playing the game has always made the pain worthwhile.

The large crowd at Esher Cricket Club groaned – the man they had come to support had been run out on 99, and they weren't pleased. Ken Barrington didn't look too happy either. It was his benefit year.

'What did you do that for, Stewpot? You know I don't like quick singles!'

'Sorry, Ken … I was trying to get you to the other end so you could have the bowling,' I answered rather shamefully,

'And another thing … who taught you to bat like that?'

'You did, Ken.'

Ken Barrington's face was incredulous.

'In the nets at the Oval when I was a schoolboy member. The Bedser twins, Peter Loader and Tony Lock were all firing them down at me, and you were there, coaching me!'

'I must have had an off day then!' he laughed, and then, with that special twinkle in his eye that I would get to know so well, he added, 'Never mind … it's all for charity.'

It's amazing, sometimes, what you'll put yourself through for charity. Suffering at the hands of demon fast bowlers, and being on the receiving end of a tongue-lashing from demanding captains wasn't uncommon.

'Eeh, lad, that was your catch … as a wicket keeper, you should be more dominant than that … like a goalkeeper in football. And tuck your shirt in!'

We laughed as we crouched low for the next delivery from fiery Fred Rumsey. He was to knock me out cold years later with a ball, which I never saw, cutting my eyebrow to the bone, and sending me off to the John Radcliffe Hospital in Oxford for repairs, which needed 32 stitches.

Vic Lewis was a name well known to cricket lovers in the 70s and 80s as an organiser of memorable charity matches. One particular match, we were playing at a favourite venue just south of London at Kew Green: the year was 1973. That particular day was Vic Lewis's 50th birthday, so it had been agreed with the opposition that he would be 'allowed' to score his maiden half-century. He toiled on and on, eventually snicking one through the slips for 4 – and his 50. He was promptly run out the next ball. By this time, the rest of us had opened the Sunday papers, pretending to read. As he approached the pavilion, and expecting thunderous applause, we all blithely looked up from our papers and said, 'How did it go, Vic?' or 'How many did you make, Vic?' or 'Bad luck, Vic, we thought you'd make a few on that wicket today!' Poor Vic – he was mortified, but took it in good heart.

But the tables were turned a couple of hours later. As I was coming in to bowl, I felt something give in my knee and I went tumbling to the ground, taking no further part in the match … or any other match that year. I had torn a cartilage, and my sporting days would never be the same again. I had the operation the following spring, spending three weeks in hospital, but still managing to be there in the studio for my weekend programme. An ambulance would deliver me to BH, where my producer Don George had arranged a wheelchair to push me to the studio. Since the hospital had told me to keep my leg straight at all times, I presented the show lying on the floor and reading out the requests flat on my back. Well, I needed the money. No work, no pay – there's no such thing as sick-leave for freelancers!

Vic was also involved in another cricket match that has lived long in the memory, this time at Lords. The beneficiary for Middlesex that year was Norman Featherstone, a fine left-handed batsman from Zimbabwe. His team of county colleagues were to play a Vic Lewis XI including David Frost, Brian Rix, Ed Stewart and other fine athletes, among them the great West Indian fast bowler, Wes Hall. David Frost was keeping wicket, and Wes Hall opened the bowling. I was fielding at leg slip, and Mr Hall said he would just limber up for an over, as he was a bit stiff. His first ball was a bouncer, and went over David Frost's head for six byes. I kid you not – *six byes*. We weren't playing on the Test match square, so the boundaries were a little closer in. Back at leg slip, I prayed hard that I wouldn't get a snick – I knew I would never have seen it!

Wes Hall finished his first over, and Captain Vic threw me the ball. 'Come on, Ed, have a few overs … show these Test chaps how to do it.' I did. It was one of my proudest moments. The image of my favourite cricket commentator appeared before me – the incomparable John Arlott. His Hampshire burr, plus his almost bewitching choice of words, made him unique. So, John Arlott, if you had been there that Sunday afternoon, in your customary position high up in the Pavilion at Lord's, you would probably have said something along the lines of, 'And it's Stewart from the Pavilion End, with his long loping run, the best impersonation of a giraffe I've seen outside of the veldt, bowling to someone who's seen plenty of them in his time, Norman Featherstone from Rhodesia …' JA would never have recognised Zimbabwe! 'Up comes Stewart, with a good delivery rising sharply on the off stump … and Featherstone tries to fend it off his chin … and it's gone … and he's out caught in the gully! It looks like Brian Rix is fielding there, and there's nothing farcical about this … he's held on to the ball! You might expect to see this billing at the Whitehall Theatre, but not at the home of cricket! Featherstone is trudging off the hallowed turf of Lord's, caught by an actor off the bowling of a disc jockey … and in his benefit year too. They'll be talking about this in Bulawayo for a long time … if Norman ever dares tell them!'

Nearly 30 years later and dear old Vic is still leading his own side out at Windsor Castle, playing in the annual matches with the Royal Household Cricket Team, captained by another old friend, John Spurling, the very man who had organised the British Bob Hope Classic. As soon as I saw Vic, the years rolled by and he started reminiscing about what bastards we'd been when we pretended to ignore his half-century at Kew Green (or Cartilage Green, as it became known). On this occasion, he wasn't playing, being over 80, but he was still just as quick to the food tent. He knew who the chef was that day – Richard Shepherd, the owner and creator of Langan's in London.

Just about everywhere we looked, Chiara and I spied old friends. There was Mary Peters, whom we'd met when she opened her new running track on a very wet summer's day in Ulster in 1974, the year we were married. She was one of Chiara's heroines, after winning gold at the 1972 Munich Olympics, and here she was, beaming at everybody as usual, making them feel so relaxed and special. For what she's done for sport in Northern Ireland, and the rest of the world for that matter, she deserves more than just a CBE.

Then, appearing at my side, with a whispered 'I hope this one's on you, Stewpot!' was Cliff Morgan, another great sporting ambassador. We had first met when he was Head of Sport at BBC Radio and had produced several editions of *Sunday Sport* in the early 70s. After each programme, we would repair to the BBC Club, each beginning the charade of slapping our chests and stomachs pretending we'd left our wallets at home. I usually had, so he invariably ended up buying the drinks. An old trick, but it always seemed to work for me!

Richard Shepherd, meanwhile, was making sure everyone was enjoying the efforts of his sublime chef's skills. If the proof of the pudding was in the eating, then the proof was clear from the number of empty plates. And considering that he had brought his own selection of wines to the table, I was thankful I had a wife who had been teetotal for ten years. They say there should be give and take in a happy relationship, 50-50, and ours was no exception – I drove there, and Chiara drove back.

That day's charity brought it home to me that the older I get, the more it seems as though the world is getting smaller. My mother's late brother, Ian, had become headmaster of the Outward Bound School in Ashburton, Devon, after he had left the Army. The charity to benefit from the efforts of the day was the Outward Bound Trust. I turned to John Spurling to ask him who was representing the Trust that day. He was munching on a raw carrot as I asked him, so I waited for him to finish, thinking how much he was sounding like Bugs Bunny.

'What's up, Doc?' he asked. He must have been reading my mind. 'Oh, he's over there, sampling the Pimms!'

I looked over and spotted Canon Michael Irving, who had the delightful title of Rector of Minchinhampton and Box, and who was also a former Head of an Outward Bound School in Ullswater, and had known my uncle well. If the world itself isn't getting smaller, then the world of charity fundraising – and ball kicking, putting, driving and thwacking – definitely is.

12

AUNTIE'S MAKEOVER

WHILE AUNTIE'S mini-skirt has continued to rise a couple of inches on Radio 1, her listening figures have continued to drop. For the first time since her beginnings in 1967, the listening figures fell below ten million in the summer of 2003. That is sad, and is surely an indictment of both the music that is played on the station, and of the standard of its presenters.

Naff. I sometimes listen to the station on a long car journey, just to wake myself up. It's a kind of therapy. For a full minute, I'll whinge at the music, shout at the DJs who seem to be shouting at me in the first place, and moan to myself about the ghastly voices they have. That restores my concentration, and I'm as bright as a button for the next 100 miles!

But then I have to realise that this radio station is a station of today, for today's youth, as it was for the youth of the 60s and 70s. As we will have read from the press cuttings of the day then, the same things were being written and said about us by the older generation of the time. Music radio has to reflect what is being written and performed by the generation of that day. At least we have a choice of hundreds of radio stations today, whereas, in the 60s, you were lucky to find half a dozen.

Radio 1's decline started in the early 90s, when John Birt, through his mouthpiece Matthew Bannister, decided that Radio 1 had to move on. And what did they do? They decimated the audience, that's what. The DJs, with whom a whole generation had grown up, were axed in one fell swoop – not gradually, as Jim Moir did with Radio 2, but almost overnight. People woke up to the sound of a new voice – and the public didn't like it. Radio 1 has never been the same since. Although Chris Moyles is trying to change things with his breakfast show.

It all started with DLT's infamous resignation during his Sunday morning programme on 8 August 1993, during which he told listeners, 'Changes are being made which go against my principles ... and I cannot continue to work for the station under current circumstances ... the only option is for me to leave, so that is what I'm doing.' He did just that, and it has taken him nearly ten years to work for the BBC again. He now has a Sunday programme on local Three Counties Radio.

Two months later and Matthew Bannister executed his 'Night of the Long Knives'. There was indignant reaction from all quarters, especially the listeners, many of whom reached for the 'off' button. 'Senior executives and top entertainment figures are joining journalists and writers to howl in agony,' wrote Jonathan King. 'Why are they destroying the BBC I love? There must have been a moment when intelligent crew members knew the ship was going down. That moment has just been reached at the BBC. For God's sake, get rid of Birt and his foot soldiers before the BBC is brought toppling down in pieces!'

Of course, the demise of one radio station doesn't make for the demolition of the rest, and Greg Dyke saw to it that the BBC became stronger than ever. But what happened to Radio 1 shows the depth of feeling that radio listeners, as a body, have. But nothing stays the same for ever – changes have to be made. I should know that!

The sound of a good broadcaster is always in his or her voice. I feel even more flattered when somebody recognises me by my voice rather than my face. I grew up listening to highly distinctive voices: Uncle Mac, John Snagge, Frank Phillips, Freddie Grisewood, and the most exciting of them all, Raymond Glendenning, the sports commentator. Voices with accents belonged to *The Archers*, *Dick Barton*, Snowy and Jock, and the comedians on *Workers' Playtime*. Then along came Radio Luxembourg, where announcers had become disc jockeys, but the voices were still just as posh. Pete Murray, David Jacobs and Jack Jackson were not as cut-glass as the voices on the BBC, but there were still no dropped aitches and 'cor blimey' accents, which are commonplace on radio today. The invasion from the colonies was being heard as well, with Alan Freeman, Barry Alldis and Ray Orchard becoming familiar Australian and Canadian presenters. And then came Jimmy Savile. There were still many listeners who hadn't heard a Yorkshire accent before, but Sir Jimmy's was about to become as familiar as the Lancashire one of Gracie Fields.

Back at the BBC, the only rural voices you heard came from the residents of Ambridge or real-life country dwellers interviewed on *Farming Today*. With the arrival of the pirate radio stations, though, came the sound of what was to be termed the 'mid-Atlantic' accent. It was thought by many to be a British accent with an American 'twang'. Dave Cash, Tommy Vance and Johnny Walker are all British born, but in their early days they sounded decidedly mid-Atlantic. But the rest of us did try and retain our 'Queen's Englishness' with the occasional Scouse and Mancunian from Kenny Everett, John Peel and Dave Lee Travis.

But, on the whole, everybody in the days of Big L and Caroline were well spoken and that's what the audience liked. Rosko was an exception with his slightly abrasive American style, and even

Jimmy Young was to retain a very slight Gloucestershire 'burr' throughout his long career. As Radio 2 continues to attract younger audiences with younger presenters, I still find the least agreeable accents to be those of what is now termed 'Estuary' English. It's not the easiest on my ear, but Steve Wright and Jonathan Ross's talent and humour make them two of the most popular voices on Radio 2.

But it has been the Irish voice that is now as familiar as any and, with it, Terry Wogan has become the most popular male voice on radio, as shown in a recent poll in the *Radio Times* ... I was eighth!

Terry has been a modern radio phenomenon, with his unique style and sense of humour, and it is no wonder that the audience for his breakfast show stays so loyal. Everybody in the business is guessing who will replace him when he decides that he has had enough of early mornings and slow journeys to work. How often must he have sat on the M4, gazing at the empty bus lane, and wondering which bright bureaucrat originated the idea? Whoever does take over from Terry will, in the best theatrical cliché, have a hard act to follow.

Terry is unique, not only behind the microphone, but on the golf course as well. A fitting tribute came to Terry from a fellow Irishman, former snooker champion and now commentator, Dennis Taylor, who once referred to him as 'Terry Wogan – a wit and a shanker!' Read into that what you will!

In 1995, Radio 2 won the coveted title of Radio Station of the Year at the Sony Radio Awards. It was then that the Controller of Radio 2, Frances Line, decided to retire, 'while at the top' she said. Who would take her place?

Two former Radio 1 'darlings' were front-runners: Paul Robinson and the man who cleared an audience quicker than Bernard Manning at the Bagshott Women's Institute, Matthew Bannister. But it was a complete outsider, Jim Moir, who got the job. Formerly Head of Light Entertainment at BBC1, Jim came to Radio

2 with little or no experience in radio. Having been moved sideways at BBC1 to become Royal Liaison Officer, he was looking for a fresh challenge. He was about to meet it head on with Radio 2. A staunch Roman Catholic, I had first met Jim when he was organising the televising of the Pope's visit in the early 80s. How this had come about under the banner of Light Entertainment, I have yet to find out.

Jim's first job was to take a long, detailed look at the station's listening figures. They were rising only slightly, hardly compensating for natural wastage. Before she had left, Frances Line had said she thought the station was losing as many as 200,000 a year to the 'Grim Reaper' as she put it.

Jim Moir immediately signed Steve Wright to Saturday and Sunday mornings, with a view to moving him to weekday afternoons. The only trouble was, he hadn't told me of his plans ... yet! He listened long and hard to us all. One morning, as he was listening to the breakfast programme, he was amazed to hear Sarah Kennedy, who was sitting in that week for Terry Wogan, who was on holiday. Apparently, Sarah had persuaded Frances Line to write into her contract that she would always sit in for Terry when he wasn't there. Jim decided that a change of personnel was required, and I soon found myself in the happy position of sitting in Terry's seat. It was a joy – I soon found I fitted in well. His mixture of emails and letters from his audience made me realise how popular he was, and what fun it was to bounce off all that mail.

Where Tony Blackburn says his best friend is the microphone, perhaps Terry's is the camera. Even if his TV appearances are fewer today, you can still see him every morning online in his radio show. On several other occasions, I would receive phone calls at very short notice to deputise for Sarah Kennedy. I would be up at 5.00am, sometimes in a BBC car, sometimes on the train, do Sarah's programme and then hang about until my own at 3.00pm. On one occasion, when I was sitting in for a whole week, I went to the press showing of *Titanic* at the Dominion that morning – and fell asleep halfway through. I know Sarah's figures are good, and she appeals to a large swathe of Middle England, but somebody up there loves her!

In 2003, we celebrated the 36th anniversary of Radio 1. Of all places, we were in a hairdressing salon called Saks in Covent Garden, and before you start saying to yourselves, there's another example of the BBC misspending the licence fee on a social bash, we paid for it ourselves! £12.50 each, to be exact. Perhaps that's why Tony Blackburn and Mike Read hadn't made it. Probably too expensive. John Peel was at home awaiting the birth of his newest grandchild and, inexplicably, Terry Wogan hadn't been invited – he had been more Radio 2 than Radio 1. Jimmy Young was up and down the country promoting his new book. Anyway, he was still moaning about the BBC, and this was a time for celebration.

'Some enchanted evening, you may see a stranger, across a crowded room ...' so wrote Oscar Hammerstein in *South Pacific*. The salon was really crowded, with a few strangers, but there were many more who I recognised. I spied Dave Lee Travis, complete with camera. 'Are you taking pictures for *Hello* or *OK* magazine?' I asked.

The Hairy Monster replied, 'Neither – just *Exchange and Mart*!' We burst out laughing. But looking around, I saw what he meant. There was an assortment of DJs, producers, secretaries and record-pluggers who were still worth exchanging, some who had been bought and sold a few times, and others who were well past their sell-by date.

We were cosy in our camaraderie from those earlier days, and I understood why so many men and women love a reunion, the opportunity to mix again with their old friends – and remember. We'd remember how some of us once had hair; remember the excitement of being the pioneers of pop radio; and, sadly, remember those who weren't there to remember with us. Kenny

Everett, Stuart Henry, Mike Raven and Barry Alldis ... they had all departed to the great recording studio in the sky, and would never have known about CDs and computer programming.

I looked around the room again, and tried to spot some others from that famous photo taken on the steps of All Soul's Church. Keith Skues, Duncan Johnson and I were the only ones there. Keith was now working for Radio Norfolk in Norwich, and had taken the night off his programme to be there. He wouldn't be paid for it, either. The life of a freelancer never changes!

It was a good turnout, though. Duncan Johnson held the doubtful honour of being the first Radio 1 DJ to get the sack. He was there. He obviously bore no grudges. Where was David Symonds, the darling of the old Light Programme's *Easybeat* before being swept into the newfangled Radios 1 and 2? Sunning himself in Cyprus, that's where, chatting to his audience on a new radio station. How many will remember Johnny Moran on *Scene and Heard*, The Emperor Rosko and Pete Myers?

What about the former pirates who were all given a chance in the original line-up: Dave Cash, Pete Brady, Chris Denning, Mike Lennox, David Ryder and Mike Ahern? All sitting there, in that original Radio 1 photograph on the steps of All Soul's Church, smiles of hope and expectancy on their faces. Even a white-suited Ed Stewart, who was to throw that suit away barely a month later when he was pelted with eggs on a student float while taking part in a rag-week procession.

But at the anniversary, many who owed their future careers to the time they spent behind the turntables all looked as happy and fit as ever. Noel, Kid Jensen (sorry, Kid, I know you prefer to be known as David, but to me you're always 'the Kid'), DLT, Gary Davis, Paul Burnett, Andy Peebles and Colin Berry ... so many old friends, relaxed and happy, without the churning worry of who was to be next for the chop.

I expect the next reunion will be for the 40th anniversary in

2007. A few of us will be drawing our pension then. Will there still be a Radio 1? Or will the last person leaving the studio have switched off the lights for ever? It certainly won't be me – I was one of the first to have switched them on!

13

LOST

YOU WILL have noticed that I have dedicated my book to the memory of my younger brother Mike, himself a writer. He died unexpectedly in December of 2000, his latest book unedited and, as yet, unpublished. Every family has been touched by a tragedy; Mike has been ours. For many, the start of a new century and millennium would be a time of hope and celebration. For Mike it was the opposite. He had been suffering from acute depression for most of the year 2000. For him, it was a time of guilt and self-doubt, as the most intense relationship he had been having for many years broke down. Added to that, and without our knowledge, the first clutches of cancer had been ravaging his stomach.

After his young Russian lover simply disappeared from the cluttered room they were sharing in Oxford, Mike took off to our sister Sue's house in Swanage, and it was there that his profound depression started until, after much persuasion, he admitted himself to St Anne's, the local hospital for mental illness overlooking Poole Harbour, quite near to where I live now.

Not that the views or position of the building inspired him – he would lie in his room most days until he found the energy one day to come over and sit in our front room, and watch the football on TV. This continued for several weeks, and he seemed to be communicating better with us all, until something triggered off a desire to return to his single room in Oxford. He was then transferred from the care of one health authority to another. Our elder brother John lived nearby, and it was he who found Mike, early one Sunday morning, having seemingly fallen asleep while sitting up in bed, reading his book. He had spoken to him only the night before, and was going to pick him up to take him home for Sunday lunch. He had died in his sleep.

What lasers of tortured thought had pierced Mike's brain? Had this been a cry for help, which had taken a tragic turn, or was it a misjudgement – an accident? Had the pain in his stomach become so great that the thought of what he might have destroyed his will to live?

Mike had been the most gifted of us academically, and had been rewarded with more than enough O- and A-levels. He had gained entry to Merton, Oxford, which had been our father's old college, with ease. Sadly, once he got to Oxford, his life changed. Out went the dedication and studying, in came the eating and drinking clubs and the high life. He eventually left with a poor 'Second', well below expectations. That was to be the bane of his life – other people's expectations. He could seldom determine whether he was people-pleasing, or pleasing people. There is a subtle difference.

His first job after university suited him well. Nurtured by a year with Voluntary Services Overseas in Bolivia, Mike had fallen in love with South America. He was highly thought of by the British Ambassador, and he then took a job with Cambridge University Press, specialising in books on education. Everything seemed to be going well for him until, one morning, Mum received a call from some friends of his that Mike had had an accident, and had broken his back. He was becoming severely depressed, and would one of the family come out to Buenos Aires to help bring him back?

John was working for the Diamond Development Corporation in Sierra Leone at the time, and hadn't done badly for someone who had failed all his O-levels. So it was left to me to go out and fetch my brother. Freelance contracts with the BBC mean that if you don't work, you don't get paid, but the adventure of flying out to Argentina to help my brother was more important than missing out on a less-than-generous weekend fee.

Mike was not in a good way when I got there. Unbeknown to us, he had fallen in with a crowd that was being watched by the military régime that governed Argentina at the time and, because of this, had suffered a nervous breakdown. I found him in a mental hospital, and he was convinced he had been pushed out of a first-floor window by a nurse. Mike was put in a plaster cast that covered his torso, and I was advised he was well enough to travel.

British United Airlines, later to become British Caledonian, gave Mike a row to himself, with a seat on the other side of the gangway for me. After a couple of hours, the effect of the painkillers began to wear off, and Mike started moaning and groaning, and I had to keep rolling him over, to try and make him more comfortable. Then I saw that first-class was empty apart from one man sitting in the front, with his head on his chest, and an empty bottle of champagne next to him. The head steward and Ed Stewart lifted Mike on to an empty row in first class, and we hoped he would drop off to sleep in what was now a wider space. No such luck. The moans and groans started again, waking the irritable passenger up front. He pressed his call button and complained vociferously to the steward that he hadn't paid for a first-class ticket to have his journey ruined by some noisy drunk behind him. Drunk? That was choice coming from one who had finished a full bottle of Moët on his own. Little did he know anything of Mike's actual circumstances, and even less did he care. But I did – this was my injured brother, after all. But it didn't make any difference – the money talked in the end, and we had to lift Mike back to his original seats.

By the time we had reached Lisbon, Mike – and the rest of the passengers for that matter – were ready for a sleeping draught, and a doctor boarded the plane to administer the necessary shot of morphine. Once we had landed at Gatwick, we were whisked through Customs to the waiting ambulance taking Mike to Queen Mary's Roehampton. As I sat there mopping his brow, I suddenly realised that HM Customs had not asked us if we had had anything to declare. Not half, we hadn't – they're hanging on the wall as I write this, a permanent memory of that journey, and of the Argentinian artist called Berni!

At the time Mike died, I was on a tour with the Central Band of the RAF and, after the concert in Norwich, was being driven back to the hotel for something to eat. Suddenly, a mobile phone rang in the front of the car, and the tour director, Paul Bowen, changed from the affable to the anxious, and I knew there was a problem.

'Your wife has been desperately trying to contact you, and since you don't carry a mobile phone, has got through to band headquarters at Uxbridge. That was them with the message – please phone home. And it didn't come from ET!' he joked.

He wasn't to know any more than me the shock that awaited me. Chiara's voice was shaking. 'I've got some bad news for you, Ed. Your brother Mike has died. John found him this morning. Can you come home tonight? I'll wait up.' She began to cry, and hung up. She hadn't wanted to tell me before I had gone on stage.

Paul Bowen immediately arranged for a driver to take me back to Poole, and I arrived home at 3.00am. Chiara and I sat up for a while, talking about how I would break the tragic news to my mother and sister in the morning. We were only a ride on the Sandbanks ferry away, and it was best to convey the news face to face. My mother took it quietly in a strangely Scottish way that doesn't seem to allow freedom of emotion. She gazed at the window and said simply, 'I'll never see him walk up the path again.'

My sister, on the other hand, reacted quite differently. She had been closest to Mike of all her brothers, and he had been her anchor. She beat her fists on my chest, crying, 'Don't joke with me like this ... Mike can't be dead ... not my Michael!' She sobbed uncontrollably until her doctor appeared, and the injection he administered gave her a temporary respite from her anguish. We had called him on the way to Swanage to tell him the sad news.

There's an old showbiz saying – 'The show must go on'. I wonder if it was penned by someone who had been in a traumatic situation like this one. Not only was I finishing the RAF tour the following weekend but, five days later, *The Wizard of Oz* was opening at the Pier Theatre in Weymouth, and I was headlining it. Mike's funeral took place in the middle of rehearsals, and it took all my experience and discipline not only to be there, but to read what is the most emotional and emotive piece ever written for a funeral. It's the one that begins, 'Death is nothing at all, I have only slipped away into the next room ...'

The next day, I was back at rehearsals, where I found that a stupid incident which had occurred two days before had been blown out of all proportion; it made me realise that life just carries on around you, regardless of your own personal circumstances.

As you might know, in the *Wizard of Oz* there is a small dog called Toto. On the first day of rehearsals, this particular Toto had become over-enamoured of Dorothy's left leg, and had persistently tried to hump it. On about the twentieth attempt, Dorothy had become a trifle fed up with this, and had kicked the little mite across the floor in frustration. Someone in the room had contacted the local paper, which, in turn, phoned the RSPCA.

ED STEWART

Within minutes, the story became front-page news in the local paper, then the national tabloids became involved, and breakfast TV weighed in, while Ken Bruce gave me a couple of minutes of light-hearted fame on Radio 2. The story did wonders for the box office, which made you wonder how many people turned up to enjoy all manner of misbehaviour and lewd leg-humping in *The Wizard of Oz*! They were disappointed. The offending Toto was replaced with a better-behaved one – a bitch!

Despite the Pavilion Theatre telling the press about my recent bereavement, there were still a couple of reviews that criticised my opening night performance as 'the weakest link'. It was unkind and insensitive, given the circumstances, but it made convenient copy for them at the time. The TV show was huge then, and it's still popular, and there have been few quiz hosts with a profile as consistently talked about as Anne Robinson. Whatever you may think of her, you've got to take your hat off to her for sheer staying power.

If Sadam Hussein described the Iraq War in the early 1990s as the 'mother of all battles', the 'mother of all TV personalities' in the 21ˢᵗ century has to be Anne Robinson. Though, as it turned out, Anne was to show a sensitive side to me which others on her shows may not have experienced.

The experience of taking part in *The Weakest Link* was not only challenging, but faintly frightening as well. In the rehearsals, all went according to plan.

'My name is Ed Stewart, I have been presenting radio and TV programmes for over 40 years, one of which was *Crackerjack*.'

The audience bellowed back 'CRACK-ER-JAAACK!', and I was off on a roller-coaster ride of concentration. That's the nearest I can get to an appropriate metaphor for the programme.

Lionel Blair's introduction was slightly more to the point: 'I'm Lionel Blair ... and I'm a star.' He was asked to change it during the

303

dress rehearsal, or Anne would make his life even more miserable than she was about to. She really is the queen of the put-down.

For the producers to include Magnus Magnusson of *Mastermind* fame was to prove a masterstroke. Every conterstant in this edition had been associated with a quiz programme during their careers, which produced a line-up that included Lionel Blair (*Name That Tune*), Jim Bowen (*Bullseye*), (*Mr and Mrs*), Henry Kelly (*Going for Gold*), Jenny Powell (*Wheel of Fortune*), Lennie Bennett (*Punchlines*), Isla St Clair (*The Generation Game*), Magnus Magnusson (*Mastermind*) and me. We were all asked to wear bright pastel colours, informal apparel and no suits. 'This is a relaxed programme!' We were told no browns or blacks, please – they might clash with Anne Robinson's chosen outfit for that edition. Anne usually wears long dresses that are both forbidding and formless. On this occasion, she wore her usual sombre black, but cut as a figure-hugging dress which belied her years. There were four blue shirts (Jim, Henry, Derek and me), one maroon (Isla), and one neutral (Lennie). Jenny wore a pink halter top, Lionel Blair was in a light-brown shirt, and Magnus chose a fawn suit and tie.

The recording began at 6.10pm and ended at 9.30pm. They would be having fun in the editing suite later, as much as we and the audience had had on the floor at Pinewood Studios.

First of all, we were asked to gather around Anne's plinth, from where she would be conducting the programme, for a group photograph. This was to be our very first meeting – and she didn't say a word.

'Good evening, Anne,' gushed Henry. She ignored him.

'Ooops,' said another, 'she's going to be difficult!'

Again, nothing from Anne, who didn't even turn around to acknowledge the attempted jocularity. We all stared at the photographer, some with a fixed smile. Anne was as expressionless as ever.

Her manner of presentation is a brilliant act. She has prepared and researched everyone meticulously, and how she controls her expression so as not to smile is masterly (or should I say 'mistressly') in itself. I was determined to try and make her smile, or just crack her stony face. If Steve Harley had been on the panel, he could have given her a quick chorus of 'Come Up and See Me (Make Me Smile)'!

The picture taken, the contest began and we introduced ourselves.

'I'm Lionel Blair. I was team captain on *Give Us a Clue* for *twelve* years and hosted *Name That Tune* for four.'

'I'm Jim Bowen. In 1980, I introduced the nation to a game show which set the TV industry back 20 years.'

The audience laughed, which was unusual on this programme, but the atmosphere was light-hearted, and they were out to enjoy themselves. Normally, there was little or no reaction at all, which was in complete contrast to the audiences on the American editions of the show. The producers over there involve the studio audience much more. They do that by paying them $40 each. Has this ever happened in Britain? I doubt it.

'I'm Derek Batey. For almost 40 years, I asked the questions on a show called *Mr and Mrs*. My motto was 'Always be nice to people' – so what am I doing here?'

Tepid laughter.

'I'm Jenny Powell.' She was a hostess on *The Generation Game*, but I've got to say I hadn't seen her. 'I'm not a mastermind, but I'm going for gold, so if you give us a clue, you could be my wheel of fortune!' She wasn't just the youngest and most glamorous of us all, which wasn't difficult, but she was quick-witted, and reached the final.

'Who am I? My name is Henry Kelly. For ten years I presented *Going for Gold* on BBC television, and for the last ten or eleven years, I've been the morning presenter on the classical music radio station, Classic FM.'

Poor Henry. In the Green Room prior to the recording, he told me he was having contractual arguments with the Classic FM management. Two days later, he was ignominiously sacked, to be replaced by Simon Bates.

'I'm Lennie Bennett. I presented *Punchlines* and *Lucky Ladders*, and I'm on *The Weakest Link* because I wanted to meet a television icon – Lionel Blair!'

Loud laughter.

'Isla St Clair. I'm a singer, but I'm best known for co-hosting the *The Generation Game* with Larry Grayson.'

'I'm Magnus Magnusson. I used to host a programme called *Mastermind*, but not in this black chair.' The producers had decided to seat Magnus in a black leather chair, similar to the one in which his contestants had sat. He was lucky to be seated. The recording lasted over three hours!

One of the real highlights of the programme was the confrontation between Magnus and Anne. Anne tried to ace him with every question, but Magnus returned her serves with expertise. At one point, having voted for Henry to be removed, Anne asked the veteran question-master, 'Magnus, you've presided over a very important quiz show, so you won't mind if I ask you a particularly difficult question?'

'I won't mind, but I wouldn't be able to answer it, though.'

'Oh, I think you will,' leered Anne, almost foaming at the mouth with the expectation of what was to come. 'In October 2000, when *The Weakest Link* was launched, which old duffer said, "I can quite understand why Anne Robinson has been voted the rudest presenter on television because she is a dreadful woman!" The audience and contestants howled with delight. Magnus waited for the hubbub to die down.

'What was the question?'

Further laughter, but Anne raised her voice a couple of decibels above the noise.

'Three weeks later, which old duffer said, "*The Weakest Link* is the Theatre of Cruelty?"'

'I take it you mean me!'

'Two weeks after that, which old duffer said that *The Weakest Link* was an abomination ... it should be taken off the air!'

'I never realised I had been so charitable.'

More laughter and applause, and I was thinking, I hope she doesn't grill me like this when my turn comes.

'The real question is ... why is that old duffer now on my show?' Anne turned away triumphantly, and we all awaited the *coup de grâce*. But it didn't come from Anne. Magnus leant back in his chair, and dryly replied, 'Because you asked me, Anne.'

Anne didn't rise to the bait this time, and changed tack. 'How old are you, Magnus?'

'Sixty-three ... no, seventy-three,' said Magnus, hoping for a reaction.

Anne asked simply, 'Why Henry?'

'Well, he did have the bad luck to be the first person to get a question wrong.'

Anne turned her eyes to the heavens. 'Oh, dear, this is going to go on for ever,' she sighed.

'I have started, so I'll finish,' rapped Magnus. The audience bellowed, and that particular match finished even.

In a youth-orientated world, 'ageism' is a word we hear or read more and more. Hardly any radio stations play music that was made before 1960, but people generally are living longer. So why this fixation with how old we are? Because it's easier to laugh at old age rather than at youth. *The Weakest Link*, and the edition entitled 'Game Show Hosts', was no exception. Lionel Blair was the next victim.

'Lionel, what I find so fascinating is the hair,' Anne taunted, her eyes mischievously flitting from head to head. 'There are the wigs, the baldies and the ones who have had their hair dyed! And then there's you – no thatching in the front then?'

'No, look,' said Lionel, pulling at his hair.

'That's very impressive.'

'Thank you – and may I say how lovely you are looking, Anne!' What a creep!

'No ... don't waste your breath!'

'Oh, all right then.'

'How old are you, Lionel?'

'I was born in 1938.'

Anne looked disdainful. 'No, you weren't!'

'Yes, I was ... 12 December 1938.'

Sorry, Lionel, but according to *Debrett's*, you were born in 1936. Anne continued her onslaught. 'So, are you claiming to still be in your 60s?' More laughter from the audience ... and us.

'Yes ... are you?' Another battle was looming.

'Are you still acting, Lionel?'

'Yes, I've just finished a long stint on *Crossroads.*'

'Are you still acting?' Loud laughter. Time for another lamb to the slaughter. Actually, he was mutton dressed as lamb.

'So, Derek Batey, how old are you?' The woman's obsessed with age ... so might she be, at 58.

'Seventy-five, this year.'

'Where do you live?'

'Lytham St Anne's, a very clean town, where the pigeons and seagulls fly upside down.'

'If you live in St Anne's-on-Sea, do you have to wear pale-blue shirts like that one, with a short sleeve?'

'There are a lot of blue shirts around tonight.' There were four of us.

'Do you know that only men who wear pale-blue shirts also wear grey shoes?'

'No, white ones!'

'Even worse.'

Anne had an answer for everyone. Later, when Derek was knocked out, Anne continued her war of words. 'Derek, everyone's gagging to see the white shoes ... are you wearing white socks as well?'

'Yes ... and white feet underneath!'

I was going to suggest to her, 'Derek, you are the whitest link. Goodbye,' but decided against it. I was already out, drowning my sorrows in the Green Room.

'Henry,' she asked nonchalantly, 'who's Jilly?' More laughter from the audience because they remembered he had called Jenny 'Jilly'.

'Jilly ... Jenny,' he floundered, 'what's in a name?'

'No wonder you're on the radio, Henry, you are the weakest link. Goodbye.'

'Jenny,' Anne turned to the youngest contestant, and the prettiest, 'it will be difficult for you to answer this, but whom of the remaining contestants do you most lust after?'

'It would actually be Magnus.' He was about to be voted off.

'Oh, really?'

'Yes, I want him to go off to the dressing room and get ready.'

Anne, with arched eyebrow, 'He doesn't look up to it.'

'I don't mind him sitting down!'

Cheers from the audience.

Anne then turned to Jim Bowen. 'Jim, why Magnus?'

'The man's a legend, he's been doing it all sitting down, now I think he should have a lie down.'

'He's going to be doing that with Jenny!' Anne retorted and then, turning to Magnus, 'You may have started my show, but you're certainly not going to finish it. Goodbye!'

Magnus, though, was not to be outdone. In his short piece to camera, which is recorded separately when you've made the dreaded walk down the steps, he continued his fencing match of words with the Dominatrix. 'Splendid fun exchanging good-natured pleasantries with the old harridan. I think she's mellowing. She's getting too nice to people. If she had gone on *Mastermind* when she was younger, she could have chosen as her specialist subject the history of the broomstick!'

Lenny Bennett was the next to go, and his parting shot was aimed at Lionel Blair, who turned out to be the eventual winner. 'I think Lionel's got to go next ... there's no question about it. He should leave the show ... and the country!'

Jim Bowen was voted off last, with a bit of tactical voting from the other two, Lionel and Jenny. They both thought they would have a better chance of winning without him there.

Jim said, 'I wasn't robbed, but it's very difficult when you're up there. I don't know how the public handle it, because we were really on edge. The wheel's still going round, but this gerbil's left the cage!'

So Lionel Blair, to the amazement of all, was the eventual winner, beating Jenny Powell in the final. There's always more money at stake in the celebrity specials, and between them the team had raised a winning total of £15,750. It all went to Lionel's chosen charity, the showbiz arm of Help the Aged called Stage for Age. The look on Anne's face said, 'How appropriate.'

Jenny might regret what she said in 30 years' time: 'I can't believe I got pipped to the post by Lionel Blair, and then he goes and gives all that money to old people – haven't we done enough for them? They were on the programme!' Thank you, Jenny.

In the meantime, what had happened to Stewpot? Simple – his brain had seized up! In the days of *Crackerjack* and the *Accumulator Quiz* on Radio 2, it had been a doddle – the answers were in front of me. I had watched my fellow contestants on *The Weakest Link* answer their questions with ease, apart from Henry who had had no idea that a young kangaroo was called a joey.

'Stewpot,' trilled Anne, 'what slang term for smashing or breaking precedes sonic to give a word meaning faster than sound?'

What sort of question is that? I asked her to repeat it and, out of the corner of my eye, I could see Jim Bowen mouthing the answer. It wasn't my day for lip-reading, though, and rather pathetically I said, 'Through the sound barrier.'

'Wrong – super!' Off she went again, contestant by contestant, and I closed my eyes to try and concentrate better.

'Stewpot – which playwright gave us *Richard II*, *Richard III* and *Henry V*?'

'Shakespeare.'

'Well done, Ed, you've got one right.'

I thought it would be me – the ignominy of that made my suntan go ashen. But it was poor old Henry who trudged off, and I was left to fight another round. Not for long, though. Inexplicably, I couldn't remember that Roy Walker had presented a show called *Crossword*, but I managed to tell Anne that the objects you put in people's shoes to make them look taller were indeed 'lifts'.

But, by this time, it was too late – I was voted off as the weakest link – though not before I had actually made Anne Robinson *smile*! I had achieved what I thought was the impossible!

Anne, returning to the ageist theme, asked, 'So, Stewpot, is that all your own hair?'

'Absolutely.'

'Is it brushed forward like Bobby Charlton's?'

I tugged at my forelock. 'Look, there you are … that's all mine!'

'That is impressive.'

'Do you want to touch it?'

She replied with a slight grimace, 'No, no, I don't think so.'

'What about the hair?'

Loud laughter and Anne's face started to crack and, with a wry smile, she asked, 'So when did your brain go, dear?'

'Oh, it went this evening. I was terrified, having only asked questions before, to answer them was quite an ordeal.'

'Stewpot, you are the weakest link. Goodbye!'

Despite my own nervous performance, *The Weakest Link* was an experience I'm glad to have had and, as I mentioned earlier, my opinion of Anne Robinson rose considerably at the end of my recording with her. Just as Mike was before his death, Anne is a recovering alcoholic, and had met Mike at occasional meetings of Alcoholics Anonymous. After the recording, and shorn of her fierce image, she took me to one side and said how sorry she was that Mike had died. She said it in such a way that I was really touched. I'll never watch the *Weakest Link* in the same way again.

14

AFFAIRS OF
THE HEART

ALTHOUGH I was born in glorious Devon, I know Dorset much better, and I've been living on the edge of Poole and Bournemouth for the last few years. When my daily show was taken off in 1999, the need for commuting to London disappeared. Instead, I travel to Birmingham every Sunday.

Dorset is also home to the Isle of Purbeck Golf Course, where I've been a member, on and off, for 40 years. The course was once owned by the famous writer of children's books, Enid Blyton. Never mind *The Famous Five* – the eighth hole is one of the longest in Dorset, at 600 yards off the back tees. I got a par there once. Now *that* was famous.

What with the wild nature of the course, and its magnificent views, it's a perfect place for gamesmanship. Once I was playing with an old friend, George Inge, and his parents, Jack and Alison. Old Jack was a bit partial to the sherry and, on the fifth green, which has one of the most commanding views of anywhere on the south coast, I thought I'd play a trick on him. As he was about to putt, I interrupted his concentration and said, 'Look at the view,

Jack – do you ever tire of it?' He straightened himself up, put his hand to his forehead, and murmured, 'You're right, old boy, and on a day like this as well, with the sun shining and the larks singing ...' While he was delivering this poetic homage, I replaced his ball with one of those 'trick' balls with mercury in the middle, which wobbled about in every direction except straight. Jack took his time to address the ball again. He hadn't noticed my sleight of hand, although the other two had, and Alison fell into a bunker, she was laughing so much. George and I turned away, unable to control ourselves. Jack hit his ball unerringly towards the hole. It veered to the left and then to the right and missed the hole by a foot! Jack turned towards us and exploded, 'You rascal, Ed!' We were prostrate with laughter. Jack promptly took another swig from the bottle. 'I'm going to take more water with it in future!' he gasped.

It was also golf that gave me an opportunity to step back in time – to Caroline House, the home near Exmouth in Devon where I was born. I was playing in a charity day at Woodbury Park in Devon hosted by Nigel Mansell, who owned the course. He played golf slower than he raced cars, but almost as well. He could be good enough to join the ranks of the Senior Tour, when he comes of age! In between playing golf that day and getting ready for the dinner in the evening, I had a bit of time so I thought I'd go and visit Caroline House, which I had left 58 years earlier.

I made my way to the general area ... and there was my birthplace, still standing. It was a large extended house, now an old people's home. I pressed the bell. A large lady dressed as Matron from the *Carry On* series opened the door. 'Can I help?' she asked, in a broad Irish accent.

I introduced myself, explaining that I'd been born there and would like to look around. She took me everywhere, ending up in the very room where my mother had given birth to me. I stood mesmerised. My mother had told me that she had been quite alone at the time – all the others were under the stairs in case of a hit – that was always considered the safest place to be if you didn't have shelter. So my timing had been impeccable – I appeared right in the middle of an air raid!

Matron had asked me my name and when I was born.

'23 April 1941,' I replied, 'St George's Day.'

She went into her office and produced some newspaper cuttings from the time. They were somewhat faded and torn. BOMBS IN EXMOUTH ... read one, ... SOME DEATHS. I wasn't one of them – I had survived and was still here.

Matron interrupted my thoughts. 'They should put up a blue plaque for you,' she said.

'But I am not dead yet,' I laughed.

'Well, you were born here, so why don't you book your place and come back and die here?'

'Do you mean I should book early to avoid disappointment?' I laughed, and so did she. She threw her head back and cackled in that uniquely Irish way – and one of her teeth fell out. As she scrabbled about on the floor to pick it up, I decided, there and then, I wouldn't be going back to Caroline House. I was still much too young!

As children, we were taken to holiday in Studland on the beautiful Isle of Purbeck, so it's a real treat being part of the local community now, and having all this on our doorstep. It's not an island as such; you can reach that stretch of coast by crossing on the Sandbanks chain ferry, or driving around Poole Harbour to Wareham where you cross the River Frome. Then you pass through the eternally quaint Corfe Castle, and when you reach Swanage, you can spy a real island, the Isle of Wight. This is the sort of environment I enjoy now, and the much more relaxed approach to life is a far cry from the pace of the Home Counties, London and the dreaded M25. My mother and sister live in Swanage, and Chiara's mother moved down to Poole to live just a ten-minute walk away. Too close for a mother-in-law, some would say, but I'm one of the lucky ones who enjoys a close and loving relationship with his. We have quiet and peaceful neighbours ... apart from the seagulls, that is, but you get used to them.

Poole Harbour is not far from us, and it was there, on a hot summer's day, that I suddenly heard a woman's voice gasping, 'Water, water ... somebody give me water, please!' The sun was beating remorselessly down on the deck of *Haven Voyager 2* as the young man next to her produced a bottle. He unscrewed the top of the gently carbonated mountain spring water, and she almost choked as she gulped it down. It had been such a brilliant barbecue on the beach the night before, but now she was paying the price of too many Tequila Sunrises. The yacht's sails were filling with a fresh southwesterly as we made our way out of Poole Harbour, carefully avoiding the Sandbanks chain ferry. Then we were out into the open sea towards the Old Harry rocks and Swanage Bay.

The young man who had helped slake the woman's thirst was our son, Marco, and we had decided to take advantage of a couple of hours' sailing aboard the *Haven Voyager*. As we made our way past Studland Bay, a mobile phone rang – you can't get away from them nowadays, can you?

'Yes, Carrie ... where are you? You're waving a yellow towel, are you? Oh, yes, I can see you now!' The lady with the hangover was waving to a young girl on the beach. 'My granddaughter's on holiday!' she cried to everyone.

I hoped the young girl hadn't seen Granny the night before, or even worse, the state of her this morning. That phone call gave me an idea. My mother's flat in Swanage overlooked the bay and, when we arrived there, I suggested to Marco that he phoned his grandmother so that we could all wave to each other. (These childish thrills never leave us, do they?) An hour later we dropped anchor in the Bay, and Marco phoned his Nonna Peg, as they had called her since childhood, to tell her to look out for the blue hull and red sail. I focused my binoculars on the Needles and white chalk cliffs of the Isle of Wight, and tried to guess how many miles away they were. About ten, I thought – but it was actually probably closer to twenty. While I was musing, Marco had borrowed a mirror from one of the women (the captain had left his behind), and was on the phone explaining to Nonna Peg that he was about to flash his mirror in the sunlight, so that she could pinpoint where we were. After several minutes search, and using most of the credit on his pay-as-you-go phone, she saw us. We all waved furiously, including the other passengers and crew, so that she couldn't possibly have missed us.

We set off again for the journey back to Poole, the stiff breeze helping us on our way. Marco waved at some of the other boats, which included a fully sailed schooner, a couple of gin palaces and a large inflatable with HM Customs on the side. I carefully made my way to the bow, to stretch out and get a bit of sun on my body. Marco did the same. Then we noticed the Customs boat churning its way steadily towards us. As it pulled up beside us, the Customs officials realised it would be impossible to board with our sails still hoisted – we were moving too fast. Our captain was ordered to take them down, which he did with the help of his crew, who happened to be the lady with the hangover. It took longer than it should have.

'What is the problem, officer?' asked the skipper.

'We have to search you,' came the reply.

'What for?'

'We're looking for drugs,' said a Customs officer. We were aghast. Us? Drugs? The lady with the hangover produced some paracetamol and handed them over.

'Don't be funny, madam!'

'Do we look like drug smugglers, officer?' I asked

'We received a phone call from a policeman who was holidaying with his family that he had seen some signals flashing from a boat, and thought they might be suspect.'

So Marco's attempts at attracting his grandmother's attention had been construed as furtive messages from drug runners!

'I'm sorry to have scared you,' said an officer with a strong Scouse accent, 'but we've had quite a problem with innocent-looking boats full of guilty contraband.'

They then searched the boat, finding nothing, of course. Then the Scouser looked at us, and asked, 'Who's going to be first for the body search?' I noticed a twinkle in his eye.

'You would have to be a Liverpool supporter to frisk an innocent Evertonian,' I joked.

'I do support Everton, like you, Mr Stewart ... and we've had a good season, haven't we? You see, it helps being a Blue sometimes, doesn't it?'

'Sometimes,' I said. 'If we'd come sixth instead of seventh, I would have won £1,000 with a bet I had at the start of the season!'

'That would have been a flash in the pan,' he laughed, looking at Marco. Marco blushed. It would be a long time before he flashed mirrors at sea again.

The next day, Nonna Peg told us she'd never seen us at all – she said she'd only said that to keep us happy!

More recently, keeping loved ones happy, and being happy oneself, has been a little more of a struggle. 'Some people never say "I love you ...", it's not their style to be so bold ...' Remembering part of the lyric to Paul Simon's song 'Something So Strong', I've often asked myself why I've found it so difficult to say those three magic words – 'I love you'. It's not that we weren't brought up with lots love when we were growing up – we were. But I don't seem to remember many tactile shows of affection; Mum would kiss us, but she wasn't the type to throw her arms around us and smother us half to death. Dad might put his hand on our shoulders and possibly shake us by the hands, but nothing else.

Once, I remember, our friends Jonnie and George were saying goodbye to their father Jack at the railway station at Corfe Castle, when he kissed and cuddled them both. I was so shocked, I nearly fell off the platform! And in front of all those other passengers as well. Later, when I married Chiara and met all her uncles and aunts in Italy, it seemed quite natural to kiss everybody on both cheeks, including the women! All of a sudden, British *sang froid* became *sangue caldo*, and it seemed perfectly natural.

But I've always retained a certain aloofness and an inability to show affection. Perhaps that cost me my marriage. Chiara needed more love, attention and TLC than I was giving – so she found it with another man. Ironically, that man was to be a professional golfer who had been our teacher for some time. We ate, drank and were merry together, but I hadn't noticed that their feelings had deepened beyond friendship. When I realised what was happening, I hesitated to do anything about it. She was so happy and, in a perverse way, I welcomed a situation in which I didn't have to make the decision to part. Talk about cowardice. Even our daughter Francesca said she had seen it coming for a while. 'Dad, Mum has done you a favour. If you had left her for another woman, she might have ended up in a nut house.' A woman's intuition, or a daughter's logic, call it what you will!

The only thing that was not part of our plans was the timing. The penny dropped the night before I was due to start rehearsals for the 2003 pantomime season in *Cinderella* at Windsor. As you can imagine, those following eight weeks were not easy for me. I hardly told a soul that my wife had left me. I couldn't. A similar thing had happened to Bobby Davro and he had broken down on stage, whereupon the *News of the World* had printed the story. Enough said.

I was going to be staying with my friends Rocky and Pammy for the run, and they had spotted that all was not well months before. Chiara and I used to spend many a weekend there. 'It's not the golfer, is it?' cried Pammy, when I had told her on the second morning of my stay. She understood the ignominy of it. A woman's intuition again. Rocky, a big bear of a man, just hugged me, and we both cried our eyes out. A typically male response – and then he laughed. 'Remember the old gag, Ed? My wife has left me for my best friend – and I don't half miss him!' Laughter – how can we live without it?

I spent Christmas Day with them, first at the pub and then around the table for a rather late lunch. Halfway through the turkey, I staggered upstairs, echoing Captain Oates's words to Captain Scott in the Antarctic: 'I may be some time ...'

I awoke at 7.00am the next morning, 12 hours after leaving the table. When I eventually appeared for breakfast, my Christmas pudding was sitting in a pool of melted brandy butter. I had to eat it – you can't waste anything when you're a war baby!

New Year's Eve was spent quite differently. Most of the cast of *Cinderella* were staying in or around Windsor and would be celebrating in the local hostelries, and although they urged me to stay, I said I was going home. Still nobody knew of my situation at home, except the Ugly Sisters. We had several scenes together, and when I broke down at rehearsals, they swore themselves to secrecy. Thank you, Michael and Chris – you kept to your word. And I didn't know at that time, either, that Chiara and Norman had gone to Francesca's house in Spain.

But I wasn't going to sit around feeling sorry for myself at Rocky's. So off I went to the pub in Oatlands Village, which had become my local, the Prince of Wales. As I approached it, I could hear the usual New Year's Eve raucous sounds of merriment, and saw the happy red faces of the revellers. Then I just caught the strident jangle of electric guitars, not one of my favourite sounds. I hesitated. At the door, to my chagrin, I spotted a notice saying

'Entry by ticket only – £15'. All of a sudden, I wasn't that keen. A burly doorman, whom I didn't recognise, politely told me, 'You can't come in here without a ticket.'

I laughed.

'Who are you laughing at?' he asked, not quite so politely this time.

'That's what I'm told in my pantomime, when, as Baron Stoneybroke, I'm trying to get into the ball!'

Gaining little response, I thought, 'Sod it!', turned on my heel and went back to my digs. Everybody had gone out on the town. I finished a half-empty bottle of champagne somebody had left on the kitchen table, watched the midnight countdown on the TV and went to bed, humming Gilbert O'Sullivan's 'Alone Again, Naturally'. The only consolation in the morning was being the only one without a hangover.

The words of songs become even more meaningful at a time of stress or unhappiness. I played two during the first programme of 2004 that had the programme team, Lisa and Lynne, wondering why on earth I had included them. They didn't know I was feeling a bit sorry for myself. Why should they? I hadn't told them about my troubled marriage. The words of 'Free Again' by Jack Jones and Josh Groban's 'I Let Her Go' were the choice of a sad old git who needed to wallow for a while in self-pity. But I dedicated the records to those who had no cause for celebration in their lives that New Year. Perhaps they had found themselves alone while others around them were celebrating happily as the New Year was ushered in.

The response was instantaneous. I had unwittingly struck a nerve and thousands of emails and letters arrived at the offices at Pebble Mill from people expressing their own feelings of solitude and unhappiness, even thanking me for remembering them at what is perversely an unhappy time of year for so many. It showed, most importantly, what a comfort the radio is to so many who have a need for friendship.

Chiara and I reacted in different ways to the split. Chiara had extreme feelings of guilt and became seriously traumatised by what had happened. We are a very close-knit family, and only her mother, daughter and son knew what was going on. Ginetta and I phoned each other every day to keep our spirits up. My mother-in-law and I are very close. I told my brother John but no one else in my own family. I didn't tell my mother and sister for three months. The immediate reaction was one I might have expected – *how dare she*! But I urged friends, as well as family, not to be judgemental. There are two sides to every story.

When I returned from Windsor in January 2004, Chiara and Norman were still in the house. On the morning of her 47th birthday, on 28 January, Chiara knocked on my door, looking and sounding awful. We rushed her to the doctor's. Having examined her, Dr Scales immediately called the hospital, where she was found to have contracted a very severe strain of pneumonia. The previous few weeks had taken their toll, and Chiara was very, very sick. What had she done for love?

I didn't have the heart to throw them out; Chiara was too unwell. Because of the design of our house, we could easily live separate lives. And, for a while, it worked. How? It just did. They are both good cooks, both of them practical and tidy. It just seemed the most civilised way of getting on with our lives.

Fortunately, Chiara made a steady recovery and, eventually, they moved in with a friend, and then would return for the long periods I spent away that summer. They, and the house and garden, were looked after. It was just as well.

Now the two of them have their own place a few miles away, after I'd loaned them the deposit against her half-share of the house. I just wanted to keep it all as amicable as possible. To return to the words of the Jack Jones song, I'm 'free again', and enjoying it more and more. I hadn't realised there were so many beautiful women in similar circumstances.

One Sunday, I checked the messages on my mobile phone to hear a strange voice telling me that my son Marco had been in an accident on his scooter, and had been taken to Bournemouth Hospital. I phoned the hospital immediately. No Marco Mainwaring there. I tried Poole. 'Yes, he's in Casualty ... a suspected broken thigh bone, and two broken wrists.'

Apparently, he'd run into the back of a slow-moving line of traffic, hitting a Range Rover full on. He was operated on that night. He had been very lucky. If he had fallen to the right, as opposed to the left, he would have been hit by the oncoming traffic. He had survived.

In the hospital, he found himself one floor below my mother, who was due to have a knee replacement. At least they were in the same hospital. In the words of Her Majesty, 2004 was fast becoming my personal 'annus horribilis', and would not be one I'd look back on with any great fondness.

Marco now lives with me in the house, so hopefully now he'll be able to have access to his children after splitting from his wife. Like father, like son. Our daughter Francesca is, as I write this, expecting her first.

The family unit is still strong.

Life goes on and I have found happiness with someone new.